THE MODERNIST SELF IN TWENTIETH-CENTURY ENGLISH LITERATURE

By the same author

A novel

Ms. Moffatt
(*under the pen-name Ned Brown*)

The Modernist Self in Twentieth-Century English Literature

A Study in Self-Fragmentation

Dennis Brown
*Principal Lecturer in English Literature
Hatfield Polytechnic*

St. Martin's Press   New York

© Dennis Brown, 1989

All rights reserved. For information, write:
Scholarly & Reference Division,
St. Martin's Press, Inc., 175 Fifth Avenue, New York, NY 10010

First published in the United States of America in 1989

Printed in Hong Kong

ISBN 0–312–02439–8

Library of Congress Cataloging-in-Publication Data
Brown, Dennis, 1940–
The modernist self in twentieth-century English literature: a study in self-fragmentation/Dennis Brown.
p. cm.
Includes index.
ISBN 0–312–02439–8: $35.00 (est.)
1. English literature—20th century—History and criticism.
2. Modernism (Literature)—Great Britain. 3. Self in literature.
I. Title.
PR478.M6B7 1989   88–18835
820'.9'1—dc19   CIP

For my Colleagues and Students:

> *the quality*
> *of the affection . . .*
> *that has carved the trace in the mind*
>
> Ezra Pound
> (Canto LXXVI)

Contents

Preface		ix
1	Introduction	1
2	Dissolving Self	14
3	Self at War	43
4	Fragmentary Self	74
5	Self-deception and Self-conflict	108
6	Discontinuous Self	141
7	Conclusion	174
Notes		185
Index		201

Preface

The book results from many years of thinking about and teaching Modernist literature. It is dedicated to my colleagues and students (past, present and future) because my readings of specific texts, and my general notion of the 'Modernist Self', developed through interchange with them, and will doubtless develop further through their responses to this study. Particularly relevant here has been teaching (and co-teaching) Modernism courses on Hatfield multi-disciplinary degrees – the BAs in Humanities, English with Historical Studies and Contemporary Studies, and our part-time MA in English ('Literature in Crisis, 1890–1930'). Since my first thoughts on Modernist representations of selfhood, and my early sense that a deconstruction of self-unity was centrally at issue, it has become commonplace to talk about 'the decentred self', 'self-fragmentation' and so forth. However, to my knowledge, no one has yet mapped this phenomenon across disparate Modernist authors as a shared discursive project. This I have attempted to do – and in my own terms. Without arguing from a specific theoretical perspective, I have tried to show that Modernist texts were involved in a revolutionary project of self-representation long before there were Poststructuralist or Postmodernist theorisations to help translate their experiments into general intellectual parlance. The interpsychic mechanisms through which such a project evolved will be the theme of my next book.

All books owe more to the thinking of others than to a single originating author, and this is no exception. In general terms, this book owes most to certain texts, and texts about those texts, and texts related to the latter, in turn. But there are people outside texts – and the final version of my book is indebted to specific people. Most particularly, I wish to thank Patrick Grant (of the University of Victoria) and Eric Trudgill (of The Hatfield Polytechnic) for helpful comments on drafts of the entire work. I also thank Margaret Carpenter, Further Education teacher and student on the Hatfield MA in English, for her attention to details, in thought and wording, while typing the final version and for her composition of the index. Many colleagues at

Hatfield have commented helpfully on specific parts of the book, or the ideas behind them, as well as offering general encouragement. I want, especially, to thank the following: Gill Davies, Paul Fletcher, Sarah Hutton, Keith Page, Graham Pechey, Jean Radford, Judith Thompson, George Wotton (English); Paul Coates, Tony McWalter, Jane Singleton, Alan Weir, Sue Wilsmore (Philosophy); Winnie Crombie, Geoffrey Turner, Eugene Winter (Linguistics); Dorothy Koenigsberger (Historical Studies); Daniel Hutchinson (Dean of Humanities). For advice, support or commentary on various stages of the project, I wish, also, to thank Professor John Chapple, Viv Graveson, J. E. Lindsay, Lyvia Morgan, Sam Murley, Marilyn Miller-Pietroni and Anne Wright. I am also grateful to the Polytechnic Research Committee for helping to fund a consultancy visit to Canada during the early stages of writing the book.

I am indebted to Faber and Faber Ltd and Harcourt Brace Jovanovich Inc for permission to quote lines from the poetry of T. S. Eliot.

Dennis Brown

1
Introduction

'That I lost my center'[1]

This book is about the literary representation of selfhood in the Modernist period. It explores developments and interrelationships within a twentieth-century discourse about the self which is both specialised and experimentalist. It is concerned with new ways of representing self-experience in both fiction and poetry, all of which are construed as part of a shared ongoing project. So implied in the discussion will be one kind of description of Modernism itself: Modernism in literature was a movement that radically probed the nature of selfhood and problematised the means whereby 'self' could be expressed. This phenomenon may be most easily evidenced in terms of key instances: Conrad's *Lord Jim* and Eliot's Prufrock; James's Lambert Strether and Pound's Hugh Selwyn Mauberley; Joyce's Leopold Bloom and Woolf's Mrs Dalloway; Ford's Christopher Tietjens and Jones's John Ball; Eliot's 'Tiresias'[2] and Pound's *Ego Scriptor*.[3] Each instance signifies a literary site where the complexities of self-experience and the problems of their expression are activated and engaged. It is clear that such literary exploration did not take place in a vacuum: a variety of factors are involved in the phenomenon – most obviously, the general diffusion of social alienation, the rise of the psychoanalytic movement, the disorientation brought about by the shock of the Great War and the increasing experimentalism of almost all the contemporary artistic movements. Nevertheless the specificity of the literary discourse of selfhood is at the core of the book. My aim, above all, is to bear witness to this quite unique literary manifestation, which has its own meaning and cultural significance.

As the sub-title indicates, I view the Modernist representation of selfhood as characteristically deconstructive. What is finally meant by 'self-fragmentation' can only emerge in terms of the developing argument. But the general implication is evident. Works such as *Ulysses, The Waste Land, The Waves*, the Pisan *Cantos* and *Four Quartets* represent, through experimental means, a selfhood which is pluralist, heterogeneous and discontinuous. The term 'fragmentation' may bear a double implication. Writers represent fragmentary selves, and such representations constitute selfhood as inherently fragmentary. There is a subtle complicity between perceived reality and constructed description. And this complicity is not a static relationship but a developing torsion. Hence my frequent use of an adjective which is simultaneously a present participle – a trope much favoured by Modernist writers because it signifies ongoing process: 'fragmenting' is used here to express not a fixed conceptualisation but an active, exploratory process.

My full title also presupposes some kind of pre-existent unity which is in the process of being broken down. That unity constitutes a model of selfhood which is autonomous, integral and continuous – what Eliot in 'Tradition and the Individual Talent' called the 'substantial unity of the soul'.[4] The Modernist discourse of selfhood is haunted by the ghost of some lost self which was once coherent and self-sufficient – Joyce's Ulysses, Pound's heroes of the Renaissance virtú, Yeats's men of 'pride', Ford's pre-war Tietjens, Eliot's Fisher King (before the curse), Woolf's Percival in *The Waves*. When Bloom meditates on the baffling discontinuity 'me – and me now', or when Eliot's Thames maiden laments her desolate estrangement, 'I can connect / Nothing with nothing', they are expressing an experiential Fall from some mythic self-wholeness.

Such self-wholeness had been a normative assumption (and indeed a construction) of most cultural discourse up until the Modernist movement. In literature this was particularly so in representations of selfhood since the seventeenth century. Selfhood in *Hamlet*, *King Lear* or the poems of John Donne could be represented as variable and complex,[5] but by the time of Milton an integrating, unitary pressure is at work. The writing subject constitutes its self-experience as a bounded, coherent whole:

> When I consider how my light is spent,
>   Ere half my days, in this dark world and wide,
>   And that one talent which is death to hide.
>   Lodged with me useless, though my soul more bent
> To serve therewith my maker, and present
>   My true account, lest he returning chide,
>   Doth God exact day-labour, light denied,
> I fondly ask . . .[6]

This is an afflicted self, but it is totally in possession of itself. The question concerns what is owed to God, granted the poet's infirmity, and the poem proceeds to resolve this: 'They also serve who only stand and wait'. The serving-self is the robust Protestant soul, secure in its own integrity and assured of its identity in relation to its maker. Selfhood here is taken for granted as an integral entity. And this model endures as the norm in the Augustan period:

> Oh let me live my own, and die so too!
> (To live and die is all I have to do:)
> Maintain a Poet's Dignity and Ease,
> And see my friends, and read what books I please.[7]

Robinson Crusoe is a classic exemplification of the integral and consistent self. We first meet Robinson at a time when he is rebelling against the paternal law and determining to go to sea – in short, to 'find himself' as independent adult. He embarks and, after a variety of adventures, is shipwrecked alone on the legendary island. At first Crusoe is moody, and at times desperate – alternating between anguish at his predicament and gratitude that he has been spared alive. But at no time – whether half-drowned, terrified by his isolation or chronically sick with fever – is there any sense of his basic self-identity being at issue, as the identity of Conrad's Decoud is after only hours on the Great Isabella (see below, p. 17). It is to a coherent self that these misfortunes occur and it is a coherent self which comes to terms with them. The construction of his dwelling (with its careful defences) and his exploration and 'colonisation' of the island operate metaphorically to indicate a systematically expanding (and carefully controlled) selfhood. The self-sufficient order he creates in an initially unknown environment is a natural projection of his integral identity. As narrator he wishes to impress upon us a moral development within himself: he arrives a thoughtless sinner, but adversity teaches him the ways of providence, and hence piety. But this conversion is not a unification of hitherto diverse self-parts, but merely a spiritual transformation of his continuous egoism. Whether evil or good, Crusoe's integral soul has been pre-formed by God. Hence – from a Postmodernist standpoint – the extraordinary ontological insouciance of Robinson the chronicler:

But something always returned swift upon me to check these thoughts and to reprove me; and particularly one day, walking with my gun in my hand by the seaside, I was very pensive upon the subject of my present condition, when Reason, as it were, put in, expostulating with me t'other way, thus: 'well, you are in a desolate condition, 'tis true, but pray remember, where are the rest of you? Did you not come eleven of you in the boat? Where are the ten? Why were not they saved, and you lost? Why were you singled out? Is it better to be here or there?' And then I pointed to the sea. All evils are to be considered with the good that is in them, and with what worse attends them.[8]

Thus Crusoe, keeping moral order in the kingdom of his ego! Throughout the whole book his selfhood is very much 'singled out'.

It has become accepted practice to see in the Romantic movement a decisive shift in the sense of secure selfhood. In his book *The Mysteries of Identity*, Robert Langbaum traces the modern self back to Wordsworth, and in *Doubles* Karl Miller begins with Hogg's *Confessions of a Justified Sinner*.[9] While there are important aspects of continuity from Romanticism to Modernism, Langbaum himself suggests the ground on which a significant contrast may be established for my purposes. He writes: 'thus Wordsworth establishes, on naturalistic, psychological grounds, a self as transcendent as the old Christian self created and sustained by God'.[10] It is precisely this self which Modernism sought to explode. In this the Modernists are nearer to the scepticism of Locke and Hume which Wordsworth opposed. His model of the organically unified, developmental self provides merely a fuller and more humanised version of the integral self of the seventeenth and eighteenth centuries. It is this unified transcendent 'soul' which Modernist poetic texts like *The Waste Land* and the Pisan *Cantos* radically dismantle. So in many ways nineteenth-century literature constitutes the discourse *par excellence* of the 'Egotistical Sublime' and Keats was quite unusual in suggesting that 'the poet has . . . no identity'.[11] But Karl Miller's book indicates the transitional aspect of Romanticism in the creation of the Double. Throughout the nineteenth century the 'Egotistical Sublime' co-exists uneasily with the spectre of a divided self: Hogg's *alter ego*, Tennyson's 'Two Voices', Clough's 'Dipsychus', Dickens's Wemmick, Stevenson's Dr Jekyll and Mr Hyde. On the one hand the Double looks back to orthodox Christian dualism; good and evil have become psychologised: but on the other, the divided self helps prepare the way for the fragmentary self, and in works like *Heart of Darkness*, 'Prufrock' or Yeats's *Responsibilities* we see the one disperse into the other as the binary formula proves inadequate to the self-realities expressed. However, in the nineteenth century itself, the Double-motif arguably confirms integral selfhood as much as it unsettles it. Paradox can become conceptually reaffirming as antinomy. And in literary figures the Double tends to represent a dark usurper which the action of the text works to eliminate so that the 'real' self is confirmed – even if, as in the case of Dr Jekyll, this can only be resolved by death.

From the standpoint of my argument, then, the modern fragmentary self is not in a direct line back to either Hogg or Wordsworth. If it has a nineteenth-century forerunner it would probably be Browning. On the face of it, Browning's dramatic monologues, with some interesting exceptions,[12] assert a strongly unitary selfhood: the self-exuberant Lippo Lippi, the immensely self-confident Blougram or the egomaniac Duke of 'My Last Duchess'. But the significance of Browning to Moderns like Eliot and Pound lies in the relation of such characters to the author himself. In Browning the absolute subjectivism of Shelley filters through the 'objective' method to resolve as the relativistic 'prismatic hues'[13] of authorial self-dispersal. So J. Hillis Miller can write:

> Nowadays, in the epoch of Gide and Sartre, we are accustomed to the idea that a man may have no given 'nature', as does a stone or a tree. But in Browning's day, and in England, the idea of the indeterminacy of selfhood was a scandalous notion, contrary to the traditional British conviction that each man has a substantial inner core of self . . . We are forced to conclude that his 'selfhood' must be defined as the failure to have any one self, and as the need to enact, in imagination, the roles of the most diverse people in order to satisfy all the impulses of his being.[14]

Browning's example, then, was able to suggest both the plurality and the relativity of selfhood, without any passage through the paradoxicality of the Double. And his high literary reputation at the turn of the century may have served to reinforce the Modernist self-exploration which was to follow.

Nevertheless, fragmenting selfhood is rather a different matter from the creation of *dramatis personae*, and my contention is that, in spite of exceptions to the norm – Hume's scepticism, Sterne's deconstructive wit, Blake's dualism, Keats's 'negative capability' or even Browning's authorial self-dispersal – the convention of unitary selfhood remained central in literary discourse until the turn of the century. In her book *Darwin's Plots* Gillian Beer identifies in the late nineteenth century an 'approaching *Götterdämmerung* for autonomous egos'.[15] The Modernists were its agents – obsessed with destroying the concept at the same time as they were haunted by it. When in *Nostromo* Charles Gould is described as 'extremely sure of himself' the canny Dr Moynighan replies 'if that's all he is sure of, then he is sure of nothing'.[16] In *The Waves* Virginia Woolf suggests the inadequacy of the concept to extreme personal experience: 'alone I often fall down into nothingness'.[17] And Wyndham Lewis sees unitary selfhood as merely a pose: 'Why try and give the impression of a consistent and indivisible personality?' and *'never* fall into the vulgarity of being or assuming yourself to be one ego'.[18] Here the Wildean notion of constructed mask is married to the beginnings of psychoanalytic awareness. But such scepticism should not blind us to the severity of the task that lay ahead for modern writers. The self as integral 'ego' was far easier to mock than to dethrone, and the following chapters record a continuing struggle rather than a completed revolution.

However, it remains tempting to construe the Modernist discourse of selfhood as effecting a virtual paradigm shift. As the classical atom, which had been the foundation of traditional physics, dissolved into its mysterious parts, so the unitary self, which had been the final hero of post-Renaissance literature, began to dissolve and disintegrate. And just as the new quantum physics evolved its arcane terminology of 'indeterminacy', 'complementarity' and 'uncertainty', so Modernism developed its rarified experimental discourse to map the fragmentary realities of selfhood. It was, at the least, a revolutionary *venture*, as Anthony Easthope has testified:

> This essay . . . will argue that in the West the twentieth century has witnessed a crisis over 'the individual' (or subject as I will prefer to say); that the 'new orthodoxy' of post-structuralism or deconstruction or whatever one chooses to call the 'new' criticism is necessary and correct in denying the sentimental, liberal–

humanist notion of 'the self' and the Romantic conception of 'individual imaginative experience'; that an acknowledgement of the end of liberalism informs Modernist poetry but that this has been ignored by poetry in England since the 1930s.[19]

I do not agree that the 'end of liberalism' is necessarily at issue in Modernist discourse, and I think the case of poetry after the 1930s is more complicated than is represented here (see my Conclusion, Chapter 7), but Easthope is surely right in seeing the Modernist 'moment' as one of crisis and disintegration for the old notions of selfhood. And while the tendency is to see such crisis in negative terms ('things fall apart'), there is also a liberating aspect of the Modernist revolutionary venture, hymned by Joyce in 'Welcome O life!'.

Easthope's placement of Poststructuralism in relation to Modernism raises a key problem about method for a book such as this. He is quite right that 'the post-structuralism of Althusser, Barthes, Lacan, Derrida, and others . . . derives precisely from Modernism, is predicated on Modernism and may valuably be read as a later "philosophical" understanding of what was first encountered in art'. But does this mean that we must necessarily construe Modernism in specifically Poststructuralist terms? If so, there are virtually insurmountable obstacles unless we are prepared to abandon any sense that what Modernists represent in their texts are realities about experience – new truths about selfhood which the conventional 'self' had suppressed. For Poststructuralism does not so much fragment selfhood as abolish it altogether, save as signifier. Consider for instance:

> it is literally true that the basis of subjectivity is in the exercise of language. If one really thinks about it, one will see that there is no other objective testimony to the identity of the subject except that which he himself thus gives about himself.
> (Emile Benveniste)[20]

> Where is the subject? It is necessary to find the subject as a lost object. More precisely this lost object is the support of the subject . . . The question of desire is that the fading subject yearns to find itself again by means of some sort of encounter with this miraculous thing defined by the phantasm. In its endeavour it

is sustained by that which I call the lost object . . . which is such a terrible thing for the imagination.

(Jacques Lacan)[21]

. . . what was it that Saussure in particular reminded us of? That 'Language (which consists only of differences) is not a function of the speaking subject'. This implies that the subject (self-identical or even conscious of self-identity, self-conscious) is inscribed in the language, that he is a function of language.

(Jacques Derrida)[22]

I cannot challenge such formulations directly. However, it does seem that, if for out-and-out Poststructuralists the denoted world has disappeared except as a collocation of 'traces', then even their own texts become merely variants on the paradox of the Cretan liar.[23] The possibility that 'the rest is silence' is the ghost which haunts the neo-Derridean banquet of *jouissance*. Common sense, and much Anglo-American philosophy, will insist that the self is more than a subject position in language and that the 'I' of Napoleon or T. S. Eliot (or even of Derrida) denotes some reality outside the self-sealed circularity of writing, the nature of whose experiences is worth discussing. So while this book is inevitably written out of a Poststructuralist ethos, it will not relegate all issues concerning selfhood to a knowing meta-discourse on the merry dance of *differance*.[24] In the Postmodernist situation, many different language games may have their specific forms of legitimacy.

But the radicalism of Poststructuralists is valuable in helping point up the specifically deconstructive emphasis of Modernism. The key texts of Modernism were originally experienced as shocking, barely intelligible and disruptive. The slow process of canonisation, and the constitution of a 'Modernist Movement', has rather had the effect of smoothing over its radical implications and translating its revolutionary tropes into the safe discourse of literary criticism. With respect to the issue of selfhood, this normalising process has tended to transmute an unprecedented fragmentary self into a special case of the familiar integral self. So the ontological chaos within Kurtz is redescribed as a dualistic conflict between ego and id (see p. 25); the self-heterogeneity of Prufrock is resolved as straightforward neurosis or alienation; Tiresias is dug out of Eliot's wishful footnote to 'unify' that disintegrated 'mind of Europe' which is *The Waste Land*; and the hilarious balance of self-

Introduction 9

parts which is Bloom is reduced to a humane version of the 'normal', everyday self. A 'vulgar' liberal–humanism has nearly succeeded in a process of intellectual revisionism which negates the whole challenge of the Modernist version of selfhood.

Poststructuralism has also been useful in putting the whole problem of language firmly on the agenda. For Modernism shows the problem of the literary self as always being involved with the problem of discourse. Where the Wordsworthian subject of, say, 'Strange Fits of Passion' is quite at home in language, and implicitly presupposes that experience can be quite fully expressed in conventional discourse, the Modernist (dramatic) subject is typically uneasy in language and self-aware of the games language plays:

It is impossible to say just what I mean!
But as if a magic lantern threw the nerves in patterns on a screen:
Would it have been worth while
If one, settling a pillow or throwing off a shawl,
And turning toward the window, should say:
 'That is not it at all
 That is not what I meant, at all'.[25]

The uneasy linguistic awareness here is demonstrated not only in overt protestation ('impossible to say' or 'That is not it'), but also in the tentative 'as if' and the typically Prufrockian strategy of talking in elaborate hypothesis ('Would it have been worth while / If . . .'). And this linguistic awareness is the property not only of the authorial subject but also of the Modernist character. Bloom, for instance, as advertisement canvasser, is familiar with the tricks of rhetoric and of the playful gap between word and world. Throughout the day he toys with puns, jingles and aphorisms, and is often aware, as Joyce is, of the strange coding of experience itself: 'Flower to console me and a pin cuts lo. Means something, language of flow.'[26] And we can add to Bloom's example that of Woolf's would-be writer Bernard, who finally abandons his notebook, sensing: 'I need a little language such as lovers use, words of one syllable such as children speak . . . a howl: a cry.'[27]

The language-scepticism of Modernist writing will be a constant theme in this book. But what does that imply in terms of the discourse of my own discussion? I must simultaneously acknowledge the relativity of language, as enacted by the texts, and hope that my discourse will be adequate to demonstrate the issues. Total success is clearly impossible. On a quite ordinary level there is the struggle with contested and imprecise terms – 'identity', 'experience', 'ego', 'consciousness' and that awkward key word 'self' with both its colloquial associations (coherent centre?) and its specialised uses, as in Jung's writings[28] – not to mention its irritating reflexivity ('self-conscious self'; 'self itself', 'experience itself' etc.). At a deeper level there is the constant awareness that 'my' book is in a sense making itself (self!) out of the current jargon ('representation', 'construction', 'signification' and so on) without my being able to do much about it, except reach occasionally for some defamiliarising metaphor or aphorism. After Modernism all discourse is suspect, and I do not pretend ('I'? – 'pretend'?) to be wholly at ease in the discourse which has here written me. Indeed, on re-reading drafts, I have sometimes wondered how far my writing position has been infected by the very fragmenting process it seeks to address. I have tried to even out such disjunctiveness to conform to convention. But I have also tried to retain some stylistic signs of life behind, within or above the text, if only to witness my engagement with the works and issues involved.

The chapter scheme is intended to suggest a growing development of shared discourse as well as interconnections between texts on specific issues. Each main chapter begins with a general description of representations of selfhood relevant to the chapter's focus and then examines, in turn, three writers' texts. 'Dissolving Self' (Chapter 2), for instance, describes initial attempts to break down the unitary construction of selfhood and then examines, in some detail, *Heart of Darkness*, 'The Love Song of J. Alfred Prufrock' and *Portrait of the Artist as a Young Man*. 'Self at War' (Chapter 3) discusses the importance of battle neurosis as an experience which combatant writers helped establish as quite central to Modernist representations of selfhood, and then examines Sassoon's poems, Ford's *Parade's End* and Jones's *In Parenthesis*. 'Fragmentary Self' (Chapter 4) focuses on the variety of experimental styles which most fully demonstrate the achieved Modernist discourse of the self. There is then an account of three key texts: *Ulysses*, *The Waste Land* and *Mrs Dalloway*. The main argument having been established, 'Self-deception and Self-conflict' (Chapter 5) discusses a central theme of self-fragmenting texts. The discussion focuses on the way Modernist texts problematise relationships between self-parts in terms of self-deception and internal conflict. The main texts examined are *Lord Jim*, Yeats's later poems and, again, *Ulysses*. 'Discontinuous Self' (Chapter 6) completes the main body of the argument by considering self-fragmentation on the temporal plane in terms of discontinuity and metamorphosis. The main texts for this chapter are *The Waves, Four Quartets* and the *Cantos*. The Conclusion (Chapter 7) then briefly describes the literary aftermath of the Modernist project and discusses the implications of a fragmentary model of selfhood for our current understanding of self-experience, within a Postmodernist world.

As is evident, most of the texts discussed in my argument have become canonised as representative of the mainstream of twentieth-century English literature, and a great deal has already been written about them. My chief concern has been to integrate these texts into a developing discussion about self-representation, and I have not attempted to recapitulate the familiar critical views about them. Within the bounds of the argument, I have preferred to offer my own readings in the hope of provoking fresh insights into the texts. My aim has not been to consolidate received understandings but to help reactivate the revolutionary implications of the Modernist project.

My argument inevitably reveals the limitations of its specific focus. For instance, I have restricted it to the accepted 'English' Modernist movement.[29] There are obvious parallels with the discourse of European Modernism (most notably Proust) and American Modernism (particularly Faulkner), but I did not want to treble the size of the book. Marxist critics will find I have little to say about the socio-economic and ideological placement of Modernist selfhood, because I have focused on representations themselves rather than their social determination. Feminist critics may feel I have blurred gender and sexual differences in not distinguishing between male and female writers but treating their works as part of one developing discourse (see below, p. 179). Historians of Ideas might object that I have not sufficiently considered the Modernist discourse of self in terms of specific influences, such as the development of psychoanalytic thinking. The focus of the book is on Modernist literary discourse itself and is necessarily restricted. It seeks to make a specific, if limited, contribution in a field where other books have been, and will be, written to fill out the picture.

Nevertheless, any book about the self locates itself at a crossroads where many competing interests, disciplines and discourses meet – and perhaps part again. Philosophical and psychological thinking has been especially relevant to my study, and I have tried, where the focus allows, to set the literary argument within the larger context. Selfhood is theoretically of interest to everyone, since we all experience our 'selves' all day, every day, and usually want to make some kind of sense out of them. The claim to importance of literary Modernism is partly that it deals with this common interest in everyday selves in a radically new way, and that it has developed its representations, to a considerable degree, out of other relevant discourses. Lawrence's bizarre *Psychoanalysis and the Unconscious* is merely a somewhat flagrant expression of the contemporary vortex of ideas and discourses out of which were written such key works as *The Good Soldier*, 'Hugh Selwyn Mauberley', *Women in Love, To the Lighthouse, Finnegans Wake* or *Four Quartets*. The importance of this literature, then, springs from its role as a site for the interpenetration of diverse new notions about the self and its ability to act as cultural transmitter and mapper of the modern 'post-Copernican'[30] self. In this, its linguistic scepticism is of vital significance. For its experimental, defamiliarising devices constantly jar us out of that linguistic hypnotism which the rationalist texts of philosophy and psychology typically induce. In Modernist texts insights are communicated through and under the overt progression of meaning, and hence interrogate and convey the experience of selfhood more directly than any other form of discourse. Hence I believe that we can understand more about selfhood by reading 'Prufrock' or *Ulysses* than by reading, say, *The Case of Dora* or Lacan's *Ecrits*. (The experience of psychoanalytic *therapy* is, of course, another matter.)

So I claim a high importance for my theme – and I believe it is relevant not only to students of literature but also to all who try to understand the nature of selfhood. But it is also a complicated and sometimes distressing theme. Modernist texts are quite 'difficult' and this book is necessarily in the business of explanation and exposition. At the same time they can be distressing because they frequently construe selfhood in terms of anguish and desperation. The book acknowledges this, and testifies how the project of literary self-fragmentation necessarily involved testing the unitary model by representations of extreme experience, including madness. But I have also tried to show how self-liberation is also on the agenda of Modernism. Works such as *Ulysses, Mrs Dalloway* and *Four Quartets* demonstrate how self-fragmentation can be reassessed as a form of self-diversification and self-plenitude. By dismantling integral selfhood, the Modernists also deconstruct egoic repression and suggest that self-wholeness consists in the acknowledgement and balancing of disparate self-parts. Fragmenting self helped open the way for a new self-at-play. My book, then, seeks to witness both the negative and the positive implications of the Modernist project, and to suggest that the fear involved in the perception 'the centre cannot hold' may ultimately be resolved into an educated reaffirmation of selfhood, as 'Look we've come through'.

2
Dissolving Self

'A Consciousness Disjunct'[1]

In his farewell poem to London of 1920, 'Hugh Selwyn Mauberley', Ezra Pound sketched an extraordinary portrait of a turn-of-the-century poet. Through a pastiche of Jamesian prose, he effects an almost Cubist dissipation of essence:

> Nothing, in brief, but maudlin confession,
> Irresponse to human aggression,
> Amid the precipitation, down-float
> Of insubstantial manna,
> Lifting the faint susurrus
> Of his subjective hosannah.[2]

The spectre of J. Alfred Prufrock hovers behind this presentation: 'Drifted . . . precipitate / Asking time to be rid of . . . / Of his bewilderment.' 'Anaesthesis' is Mauberley's defence in a world shaken by 'current exacerbations'. But in the end he retires to the Moluccas islands, a 'hedonist' reduced to 'this overblotted / Series / Of intermittences'. Pound's satirical poem encapsulates the indifference of Edwardian society to the aesthetic venture: it also makes exemplary the sensitive modern man as dissolved and disjunctive selfhood. It is Modernist characterisation in terms of the historical ambivalences Pound had perceived in the heroine of 'Near Perigord': 'a shifting change, / A broken bundle of mirrors'.[3] From his post-war perspective he had written the modern anti-hero as a collocation of split-off self-parts.

However, the dominant literary discourse of the era Mauberley is supposed to represent – late Victorian and Edwardian society – expressed selfhood in a different and quite traditional way. The dramatic division of self into Jekyll and Hyde, or the projection of a contrary self as double, were the only familiar variants on the model of unitary selfhood – and in a paradoxical way confirmed the normal validity of that model. Poetic response to adversity was frequently a shoring up of the integral persona: 'Play up, play up, and play the game'; 'If you can keep your head when all about you / Are losing theirs and blaming it on you'; 'I am the master of my fate, / I am the captain of my soul.'[4] More sensitively aesthetic verse tended to centre selfhood around some emotional node: 'Thus I; faltering forward, / . . . And the woman calling'; 'Into my heart an air that kills / From yon far country blows': 'I hear it in the deep heart's core.'[5] Both types of self-construction were inherited by the War Poets and, despite personal experiences of self-fragmentation through breakdown, developed into the characteristic postures of war poetry – defiance of modern war and grieving pity for its victims. In fiction, too, the traditional representation of selfhood was the norm. The hero or heroine of turn-of-the-century novels constituted, in fact, precisely Western selfhood – itself: what Lawrence would call the 'old stable ego.'[6] If, as Virginia Woolf asserted, 'on or about December 1910 human nature changed,'[7] then even in her own fiction it was not until some years later that the expression of that change could be adequately expressed in a revolutionary literary discourse. Hardy's tragic victims of fate, Wells' perky protagonists, Bennett's town-made hero(in)es, are all bounded and coherent entities – 'characters' in the established unitary sense. However afflicted or distressed, they remain themselves – integral, self-consistent, susceptible to change only in terms of overt causal development. They are fictional idealisations of the self-coherence we all insist we possess and obscurely dread losing. So the consensus of Edwardian discourse constructed selfhood as a slightly updated version of the post-seventeenth-century norm. Nevertheless, from the nineties onwards, some writers were beginning to dissolve this model, initiating a process which led beyond Mauberley's dissociations to the interior disintegrations of Eliot's 'Tiresias' or Joyce's Molly Bloom.

On the poetic front, Yeats was the older-generation writer in whom lay the seeds of future possibility. His sense of the fluidity and paradoxicality of self is expressed in essays that portray his own early mental states: 'Then . . . came the thought that a man always tried to become his opposite, to become what he would abhor if he did not desire it.'[8] Or again: 'all happiness depends on the energy to assume that mask of some other life, or a re-birth as something not one's self, something created in a moment and perpetually renewed.'[9] For Yeats, the tension between rival 'selves' was essentially creative and he stressed, in particular, the struggle between opposites in the search for a higher selfhood (see pp. 124–30 below). However, what most strikes us about the early poems is how little all of this is given direct representation. The doctrine of the mask (modified from Wilde), his sense of 'phantasmagoria', the self-identification with great historical characters, his awareness of the 'shifting' borders of our minds – these do not register in his verse as radical expressions of selfhood until the later period. It is not just a matter of preferring mythological 'embroideries' to walking 'naked'[10] at that time. Until he met Pound and came to terms with the new literary developments, Yeats lacked a discourse in which his sense of the 'congeries of being' in selfhood could be represented.

The precursors of the fragmentary self, then, are to be found in fiction rather than in verse. Both James's heroes of paralysed sensitivity and Conrad's men of tortured introspection are the true heralds of the early modern dissipation of selfhood. It is no accident that Eliot, for instance, was influenced by both. *The Ambassadors* (1903)[11] is probably the most relevant novel of James. Its protagonist, Lambert Strether, who also provides the narrative viewpoint, has been likened to Prufrock (and may well have helped shape Eliot's conception); at the same time aspects of Mauberley are reminiscent of him, while some of the work's Parisian atmospherics are evoked in Pound's *Cantos*.[12] James's interest in the complexities of selfhood was doubtless partly informed by his sister's 'hysterical' phases and his famous brother William's psychological explorations[13] (themselves indebted to Janet's studies of split personality). Yet Strether is no dramatic exemplum of self-disintegration. He is rather an instance of the integral self reengaging with lost self-possibilities before returning at last to his allotted persona. Released from American values to savour the rich ambivalences of French culture, Strether offers a strange parallel and contrast to Conrad's Marlow, in *Heart of Darkness*, who relinquishes European values to encounter the sinister turbulence of 'primitivism'. Conrad's hero is more radically affected by self-dissolution (see below, pp. 22–9), but Strether himself is torn between his 'stiffer self' and 'let[ting] himself go' (*The Ambassadors* p. 49), encounters 'germs' which had been 'buried for long years in dark corners' (p. 55), is 'liable to strange outbreaks' (p. 248), and acknowledges eventually the confusion of 'his perceptions and his mistakes, his concessions and his reserves, the ridiculous mixing . . . of his braveries and his fears' p. 347). In the course of the work Strether avows many aspects of himself that his American self has denied and repressed for most of his life. It is, perhaps, because he feels old that he renounces the possibilities of such aspects at the end. By contrast, Joyce's Stephen in *Portrait of the Artist* is able to utilise all the resources of 'a young man' to rebut the persona Ireland would force onto him and elect to live in fluidly creative freedom.

Much of Conrad's fiction directly pioneers the Modernist representation of the fragmented self. At the same time it hints at precedents in the brooding self-doubters of the American tradition, as well as in Dickens's psychological grotesques and Dostoyevsky's obsessional outsiders. As we shall see, *Heart of Darkness* was a seminal work in transforming the traditional adventure narrative into an exploration of tormented inner space. In the figure of Kurtz, Marlow meets a representative Western self who has disintegrated into the random 'lusts' that his persona had previously denied. The hero of *Lord Jim* (see below, pp. 117-24) embodies a slightly different but related predicament – that of the self wrestling to refound itself after a fatal lapse. The book is a study of self-deception and self-conflict arising from divisions within that the hero cannot resolve. In this case, as in *Heart of Darkness*, the theme of self-dissolution is reinforced by the manifest uncertainties (at times unreliabilities) of a dramatic narrator himself in search of a founding self-integrity. Conrad's ontological scepticism is more than equalled by the emotional horror of a self-disintegration that these works express. This is perhaps most directly exemplified in the later *Nostromo*.[14] Martin Decoud, whose social persona has collapsed into nothingness on his lonely island, succumbs to a sense of the utter unreality of self:

> The brilliant 'Son Decoud', the spoiled darling of the family, the lover of Antonia and journalist of Sulaco, was not fit to grapple with himself single-handed. Solitude from mere outward condition of existence becomes very swiftly a state of soul in which the affectations of irony and scepticism have no place . . . After three days of waiting for the sight of some human face, Decoud caught himself entertaining a doubt of his own individuality . . . Decoud lost all belief in the reality of his action past and to come . . . He beheld the universe as a succession of incomprehensible images . . . (it had occurred to him that Antonia could not possibly have ever loved a being so impalpable as himself) . . .
> (pp. 408–9)

The result is suicide. Conrad, among the very first to represent selfhood as dissoluble, helped stamp the relativistic self with his own pessimistic terror. With exceptions, such as Stephen's self-generative fluidity in *Portrait of the Artist* (see below, pp. 36–42), the dissolving self was to be represented as a site of acute anxiety and deprivation. And after the realities of the Great War it was all too easy to portray the heterogeneous self in terms of trauma, fragmentation from without and total breakdown.

In Lawrence's *Sons and Lovers*,[15] published a year before the outbreak of war, anxiety also characterises the dissolution of selfhood. It is true that Lawrence also attempts to suggest the fluid freedom of selfhood, its ongoing transcendence – like the Norman arches Paul admires. However, the most dramatic and memorable moments occur when consciousness falls under the impact of emotional shock and begins to disintegrate. Such moments are not merely represented as extremities of feeling, as they might be in any nineteenth-century fiction: rather the whole ontological status of the self becomes at issue, and the protagonist is in danger of acute psychological breakdown. It is less that the self is grievously wounded than that there is a chaos of conflicting elements where once was the sense of self. This typically results in a temporary loss of self. Such a moment occurs early on when Mrs Morel is turned out of the house by her husband:

> Mrs Morel leaned on the garden gate, looking out, and she lost herself awhile. She did not know what she thought. Except for a slight feeling of sickness, and her consciousness in the child, herself melted out like scent into the shiny, pale air. After a time the child, too, melted with her in the mixing-pot of moonlight, and she rested with the hills and lilies and houses, all swum together in a kind of swoon.
>
> (p. 35)

Like Conrad, Lawrence tests the actual substance of Western selfhood in terms of highly symbolistic descriptions of unusual psychic states. Again, the representation depends not on intellectual theory (even if Lawrence was aware of basic Freudian concepts), but on the existential experience of self-dissolution and self-loss. The most striking instance of this is at the end of the book when Paul feels the reality of his mother's death:

Dissolving Self

Always alone, his soul oscillated, first on the side of death, then on the side of life, doggedly. The real agony was that he had nowhere to go, nothing to do, nothing to say, and *was* nothing himself. Sometimes he ran down the streets as if he were mad: sometimes he was mad; things weren't there, things were there. It made him pant. Sometimes he stood for a drink before the bar of the public-house where he had called for a drink. Everything stood back away from him . . . He could not get in touch . . . On the threshold he stood and looked at the lighted street. But he was not of it or in it. Something separated him . . . He felt stifled. There was nowhere for him. The stress grew inside him; he felt he should smash.

(p. 501)

Lawrence resolves Paul's desperation with an ambivalent but finally optimistic paragraph. Yet already, in this his first really characteristic novel, he has served warning that the conventional notion of selfhood is on trial and that he will try to explode its smug security by probing the extremes of experience and expression.

Ford Madox Ford's *The Good Soldier*,[16] begun in the year of publication of his Nottinghamshire protegé's first major fiction, also takes a place in the developing discourse of dissolving self. Its focus is on the destructive passions that underlay polite Edwardian society and the effects these have on the four main characters involved in the 'minuet' of relationships described. But in this exposure of hidden lusts, greeds, jealousies and hatreds, Ford quite consciously expresses the new psychoanalytic ethos and makes a play of using such terms as 'breakdown', 'hysteric', 'unconscious', 'analysis', 'pathological' and so on. The book develops strong polarities to enforce the dichotomy between social and inner realities. On the one hand, 'our friendship has been a young-middle-aged affair, since we were all of us of quite quiet dispositions' (p. 12); on the other, 'broken, tumultuous, agonised, and unromantic lives, periods punctuated by screams, by imbecilities, by deaths, by agonies' (p. 213). This is most clearly centred in the figure of Edward Ashburnham who appears as an exemplary active, responsible and respectable soldier-squire, but who is, in fact, sexually obsessive and whose passions wreak havoc throughout the book. Like Tietjens in *Parade's End*, he stands as a model of the English integral self – a model which is there to be split down: 'Edward went mad: his world stood on its head: the palms in front of the blue sea danced grotesque dances' (p. 148). Yet he is not alone in this. His conduct also drives his wife over the edge: 'Leonora had completely broken down . . . It is after a husband's long illness and death that a widow goes to pieces' (p. 183). The whole text is obsessed with the fear of madness, and its final eloquent symbol is the reduction of Ashburnham's infatuated ward to a beautiful invalid who can utter only 'shuttlecocks' and 'Credo in unum deum omnipotentum' over and over again. But the very textual unravelling of events is itself obsessional. The celebrated indirect narration elaborates a persona broken down into desperate ramblings, repetitions and exclamations. Dowell, the narrator, has had his whole world broken up by the events he tries to describe and the very manner of his telling signals a radically disintegrated self-world: 'I know nothing – nothing in the world – of the hearts of men. I only know that I am alone – horribly alone' (p. 14); 'It is all a darkness' (p. 18); 'I would be in hell. In hell, I tell you' (p. 50); 'It is as if one had a dual personality, the one I being entirely unconscious of the other' (p. 99); 'I have, I am aware, told this story in a very rambling way so that it may be difficult for anyone to find their path through what may be a sort of maze. I cannot help it' (p. 167); 'Yes, no doubt I am jealous. In my fainter sort of way I seem to perceive myself following the lines of Edward Ashburnham. I suppose that I should really like to be a polygamist; with Nancy, and with Leonora, and with Maisie Maidan and possibly even with Florence' (p. 213). Of course, Ford uses Dowell's dislocations and free associations to build up an overall aesthetic pattern: but the pattern is still built out of the intense dissociations of the represented self. The neo-Conradian dramatic introspection is what makes the book a psychological as well as a formal masterpiece. Finally published in the war climate of 1915, Ford's title *The Saddest Story* was changed to *The Good Soldier*[17] – a symptomatic transmogrification, in that it was above all the recognition of 'shell-shock' which transformed the dissolving self of prewar literature into the chronically fragmented self of the twenties.

But if the dissolution of integral self was begun in fictional discourse, contemporary experimental poetics was clearing the ground for its own demolition work. The Imagist group, in particular, helped drain away the ebbing Postromantic tide of poetic self-expression. T. E. Hulme's denunciation of the cult of *'Personality'* (which he traced back to the Renaissance), and his connoisseurship of the real as 'cinders'[18] helped make possible a poetry devoted not to the construction of selfhood but to the expression of experiential variety. The wider Imagist circle – which in England included Ford, Lawrence and even Joyce, as well as Pound and (later) Eliot – effected a liberation from the pursuit of Western selfhood and focused poetic perception on relationships within heterogeneity. The verse reached out to things rather than attempted to appropriate them for self, and sought to relate feelings to the diversity of the natural world. It was perhaps workshop verse rather than the expression of a major new movement, but the insistence on specifics and a detached stance provided the means to portray things afresh. This remained true when the subject was selfhood. So Pound could render the bourgeois self as 'a code and not a core', lacking 'affections' and so entitled 'An Object'.[19] Or, in a more appreciative vein, he could dissolve selfhood into the variety of its contents:

> For all this sea-hoard of deciduous things,
> Strange woods half sodden, and new brighter stuff:
> In the slow float of different light and deep,
> No! there is nothing! In the whole and all,
> Nothing that's quite your own.
>   Yet this is you.
>
> ('Portrait d'une femme')[20]

Specifics, rendered imagistically, provided the basis of a discourse that could later express the fragmentariness of self-experience in such larger works as *The Waste Land* or the Pisan *Cantos*. Meanwhile, on another continent,[21] Eliot had already been pioneering that blend of novelistic satire and proto-Imagistic concreteness on which his life-long analysis of selfhood was founded:

> And I must borrow every changing shape
> To find expression . . .
>
> ('Portrait of a Lady')

> Whispering lunar incantations
> Dissolve the floors of memory

> And all its clear relations,
> Its divisions and precisions . . .
>
> ('Rhapsody on a Windy Night')
>
> The thousand sordid images
> Of which your soul was constituted.
>
> ('Preludes')[22]

'HIS SOUL WAS MAD'

Heart of Darkness, published at the beginning of the century,[23] still strikes us as an extraordinarily innovative and prophetic intervention in the tradition of English story-writing at that time.[24] Its essentially negative view of the imperialist project (and the myth of *pax Romana* which helped sustain its ideology),[25] its bleak vision of human motives and obsessions and the portentous implications of its dream scenario (almost crying out for psychoanalytic explication), all point forward to the chief works of Modernism rather than back to the assumptions and conventions of Victorian fiction. In particular, the tale constitutes a provisional attempt at deconstructing Western selfhood. Where *Lord Jim* represents self in terms of the intricacies of self-deception (see below, pp. 117–24) and 'The Secret Sharer' constructs a divided self through the mechanism of a doppelgänger, *Heart of Darkness* combines aspects of both techniques in an attempt to dissolve the very concept of the integral self: 'he was hollow at the core' (p. 83). This hollowness is no mere vacuum, but rather a central chaos where conflicting desires, intentions and conceptions whirl about in a dark vortex. We have the spectacle in Kurtz of supreme 'egotism' in the absence of any coherent ego.[26]

The tale is littered with sketchy representations of the unitary self – many of them parodic. Right at the beginning we have typecasting in the figures under the mast – the Director of Companies, the Lawyer and the Accountant. In the spectral European city we find the 'great man' in charge of the African trade and the 'old doctor' with his 'scientific' interest in the shape of skulls. In the African station there are the impeccably dressed clerk, the disease-proof manager ('perhaps there was nothing within him', p. 31), the aristocratic brick-maker ('this papier-mâché Mephistopheles', p. 37) and the various undistinguishable 'pilgrims'. Back in London we have the company official and Kurtz's 'cousin'. Such characters define themselves in terms of basic social roles: they maintain the fiction of self-wholeness by superficiality, security or complacency. Like Kurtz's Fiancée they typically protect themselves from extreme experience and consequent self-knowledge by living in some 'great and saving illusion'. Thus they can posture as integrated persons only through self-ignorance – the stuff of brief caricature.[27] As Marlow notes, 'you may be too much of a fool to go wrong' (p. 70): in this way the white traders evade the message of the 'heart of darkness'. The listeners around the mast, however, like the tale's readers, are given a chance to surmount the world of 'policeman and pork-butcher' by sympathetic identification with Marlow's story and its varied implications, and consequent self-examination. In this sense the tale is very much an appeal to authenticity: a challenge to its listeners to contemplate and acknowledge the complexities of experience – 'Do you see him? Do you see the story? Do you see anything? It seems to me I am trying to tell you a dream . . .' (p. 39).

As contrast to the hollow egotism of the Imperialists, the native Africans of the tale assert a dignified form of 'natural' selfhood – when they are uncorrupted by Western culture. They are represented in terms of mystery, simplicity, otherness. They are neither unitary selves nor fragmented selves but suggest a tribal self-in-community quite outside Western conceptions. So, where the egotism of the whites causes them to inhabit a social realm of constant intrigue and backbiting – each wilful self plotting to reorder affairs to its own maximum advantage – the natives on the river-bank merge into harmonious communality, expressed in drumming, dancing and shared gesticulation whose meaning is quite closed to Western observation: 'The prehistoric man was cursing us, praying to us, welcoming us – who could tell?' (p. 51). Those unlucky enough to have fallen foul of the Imperialist endeavour sink, with bleak dignity, into a deathly despair, cut off from their tribal relationship and so drained of all sense of self or even life; 'they were nothing earthly now – nothing but black shadows of disease and starvation, lying confusedly in the greenish gloom' (p. 24). The one or two who find favour with the Europeans tend to ape the Western habit of disdaining all that is not the imperial ego, one's self: 'provoking insolence' (p. 32); 'in a tone of scathing contempt' (p. 100). But the cannibals on the boat seem to have retained their communality, in spite of (frictional) contact with the white 'pilgrims': the 'restraint' that Marlow admires in them is a matter of corporate solidarity rather than individualistic self-control: 'Why in the name of all the gnawing devils of hunger they didn't go for us – they were thirty to five – and have a good tuck in at once, amazes me now when I think of it' (p. 59).

However, beyond such characterisations Conrad is careful to represent the nature of native selfhood as essentially mysterious – whether the prancing 'She' of Kurtz's desire or the trained helmsman who dies with a frown that 'gave to his black death-mask an inconceivably sombre, brooding and menacing expression' (p. 67). Conrad's concern is with the Western self – its unitary pretensions and its capacity for gruesome disintegration. And to act as a transition between the hollowness of the traders and the mad brokenness of Kurtz, we are given the bizarre figure of the Russian harlequin. He is endearing in his inconsistent enthusiasms: he represents the life-force as zany disjunction – thriving on self-contradiction, special pleading and fluid instinctuality (a little like Molly Bloom in this).[28] He is shown as a miraculous creature, so that even the experienced Marlow is 'lost in astonishment' (p. 78). Morally, of course, he appears suspect because of his unreflecting loyalty to Kurtz: and yet his naive simplicity can also be read as saint-like. He nurses Kurtz through two illnesses at great (and constant) danger to himself – he has not slept properly for ten nights. Indeed, by means of narrative manipulation, his selfless generosity is systematically contrasted, over some pages, with Kurtz's depravity. 'I heard he was lying helpless, and so I . . . took my chance' (p. 82) pivots round the description of the skulls facing Kurtz's hut and mention of the latter's 'gratification of . . . various lusts' (p. 83). In general, the harlequin represents Protean youth: neither founded nor fragmented selfhood but a freedom of self-possibilities which is like that of Stephen Dedalus or Rupert Birkin. He has successfully resisted social acculturation into integral Western selfhood: his brightly patched clothes speak his capacity for living contradictions. So, too, the smiles and frowns which chase each other over his unformed face. Thus the 'flame' of hope had 'consumed all thought of self . . . completely' (p. 79). The harlequin is the free self as openness to experience and instinctive zest in contrastive possibilities. He provides a positive model of the non-unitary self as joyous selflessness: Kurtz, whom the story focuses on immediately after the Russian's departure, provides a portentous negative model – selfhood as sheer, contradictory, unpredictable egotism.

In the space of a quite short tale, Conrad has laboured hard to establish Kurtz as a fully representative Western self. The matter of his 'reputation' becomes a touchstone of how we are to see the reality of the post-Cartesian, capitalist ego. 'All Europe contributed to the making of Kurtz' we are told (p. 71). He is associated variously with art, journalism, politics, poetry, business, music, science, exploration and philanthropy. He is a 'universal genius' (p. 103), and his plans ('What vast plans he had', p. 109) represent the rationalising and greedy will of Western man in general. If the pilgrims stand for the appearance of unitary selfhood, then Kurtz is the reality of it under the veneer. The cunningly orchestrated series of references to the man, as the tale progresses towards the heart of darkness, guide us to a meeting fateful for 'mankind's conception of itself' (*Lord Jim*, p. 75). Inevitably this resolves as something of an anticlimax on the level of fictive plot. We expect some climactic dramatic action commensurate with this encounter with the Western self. This the tale cannot fully provide because 'the changes take place inside' (p. 17). There is the fight, the vision of the heads, the midnight crawl towards the native rites, and beyond that the obsessional accumulation of heavily adjectival phrases[29] whereby Conrad's discourse endeavours to speak of the mysteries of self-interiority. The reality of Western man resolves into a collocation of hints, suggestions, symbolisations. But these tell enough to radically undermine the notion of self-coherence and self-consistency.

In his influential chapter on *Heart of Darkness*, C. B. Cox[30] falls into the trap of trying to construe the selfhood of Kurtz in terms of dualistic oppositions. It is true that Conrad's language and symbolisation at times tempt us in this direction. However, there is far too much in Conrad's complexity of explication to allow us to rest with the formulation 'a powerful fable of the divided consciousness' or 'the novel oscillates . . . between two definitions of "reality"'.[31] Conrad probes far beneath the linguistic conveniences of mere binary opposition: the tale asserts not a divided but a radically fragmentary self, and at the same time calls into question all the terms we can use to constitute the self as reality. Hence the ironic suggestivity by which Marlow attempts to convey Kurtz's condition:

there was something wanting in him – some small matter which, when the pressing need arose, could not be found in his magnificent eloquence. Whether he knew of this deficiency himself I can't say. I think the knowledge came to him at last – only at the very last. But the wilderness had found him out early, and had taken on him a terrible vengeance for the fantastic invasion. I think it had whispered to him things about himself of which he had no conception till he took counsel with this great solitude – and the whisper proved irresistibly fascinating. It echoed loudly within him because he was hollow at the core

(p. 83)

He kicked himself loose of the earth. Confound the man! he had kicked the very earth to pieces. He was alone, and I before him did not know whether I stood on the ground or floated in the air. I've been telling you what we said – repeating the phrases we pronounced – but what's the good? They were common everyday words . . . They had behind them, to my mind, the terrific suggestiveness of words heard in dreams, of phrases spoken in nightmares. Soul! If anybody had ever struggled with a soul, I am the man . . . But his soul was mad. Being alone in the wilderness, it had looked within itself, and, by heavens! I tell you, it had gone mad. I had – for my sins, I suppose – to go through the ordeal of looking into it myself.

(p. 95)

'Something wanting'; 'things about himself'; 'irresistibly fascinating'; 'hollow'; 'loose of the earth'; 'alone'; 'phrases spoken in nightmares'; 'mad' – such articulations enforce the mysteriousness of Kurtz's case; its resistence to terminological dualism. Thus, to see Kurtz as a battle-ground where 'restraint' succumbs to id is to surrender all the radical subtlety of Conrad's vision of the Western self.[32] Outside of the psychoanalytic literature which gives great complexity to the term, id takes on the appearance of a liberated version of the coherent self. But Kurtz's 'brutal instincts' and 'various lusts' have no coherence beyond their co-existence in the one man. This is what makes him so dangerously unpredictable. He may ignore you or shoot you or harangue you. He may be in the mood for 'unspeakable rites' or ivory-stealing or sexual licence or being worshipped or writing poetry or – anything. At the same time there is a purpose in many of his excesses (to control the

Dissolving Self

natives and so get more ivory) and self-indulgent passions involved in his 'plans'. He has by no means become pure id (how would that be possible?): rather, like all of us, he is caught between the opposing forces of ego, id and superego,[33] torn by disparate mechanisms of flow and release, projection and introjection, phantasy and reality-recognition and so forth. He is merely less balanced and has greater opportunities for self-indulgence than most of us because he is in a position of near-absolute power. Kurtz is 'utterly lost' because his relatively coherent self-project has broken down in the jungle into the gratification of random whims. The man who could 'get himself to believe anything' (p. 104) has become the man who believes, fantastically, that he can own everything: 'My Intended, my station, my career, my ideas . . .' (p. 70). So 'the wastes of his weary brain were haunted by shadowy images now' (p. 98) and his face shows contrastive surges of emotion: 'sombre pride . . . ruthless power . . . craven terror . . . intense and hopeless despair'. Such contradictory emotions speak his fragmented condition. Kurtz represents the Western self not as divided between neat opposites but as a finally indescribable chaos. He inhabits a living 'nightmare', with all the gallimaufry of split-off self-parts that are the stuff of dreams. Hence, for the one-time pilgrim of Western 'enlightenment', 'the horror! The horror!'

Marlow is garrulously self-conscious about the fact that Kurtz's state can only be suggested through hints and partial formulations. What he admires in the man is that he could finally acknowledge his self-disintegration and label it morally. When Marlow himself is in danger of 'sympathetically' joining the now-dead Kurtz, he too, in a feverish state, directly experiences the hollowness of the Western version of selfhood:

> an impalpable greyness, with nothing underfoot, with nothing around, without spectators, without clamour, without glory, without the great desire of victory, without the great fear of defeat, in a sickly atmosphere of tepid scepticism, without much belief in your own right, and still less in that of your adversary.
> (pp. 100–1)

Self-knowledge is here equated with 'unextinguishable regrets' and the self's life is characterised as 'that mysterious arrangement of merciless logic for a futile purpose' – 'a greater riddle than some of us think it to be'. So, after he has recovered and returned to

London, he is filled with scorn for the secure but self-ignorant lives about him: 'they could not possibly know the things I knew' (p. 102). Thus he allows the Fiancée to believe the integrity of the Kurtz she thought she knew: the truth of his self-disintegration would be 'too dark' for her to bear.

While ill, we are told, Marlow feared that 'within a hair's breadth of the last opportunity for pronouncement' he would 'have nothing to say' (p. 101) – unlike Kurtz. Kurtz's own pronouncement amounts to a single judgemental word: 'horror'. Marlow's 'inconclusive tale', years after those events, represents his real opportunity to pronounce – and he does so at length. Marlow's discourse, in fact, does far more justice to the subtleties of experience, because in addition to moral evaluation he bears witness to the complexities of self-fragmentation. His decisive encounter with Kurtz and its aftermath informs the very way he constitutes self-experience in the tale: 'in the midst of the incomprehensible' (p. 9); 'the dream-sensation, that commingling of absurdity, surprise and bewilderment' (p. 39); 'your own reality . . . what no other man can ever know' (p. 41); 'cut off from everything you had known once – somewhere – far away – in another existence perhaps' (p. 48): 'the mind of man is capable of anything – because everything is in it, all the past as well as all the future' (p. 52). Such awareness informs the manner as well as the matter of the story. If narrative purpose, coherence, rationality are founded on and speak the notion of integral selfhood, then vagueness, indirection and ambiguous symbolisation express awareness of self-fragmentation. The 'glow' versus 'kernel' opposition[34] can refer both to narrative method and the self-source that narrates – the latter defined and specific, the former a matter of 'misty halos . . . made visible by the spectral illumination of moonshine' (p. 8). Hence Marlow's narrative speaks the overdetermination and contradictoriness of modern selfhood and yields what is said up to various possibilities of interpretation. Frederick C. Crews, for instance, can read the tale as a disguised phantasy-journey into the maternal body. This is not a sufficient interpretation,[35] but it demonstrates the plenitude of possible meanings involved in Marlow's (Conrad's?) expressionistic self-dispersal into a densely connotative discourse of reverie. There are Freudian and Kleinian and Lacanian implications here, just as there are religious ones (the 'pilgrimage') and political–ideological ones which we can read through Marx and Althusser.[36] The fragmentation of Western

Dissolving Self

selfhood constitutes experience as a 'heart of darkness' and the disparate self-parts, or partial self-formulations, need to be seen through a variety of theoretical perspectives. However, to expand such theoretical implications into an exclusive, coherent allegory is precisely to negate the overwhelming message of the text: that selfhood is heterogeneous, mysterious, finally inexpressible.

Hence Marlow's own notorious self-contradictoriness. He hates a lie – but lies to the Fiancée. He loathes and abominates imperialism in general but has a good word to say about 'red' on the map. He deplores Kurtz's conduct and yet identifies himself closely with the man. He praises 'restraint' and the saving power of work and yet somehow conveys the power of 'darkness' as irresistible. He is abusively scornful of women but is obsessed with the feminine on a symbolic level.[37] He accuses his patient listeners of bourgeois superficiality and yet relies on their imaginative ability to fill out his meanings. And so on and so forth. We need not look for some coherent explanation of all this: Marlow is simply expressing the reality of self he encountered on the journey – that it is inconsistent, heterogeneous. And this is conveyed not only in Marlow's narration but in the text as a whole. We may read this as Conrad's personal confession of self-disintegration: but we can also grant him the authority of a Freud or Jung, as organising insights into universal experience – but in a specifically literary way. Thus we may see the text as the expression of a new vision of selfhood which can overflow (and undercut) the limitations of purely conceptual discourse.

But it is a profoundly sombre vision that *Heart of Darkness* conveys. Although the Russian harlequin may be said to offer a more heartening version of variable selfhood, it is Kurtz and Marlow, the pessimistic sceptic, who predominate; and the work of the tale is deconstructive rather than regenerative. Conrad's disintegration of the western self has something in common, one feels, with the fragmentation of the classical atom in modern physics – and perhaps even with its explosive fission. Darkness characterises this disintegration – and the 'dream sensation' is specifically one of nightmare. If at times the discourse overstresses restraint, this may be because, at the core, it construes self-truth in terms of apparent 'madness'. Fragmentation is here represented as breakdown. For the dreamer of self-order the implications may seem 'too dark – too dark altogether' (p. 111).

'A HUNDRED INDECISIONS'

T. S. Eliot, himself a deep admirer of *Heart of Darkness*, collaged his own prototype of self-dissolution while still a student at Harvard. The result was J. Alfred Prufrock, that notorious man-without-qualities. Prufrock's ironic love-song is a monologue in the form of a confession, and what it confesses is the inability of the self to connect, let alone act. The represented self is solipsistic and yet riven through with contrastive forces of socialisation; it is incoherent except in the consistent, obsessive reiteration of key phrases and images; it is subtly and specifically voiced, but that voice is characteristically constructed out of the discourses of others. Prufrock himself appears to resemble a 'catalytic chamber'[38] where social images, phrases, questions and allusions meet and combine in new ways – but without any rational cohesion. The poem is in the tradition of the dramatic monologue, yet Prufrock's shifting drift of interior figments is quite different from the strongly centralised characterisation of Browning and Tennyson, or the early Pound. We have less 'action in character'[39] than character in paralysed fragmentation. And the phenomenon cannot be adequately accounted for in terms either of Laforgue's Pierrots or James's heroes of over-refinement.

The uniqueness of the characterisation is signalled initially in relation to the Dantesque prefix – the only discourse, except the *humoresque* title, outside Prufrock's solipsistic field. Critics have tended to stress the similarity in situation of Prufrock and Guido da Montefeltro, but in terms of the construction of character they are in strong contrast. Guido, characterised from without, represents the self as mediaeval type, unitary in terms of its eternal spiritual state. He is simply the crooked counsellor – one hoist by his own petard, since the Pope had deceived him in turn. Prufrock, characterised from within, represents the self as Modernist vortex, fragmented in terms of an existential anguish among possibilities. His inner state resembles a 'heap of broken images' glimpsed in a 'wilderness of mirrors'. His endless 'visions and revisions' of self-parts prevent any possibility of our seeing him as an integrated whole. So if the mediaeval hell consists in the agony of perpetually remaining the self you once chose and lived, the modern hell lies in the anguish of never attaining an identity – not even an evil one.[40]

It is possible that Prufrock's characterisation owes something to

Dissolving Self

the philosophy of F. H. Bradley.[41] If not, Eliot must surely have been reminded of his own anti-hero when he read comments like the following:

> That various worlds of experience should be distinct, and, for themselves, fail to enter one into the other – where is the impossibility?
>
> (*Appearance and Reality*, p. 190)

> The universe we certainly feel is one, but that does not prevent it from appearing divided, and in separate spheres and regions. And between these diverse provinces of our life there may be no visible connection . . . The individual . . . may . . . have several worlds without rational unity, conjoined merely by co-existence in his own personality . . . It would be impossible that any man should have a world, the various provinces of which were quite rationally connected, or appeared always in system.
>
> (*Appearance and Reality*, p. 325)

At the same time, Eliot was aware both of Bergson's interest in the flux of subjective time (the intuition of which was best represented by *images*),[42] and of James's 'stream of consciousness' where at any one time the mind is 'a theatre of simultaneous possibilities'.[43] In the figure of Prufrock Eliot has already begun his deconstruction of 'the substantial unity of the soul'[44] and his representation of selves which 'can connect/Nothing with nothing'.

Prufrock's self-world is articulated in terms of suspended potentialities. Self-defining actions are hypothesised in a kind of temporal limbo: 'there will be time, there will be time'; 'Do I dare . . . ?'; 'Shall I say . . . ?'; 'And would it have been worth it . . ./If . . . ?'; 'Shall I part my hair behind?' Such self-queryings assert the self's possibilities while continually refusing actual self-commitment. Prufrock, we might say, is an existent contemplating a plenitude of possible essences. But, as Eliot was to put it in 'The Hollow Men': 'Between the idea/And the reality . . ./Falls the shadow'. It is a shadow which Prufrock can never, it seems, cross – like the young Virginia Woolf paralysed by the puddle in front of her feet.[45] Suspended in a world of hypothesis, Prufrock cannot commit himself to self-definition. Hence he characterises himself as contrastive lacks and impotences, frozen into immobility.

In addition to this he appears as a heterogeneity of passive experiences (whether fictive or factual is never quite clear). His selfhood is composed of disjunctive images: 'Narrow streets'; 'Yellow fog'; 'arms that are braceleted and white and bare'; 'coffee spoons'; 'ragged claws'; 'head . . . brought in upon a platter'; 'the eternal Footman'; 'the cups, the marmalade, the tea'; 'Lazarus, come from the dead'; 'mermaids singing, each to each'. The Imagistic method is used less in the Bergsonian manner to build up a strange wholeness than as a mode of deconstruction, which fragments a presumed whole (J. Alfred Prufrock) into disparate constitutive parts – 'the butt-ends of my days and ways'. That this is organised aesthetically – 'as if a magic lantern threw the nerves in patterns on a screen' – merely heightens, through repetition, the unlikeness of his various obsessions. The task to comprehend selfhood persists, but it can reach no end in terms of final self-establishment. As Eliot was to note in his doctoral dissertation, 'the life of a soul does not consist in the contemplation of one consistent world but in the painful task of unifying . . . jarring and incompatible ones'[46] (*Knowledge and Experience*, p. 147).

Because he is thus uncentred and fluid, Prufrock is particularly vulnerable to other people's versions of him. He speaks of preparing 'a face to meet the faces that you meet', but that does not save him from 'the eyes that fix you in a formulated phrase'. In proto-Sartrean fashion,[47] he has a mortal dread of the 'look' of others, which he feels can annihilate him. So self-conscious is he that he talks of his thinness and baldness as if they are observed by someone else and frequently collapses his train of thought into a presumed rebuff: 'that was not what I meant at all'. Above all he is frightened of the women who 'come and go' in his meandering consciousness. Lacking an identity, he is terrified of the glib identities the imagined female will attribute to him; anguished that he will be sexually rejected in terms that do not apply to the real him (whatever that might be). In the same way he is susceptible to differing cultural models of selfhood – Michelangelo, John the Baptist, Lazarus, Hamlet, the 'attendant lord': almost hypnotically, he tests them out as self-possibilities, even though his inner confusions do not remotely resemble the predicaments of these public exemplars. The 'overwhelming question' is never asked, let alone answered, but it could well be simply 'Who am I?' But just as he has no personal answer, so he will get no answer from others: whether the imaginary women, or historical and literary figures or, indeed, from the 'you' of the poem, whether as friend, alter ego, or just the reader.

And yet the open-endedness of the poem tempts the reader to try for answers. There is enough psychoanalytic material to attract the would-be therapist; enough religious allusion to tempt the amateur priest; enough urban alienation to lure the do-it-yourself sociologist. Everyone wants to put Humpty Dumpty together again; and in this sense the poem is a self-conscious tease. But no single explanation of Prufrock's state is sufficient to recuperate him as unitary self within a consistent rationale because he is overdetermined in too many ways. What we can learn from a careful study of the poem is not some final truth about his situation in the old terms, but simply that there is no final truth about selfhood, no hidden core, no (disguised) coherence. The poem effects a new type of poetic character, based on unresolved multiplicity, and a new kind of tentative discourse to help construct fragmentary man.

This novel discourse enacts the complexities of self-definition on the plane of language itself. It is less that Prufrock uses words with self-conscious subtlety to explore himself than that the machinery of words appropriates his whole experience of self and demonstrates the ultimate futility of such exploration. In short, Prufrock becomes dissolved into the structured heterogeneity of linguistic signification. His selfhood is dispersed in the variabilities of clausal positioning, dissipated in the connotative subversion of meanings, whirled away, finally, in the endless dance of 'difference'.[48] He tries to speak of himself but the words speak him, in coded signs. It is indeed 'impossible to say just what I mean'. He cannot say what he means to say: and he cannot say what the meaning of himself is. The play of words constantly takes him over. So his obsessiveness is involved in the obsessiveness of language itself – its iterative compulsion to transcend the limits of its arbitrary divisions and differences and grasp the real. His frantic search to attain self-identity mimics, and is involved in, the desperate quest of language to bridge the gap between word and world (more indeed than an 'I'!). For the reader, this double compulsion is only made tolerable by the way the writer distantiates his character's language in terms of poetic play. The celebrated Eliotic 'music' pleases intellectually because it mockingly foregrounds the capacity of words to live a life of their own and betray the intentions of the earnest speaker. Eliot's irony works through his 'auditory imagination' to expose how meaning becomes subverted by rhythmic repetition, by sound-similarities of quite different words, by the fatal attractions of rhyme. Eliot elaborates his wry melody out of the way self loses self in the entrapments of its own language habits.

Consider a short passage, for instance:

> And indeed there will be time
> To wonder, 'Do I dare?' and, 'Do I dare?'
> Time to turn back and descend the stair,
> With a bald spot in the middle of my hair –
> (They will say: 'How his hair is growing thin!')
> My morning coat, my collar mounting firmly to the chin,
> My necktie rich and modest, but asserted by a simple pin –
> (They will say: 'But how his arms and legs are thin!')
> Do I dare
> Disturb the universe?
> In a minute there is time
> For decisions and revisions which a minute will reverse.

If we consider the last line in itself, it is clear that Eliot is making play with the way one word can breed another by differential similarity and sound-attraction. 'Revision' is generated by its closeness to 'decision' rather than by a progression of pure meaning. Indeed, as meanings they cancel each other out. Further, 'reverse' is partly generated by the sound of 'revision' (with 'minute' providing the 'i'-sounds present in both prior words). On the plane of meaning, 'reverse' cancels out both the previous terms so that the whole line works in terms of the undercutting of provisional formulations. The word 'minute' here serves as a repetition of that in the previous line, just as the word 'time' there relates compulsively back to its many prior uses – a hypnotic iteration which again serves to unmake the very sense of time as sequence, flow, linearity. 'There will be time, there will be time' locates the itch to repetition and jingle at the clausal level, as does the echoed 'They will say. . .' in the quoted passage. The effect of such distantiations is to unsettle our sense of the rational adequacy of language to any question and to make us wonder how much of any discourse is, in fact, produced by the iteration of habitual rhetorical postures. It is this tendency to use the music of words to expose a stuttering or short-circuit of the sense which makes

Eliot's aesthetic play unique. When Keats used 'poesie' ('And diamonded with panes of quaint device'), the vowel music is employed to supplement the meaning – sensuous pleasure added to sense. Or when Tennyson used onomatopoeia ('The moan of doves in immemorial elms'), it is to give the illusion that in sound, as in sense, word and world are one. Eliot does the opposite. He uses the music to subvert our faith in the sense. It is a virtually Poststructuralist device. So too at times, the very child-like simplicity of the rhymes – 'Dare', 'stair', 'hair'; or 'thin', 'chin', 'pin', 'thin' – makes a satirical point about our way with language, or rather language's way with us. And such foregrounding of the constraints and traps of language is spread throughout the poem. 'Visions and revisions'; 'time for you and time for me'; 'days and ways'; 'wept and fasted, wept and prayed'; 'come back to tell you all, I shall tell you all'; 'worth it . . . worthwhile' – such self-reflexive jingles almost dominate the text. And the neurotic dependence on a continual repetition of key words like 'dare', 'time', 'all', 'question' or 'say' – frequently in repeated phrase patterns – again highlights and calls into question the way all discourse is repetitive and to a degree compulsive by its very nature.

But if all discourse is compulsive, the poem perhaps suggests that, to a sensitive mind, discourse about selfhood is liable to be even more so. It is in the attempt to account for inner states that we are most affronted and betrayed by the structural limitations of language – hence the final silence of mysticism. Prufrock's urge to get beyond 'formulated phrases' is all too human. In this he is representative, rather than some psychological freak. He aspires to a wholeness of identity that is the more fractured the more he talks about it. Like all of us he is finally overthrown by the 'intolerable wrestle/With words and meanings'.[49] Indeed, it is in 'human voices' that we 'drown'. As an idealist, Eliot would probably have resisted, in argument, the language-relative position which his poem suggests. He would have fallen back on 'immediate experience'[50] which was deemed to precede and underlie all conceptual formulations. Still, the poem poses issues that are not easily laid to rest. In what sense can the heterogeneity of experience be construed as self-wholeness? How far is even our experience constructed by language biases? How can we even talk about self without losing ourselves in the formulations of others and the arbitrary dispersals and deferrals of signification? In the light of such questions 'immediate experience' may well strike us as quite as shadowy and dubious as Bradley's Absolute.[51] If the main line of modern philosophy must now run from Bradley's denunciation of 'terms and relations',[52] through Wittgenstein's failed model of 'facts in logical space'[53] to the language-game theory of *Investigations* and so to Derrida and the deconstruction of logo-centrism,[54] then 'Prufrock' may stand as a far more substantial *philosophical* contribution than Eliot's thesis, quite apart from its aesthetic merit. In particular, it puts the whole issue of selfhood and what can be said of selfhood at issue. In this sense it is the traditional Western ego itself that is made to appear: 'Full of high sentence, but a bit obtuse;/At times, indeed, almost ridiculous –/Almost, at times, the Fool'.

'THE SMITHY OF MY SOUL'

If *Heart of Darkness* exemplifies the dissolution of a constituted self and 'Prufrock' expresses a paralysis of self-possibilities, then James Joyce's *Portrait of the Artist as a Young Man*[55] represents a progressive attempt to build a free self out of the plethora of influences, impulses and discourses which its hero experiences. The often-repeated word 'soul' bears a theologically freighted unitary implication. Yet the aesthetic soul to which Stephen aspires (and which the author himself achieves in the very writing act) is the opposite of unitary identity. Stephen's goal is total creative spontaneity. The soul is a 'smithy': and what it constantly forges and reforges is its own reality. As Stephen asserts: 'I will try to express myself in some mode of life or art as freely as I can and as wholly as I can' (p. 247). For its author *Portrait* constitutes just such an act of self-expression – or, indeed, self-creation. And the self which is founded by this existential appropriation is neither integral nor continuous, but a fluctuating plenitude of possibilities-in-anguish,[56] constantly beset by those external pressures – national, religious, familial – which seek to repress it into integrated definition.

This heterogeneous self-plenitude is perhaps most clearly expressed by the diary entries of the last few pages of the text (pp. 248–53). At this point of closure in a typical *Bildungsroman* we would expect confirmation of the hero's developed identity: in a *Künstlerroman* we might expect the 'artist' to have founded a distinctive style. *Portrait* gives us neither of these. There is not a consolidation, but a dissolving of identity; not personal narrative style, but a montage of jottings, representing variously: encounters, memories, dreams, sketches, fantasies, epiphanies, expostulations etc. The entries speak the fragmentary nature of self-experience – its resistance to unitary 'characterisation':

> *March 21, night.* Free. Soul free and fancy free. Let the dead bury their dead. Ay. And let the dead marry the dead.
>
> *March 22.* In company with Lynch followed a sizeable hospital nurse. Lynch's idea. Dislike it. Two lean hungry greyhounds walking after a heifer.
>
> *March 23.* Have not seen her since that night. Unwell? Sits at the fire perhaps with mamma's shawl on her shoulders. But not peevish. A nice bowl of gruel? Won't you now?
>
> *March 24.* Began with a discussion with my mother. Subject: B.V.M. Handicapped by my sex and youth. To escape held up relations between Jesus and Papa against those between Mary and her son . . .
>
> (pp. 248–9)

It is difficult to think of any other textual device – except mature Joycean stream-of-consciousness – which could represent the heterogeneity of interior self so graphically. In the last pages of the work, just prior to his departure from Dublin, Stephen is 'portrayed' as a Cubistic collage of miscellaneous impulses and awarenesses.

If we consider the text from this standpoint, it becomes evident that Stephen has never been represented in terms of self-coherence and self-consistency. He is continually shown in terms of rebellious and confused self-conflict: 'restless foolish impulses' (p. 67); 'den of monstrous images' (p. 90); 'the infuriated cries within him' (p. 92); 'from every part of his being unrest began to irradiate' (p. 161); 'a confused music within him as of memories and names which he was almost conscious of' (p. 168); 'his thinking was a dusk of doubt and self-mistrust, lit up at moments by the lightning of intuition' (p. 176); 'the tumults and unrest and longings in his soul' (p. 178); 'more mud, more crocodiles' (p. 250). For the commenting critic to construct such confusions in terms of a coherent value-scale – whether, say, Catholic, humanist or Freudian – would be to radically misrepresent the text's emphasis.

Stephen is not written as the centre of some theorisable predicament, but as a vortex where all possible descriptions are broken down. His struggle is not to find and found himself in any pre-given framework but to reject, in feverish struggle, all ideological pressures to constitute a self for him. The only perspectives he will avow will be wholly self-chosen; a literary founding in appropriated symbols, 'forged' out of experience.

But the struggle is not uniformly intense. Rather, it surfaces powerfully at sudden moments. A key fictive pattern is established in terms of external pressure, followed by acquiescence, resulting in unrest, which leads to rebellious reassertion of freedom. An example is the religious crisis in the central part of *Portrait*. The initial pressure arises from a previous (sexual) assertion of freedom; 'tears of joy and relief shone in his delighted eyes' (p. 101). During the Retreat Stephen's ecstasy becomes transformed into guilt as the Church attempts to recoup his selfhood into its system of values. The extended sermon (at times interiorised within Stephen's consciousness)[57] constitutes an extraordinary exemplification of discourse-as-ideology; words-as-social-power. The bulk of the sermon is directed straight at the reader, with all the weight of the Church's historical authority. Hence Stephen's repentance is initially experienced as a fictive resolution of an amplified *crise de conscience*, and the drift of the hero towards the priesthood is perceived as a *Bildungsroman* dénouement into 'maturity'. It is only with the renewed onset of Stephen's unrest, and his scorn at the priestly surrender of self-possibilities, that we realise we have participated in a false catharsis. After this comes a reiteration of selfhood as uncentred freedom:

> A feverish quickening of his pulses followed, and a din of meaningless words drove his reasoned thoughts hither and thither confusedly.
>
> (p. 161)

> He wondered . . . at the remoteness of his own soul from what he had hitherto imagined her sanctuary, at the frail hold which so many years of order and obedience had of him when once a definite and irrevocable act of his threatened to end for ever, in time and eternity, his freedom.
>
> (p. 162)

Dissolving Self

The moment is followed by his formulation of the 'symbol of the artist forging anew' (p. 169) and his vision of the girl on the strand which has him 'swooning into some new world . . . an opening flower . . . spread in endless succession to itself' (p. 173). 'Non serviam' resolves into 'Welcome, O life!'

This fictive structure typifies the major actions of the book: restriction; unrest; rebellion; reassertion. The sermon sequence is preceded (and set up) by Stephen's visit to his father's college. Here he succumbs to the pressure of the paternal past, focused in terms of Simon Dedalus's initials and the word 'Foetus'[58] – both carved in wood. It appears that Stephen will become reincorporated as an identity within the familial (indeed, Oedipal) line: 'mocking his . . . futile enthusiasms' (p. 91); 'I'm a better man than [Stephen] is any day of the week' (p. 95). But the hero's 'unrest' reasserts itself: 'an abyss of fortune or of temperament sundered him from them' (p. 96). His brief attempt to set up a renewed family 'commonwealth' dissipates along with his dwindling funds. Finally, he makes a fresh bid for freedom by going to a prostitute. A similar pattern is repeated after his break with the Church. Now it is the claims of Irish nationalism that threaten his freedom. But he gives up Gaelic lessons and foreswears the claim of 'race'. Later again, E.C. makes a bid for him but he rebels against her too. In his last meeting with her he speaks of 'his plans'. Her farewell releases him for his inchoate but determined project: 'She . . . said she hoped I would do what I said' (p. 252). Immediately after this comes a similar release from his mother and his declaration for experience and art. Stephen's progress, then, is written in terms of a recurring pattern of repression and reassertion. And each new rebellion dissolves the provisional identity that had preceded. Stephen's freedom progresses as continual self-deconstruction.

The site of this self-deconstruction is also constituted as a source. If the end-pronouncement is collated with the book's title and the dominant pattern of progression, then we see how the 'soul' that has been written proceeds out of the free authorial writing soul. The 'Artist' is the once-and-future wordsmith, split textually as, at the same time, experiencer, writer and founder of the illocutionary writing act ('to forge in the smithy of my soul'). The collagistic progression of textual styles which characterises the book[59] signals a free performer of language 'within or behind or above' the text itself. So while Joyce remains the supreme exponent of language relativism, and a major witness to the way selfhood is textually produced, he is also, in *Portrait*, the supreme advocate of the freedom which rebels and appropriates discourse for its own purposes. The last words of the book postulate a plenitude of free possibilities out of which he writes self as creative freedom.

This freedom is both delimited and deployed in the possibilities of language. In a sense, then, it is only relatively free: but Joyce freely chooses the medium (there is more than one kind of artist), and he clearly feels that the very finite rules of language constitute the condition in which he can exercise maximum self-play. As in Stephen's upbringing, freedom can only be deployed in relation to restrictions. So Stephen's world is built up out of a multiplicity of terms, images and symbols which, though rooted in common usage, create their own autonomous, free domain. Through such words, selfhood is expressed not as a centred identity but as an expanding web of interactive meanings. From the start, Stephen is represented in specific words whose contexts give them directly (and solely) personal meaning – 'baby tuckoo' contextualised in relation to 'father', the 'moocow', Betty Byrne, 'mother' and the words of his song 'O, the wild rose blossoms . . .' From this point onwards the hero's consciousness is both obsessed and expressed by the dance of words: 'he could see the names printed on the cocks. That was a queer thing' (p. 11); 'he wanted to cry quietly but not for himself: for the words' (p. 24); 'Words which he did not understand he said over and over to himself till he had learnt them by heart' (p. 62); 'his monstrous reveries came thronging into his memory. They too had sprung up before him . . . out of mere words' (p. 90); 'Did he then love the rhythmic rise and fall of words better than their associations . . . ?' (p. 167); 'vague words for a vague emotion' (p. 251). Stephen's 'character' is both created out of and dissolved within the specific words he chooses. His development is given as a continual recontextualising and reinteraction of key terms such as 'soul', 'white', 'bird', 'confess', 'father', 'green', 'water', 'girl', 'Dedalus', 'heart', 'eyes', 'Parnell', 'darkness', 'free', 'past', 'life', and so forth. The self-conscious repetition and contextual modification of such terms builds up a picture of selfhood as something various, expanding, contradictory; dispersed into the social and psychic realities out of which it effects its choices and growth. Like the epiphanic girl on the strand, Stephen is rendered as a signifying variety of symbols, vowel sounds and rhythms. Stephen, like the book, becomes the maze of Daedalus.

Portrait, we might say, both makes use of and leaves destroyed its own genre conventions. Just as *Ulysses* will employ the methods of both Realism and Symbolism to disintegrate them in the novel's wake, so the earlier work plays on *Bildungsroman* conventions only to leave them discredited. Most particularly, *Portrait* undoes the prime project of both 'life-novel' and biography – to render the development and consolidation of the integral self. The sense of selfhood is central to the book, as is the appearance of ongoing development. But the latter is ruptured by sudden metamorphoses in style, and by the way change is rendered as rebellion against influence rather than the product of it. Critics are free, of course, to reconstitute this as a subtler form of causal development, but that is not the text's representation of it. Similarly, the end result of such changes is not a coherent self founded upon its basis of conditioning, but a creative, fluid self which vows to invent the very race conscience out of which it should have proceeded. The writing self proclaims its own self-origin and chooses its own father (Daedalus), religion (art) and nation ('Bohemia'). It is the original sin of self-pride and the Oedipal project of pre-empting the father – both proclaimed as affirmative being. Involved in this existential proclamation is nothing less than the unmaking of the cardinal concepts of selfhood and development and all ways of writing or speaking which they entail. Joyce's specific use of narrative enforces the radical nature of this challenge. Instead of evolving growth we have periodic metamorphosis; instead of unfolding story we have discourse montage; instead of sequential 'argument' we have expanding recontextualisations of terms within a resonant symbolic field of textuality. By the end, even conventional grammar can be discarded: 'Free. Soul free and fancy free'; 'Cannot repent'; 'A race of clodhoppers!'; 'And mine?'; 'Eyes of girls among the leaves'; 'Away! Away! The spell of arms and voices: the white arms of roads, their promise of close embraces and the black arms of tall ships that stand against the room, their tale of distant nations.' Even before *Ulysses*, Joyce has involved breaking down the 'self' in the breaking-up of language. And by doing so, *Portrait* calls into question all the ways in which selfhood can be represented or even discussed.

The project of the book, then, is finally as heroic as it is ambitious. For Joyce, dissolving self is not surrender of sanity but expansion of possibility. Though the way is strait, and rebellion hard, Stephen and his author rejoice in refusing the legacy of identity. Security of selfhood, with all the repression it entails, is gladly left behind. The compound hero (Stephen/Joyce) embraces isolation and exile, existential anguish and the 'alterity' of language, in order to remain the creative plenitude he is. The novel expresses many moments of dark confusion and guilt, but the overall thrust is optimistic, energised and, at times, ecstatic. Where Conrad construes self-dissolution in terms of the vanity of human wishes, and Eliot as a mode of anguished paralysis, Joyce writes it as rebellion against the ideology of others and the embrace of Protean potentiality. Stephen is a hero of free consciousness and creative language performance. He accepts Modernist, heterogeneous selfhood and utters its positive challenge:

> I go to encounter for the millionth time the reality of experience and to forge in the smithy of my soul the uncreated conscience of my race.

3
Self at War

'I Found Myself Dividing into Parts'[1]

If exceptional writers like Conrad, Eliot and Joyce were beginning to 'dissolve' Western selfhood from the turn of the century onwards, it was the 1914–18 War which precipitated many less hypersensitive individuals into the existential reality of self-fragmentation. Much of the terminology which could be used about crisis in the self had a literal meaning in battle experience – an experience which in its modern, mechanised form was shared by millions of citizen–soldiers:

> To die from a bullet seems to be nothing; parts of our being remain intact; but to be dismembered, torn to pieces, reduced to pulp, this is a fear that flesh cannot support and which is fundamentally the great suffering of the bombardment.[2]

'Torn to pieces', or 'fall apart', 'break down', 'disintegrate', 'shock', 'fragmentation' – all such words found their direct combat meaning. A key metaphor was contributed by the force of the shell-burst, so much so that 'soldiers suffering from psychiatric illness were initially diagnosed as having "shell shock", in the belief that the patient's brain had been concussed by the proximity of an exploding shell'.[3] And, by a figurative extension, the neurotic brain itself could be described as 'shattered', or in a state of 'disintegration' – as if the explosion came from within. Neither the fiction of unitary selfhood nor an army bureaucracy structured to conform to it in terms of 'duty' and 'responsibility' could easily assimilate what the new warfare demonstrated about interior states. Hence 'the process of recognising that there was such a thing as psychiatric breakdown was a painful one'.[4] Nevertheless, the Great War highlighted the reality that was there to be recognised. In terms of the literary precursors examined in the last chapter, it was as if, *in extremis*, human nature was indeed imitating art.

Richard Holmes, whose book *Firing Line* I have been quoting, shows how, in spite of the prejudice against 'shell shock' cases, the engaged armies slowly came to terms with combat neurosis and developed facilities to deal with it. The change came none too soon. In 1917 psychiatric admissions in the British Expeditionary Force, for instance, were four per 1000 troops as opposed to one per 1000 for the civilian population.[5] Such instances of breakdown among the Empire's 'heroes' could least of all be ignored by literary men fighting at the front, even if their notions of selfhood had been formed by Wordsworth, Kipling or Haggard rather than the Austrian, Dr Freud. The poems, memoirs and novels generated by the Great War are strewn with descriptions, evocations and anecdotes of psychiatric cases. Three key poets – Owen, Graves and Sassoon – had direct knowledge of both the experience of battle neurosis and the work of Dr W. H. R. Rivers with 'shell shock' patients at Craiglockhart War Hospital. And yet, in most ostensible 'war literature' breakdown and neurotic symptoms are strangely distanced. They are acknowledged, with horror, as an example of the dehumanising nature of modern warfare, but – however the writer may have suffered in a similar way – these realities are seldom allowed to infect the security of the writing subject. This is not only true of the more reflective memoirs, it also characterises most of the poetry, for all its *physical* immediacy. In Ivor Gurney's 'Strange Hells', for instance, the hells 'within the minds War made' are described as 'not so humiliatingly afraid / As one would have expected'.[6] The poem then proceeds to praise the pluck of the Gloucestershires who sang under bombardment and, after a wry consideration of their post-war fates, it ends quite romantically: 'the heart burns – but has to keep out of face how heart burns'. Owen's 'Mental Cases' does not so much diminish the realities of battle neurosis as objectivise them, almost to the point of caricature. The 'cases' are depicted from a distanced viewpoint: 'what slow / Panic gouged these chasms round their fretted sockets?'; or 'this hilarious, hideous, / Awful falseness of set-smiling corpses'.[7] The poem is an important one in that it focuses on the reality of battle breakdown, and there is an attempt to connect these 'shadows' with the communal experience: 'Surely we have perished / Sleeping, and walk in hell; but who are these hellish?' Nevertheless Owen's objectivised, craft-conscious realism somehow marginalises the men's experience as extreme and grotesque. They are like Conrad's blacks in the hollow of death, but the narrator is no Marlow whose own selfhood is under threat. In such a case, Owen's very compassion seems to operate as a means of defence, even of denial. His own felt terror, loathing, confusion, hysteria or anger are all sublimated in his project: 'the poetry is in the pity'.[8]

There are, of course, exceptions to this generalisation about war literature, some of which will constitute the main matter of this chapter. However, most of the familiar texts by combatants do tend to distance the reality of battle neurosis, whether by reduction, like Gurney, or by altruistic compassion, like Owen, or by protest or satire or humorous anecdotage. There are at least two possible explanations for this: the first is that the project of many writers to condemn the Great War could not rest on a writing position which incorporated emotional splitting and confusion; the second is that, for those who suffered even partial breakdown, writing tended to become, itself, a form of therapy, asserting the reconstitution of selfhood.[9] But also there were those, like Ivor Gurney, so ravaged by their experiences at the front that they ceased writing for publication altogether, and ended their days in tragic and solitary torment.

But while combatants did not, typically, develop a discourse of self-fragmentation, their non-combatant literary colleagues (often friends) did so quite thoroughly. Many of these, of course, were among those who had previously pioneered the expression of self-dissolution. But the war seemed to increase their urgent efforts to rewrite selfhood, resulting at times in proto-Dadaist or pre-Surrealist formulations.[10] It is as if the non-combatants took upon themselves the task of representing psychic horrors which the combatant writers were fated to live and could afterwards rarely bear to face directly. It was Ezra Pound, after the death of friends like Gaudier-Brzeska and T. E. Hulme, who wrote some of the most poignant lines on self-disintegration at the front:

> fortitude as never before
> frankness as never before,
> disillusions as never told in the old days,
> hysterias, trench confessions,
> laughter out of dead bellies.[11]

Similarly, D. H. Lawrence's *Women in Love*, while largely concerned to trace back into Edwardian origins the traumas of the home front, writes into the depressions, confusions and self-doubts of his main characters something of the psychic tensions of battle.[12] In *The Waste Land* Eliot gives his passive male the words of a returned veteran:

> I think we are in rats' alley
> Where the dead men lost their bones . . .
>
> I remember
> Those are pearls that were his eyes.[13]

And in *Mrs Dalloway* Virginia Woolf creates, in the person of the traumatised ex-soldier Septimus Warren Smith, a portent resonant within twenties' society as a whole. The metaphor of incandescent blast is central:

> The violent explosion which made Mrs Dalloway jump and Miss Pym go to the window and apologize came from a motor car which had drawn to the side of the pavement . . .
> There the motor car stood, with drawn blinds, and upon them a curious pattern like a tree, Septimus thought, and this gradual drawing together of everything to one centre before his eyes, as if some horror had come almost to the surface and was about to burst into flames, terrified him. The world wavered and quivered and threatened to burst into flames.
>
> (pp. 16–18)[14]

But if it was the non-combatants who centralised battlefield breakdown, and made of it a metaphor of the modern mind in general, they were able to do so because war poetry, in particular, had established 'shell shock' as a real phenomenon.[15] In later years, too, some ex-combatants were able to write their battle experience more directly, in turn borrowing from non-combatant authors, and representing the experience of the front through specifically Modernist techniques. *Parade's End* and *In Parenthesis* were, as we shall see, full-scale attempts to express the realities of war in experimental terms. And just as Sassoon, in his trench poems, could at times suspend his aristocratic irony to express genuine neurotic confusion (see below, pp. 51–8), so Graves, in the twenties, explored psychic fragmentation in poems like 'The Pier Glass', 'Down', and 'In Procession'.[16] These poems drew directly on the 'neurasthenia' Graves acknowledged as his legacy from the war. In writing them he wanted to 'help the recovery of public health of mind, as well as my own, by the writing of "therapeutic" poems; and to increase their efficacy by a study of the nature of poetry from "subjective evidence"'.[17] The poems make use of personal dream imagery and exploit Romantic mind scenarios to achieve a near-Modernist spectacle of self-disintegration. At the core of each poem is a lifeless chaos: 'abstract, confusing welter' in 'The Pier Glass'; the 'secret void' of 'Down'; the 'rambling limitless' hell-town of 'In Procession'. Each in its way explores a 'huddle of dirty woes'. 'Down' exemplifies Graves's 'therapeutic' probing of the fragmentation within self. It is a night poem, set in a manse which symbolises the mind. A sick man is awoken in the small hours by the chime of a clock and a cock's crowing. To avoid the 'sad superstition' these set in train, he ponders childhood tales – 'half-riddles, answerless . . . / Lost bars of music tinkling with no sense'. In the next section the man is 'sinking', a younger but more desperate Gerontion, lost in the entrails of his thought. He plunges down into unconscious layers of the mind, figured as a descent through the floors of the house:

> . . . stairs, cellars,
> Through deep foundations of the manse, still sinking
> Through untamed earth.

The 'abracadabra' of rent thought and language precipitates him 'weeping, down, drowned, lost' in an earthy scenario reminiscent of Owen's 'Strange Encounter':

> . . . penetrate with sliding ease
> Dense earth, compound of all ages, granite ribs
> and groins.

There is here a weird amalgam of bayonet violence, (homo-?)sexual fantasy, the iconography of hell and wormy circumstance. It is a place where selfhood is spent, lost, dissipated into the images which haunt it. The invocation of childhood creativity cannot effect self-recovery for the sufferer. Still falling, he is whirled off in the flux of unconscious streams to the 'flame-exits of this terrible earth'. It ends inconclusively, 'O spirit . . .': as in 'The Castle',[18] there is 'no way out'. The poem, then, is one of fragmentation and, almost, of self-annihilation. War experience has acted as the detonator whereby mental surfaces are broken up, apocalypse is discovered below the 'manse' cellars and disintegration is plumbed beneath layers of defensive self-ordering.

Graves's friend T. E. Lawrence was concerned, at key moments in *Seven Pillars of Wisdom*, to account for the ravages in selfhood effected by a very different type of warfare. Most of the book is concerned to chronicle the events of the Arab revolt, but, as Andrew Rutherford has shown,[19] it is a work which straddles differing genres and a neo-Wordsworthian or Conradian element of subjective confession is vital to the richness of the whole. Lawrence defined his project in varying and contradictory ways. But although he excluded the personal and psychic element in *Revolt in the Desert* (thereby making it a less interesting book), he retained it in the longer and more famous work. He once described it as a 'sort of introspection epic' and later, in a typical outbreak of self-loathing, condemned it as 'hysterical' and 'full of the neurosis of the war'.[20] For most readers, surely, Lawrence's fluctuating self-revelations are at least as interesting as his depictions of the excitement and horror of the campaign. Yet this division is largely false, in that the tormented confessions result from the nature of the action he undertook, and the specifics of battle experience were the stuff out of which his avowed self-divisions were made. As he admitted, there was an inherent ambivalence in his chosen role as Englishman among Arabs, and artistically inclined intellectual among fighting men which, in the cockpit of battle, could only be self-disjunctive. Hence the brooding high rhetoric, the simultaneous presence of confession and suppression, in his first chapter:

> By day the hot sun fermented us; and we were dizzied by the beating wind . . . We were a self-centred army . . . devoted to freedom . . . We had sold ourselves into its slavery . . . We lived always in the stretch or sag of nerves, either on the crest or in the trough of feeling . . . Gusts of cruelty, perversions, lusts ran lightly over the surface without troubling us . . . What now looks wanton or sadic seemed in the field inevitable . . . Bedouin ways were . . . a death in life . . . (there are things not to be repeated in cold blood for very shame) . . . Sometimes these selves would converse in the void; and then madness was very near.[21]

In the general narrative such renderings of action through a charged self-consciousness occur at specific points: his description of the dead Turks at Aba el Lissan, for instance, or of the bodies in the hospital at Damascus. But at times, too, the authorial self emerges out of description to effect, as Lawrence put it, 'a standing court martial on myself' (p. 583). Such a moment occurs in Chapter LXXX:

> Now I found myself dividing into parts. There was one which went on riding wisely, sparing or helping every pace of the wearied camel. Another hovering above and to the right bent down curiously, and asked what the flesh was doing. The flesh gave no answer, for, indeed, it was conscious only of a ruling impulse to keep on and on; but a third garrulous one talked and wondered, critical of the body's self-inflicted labour, and contemptuous of the reason for effort.
>
> (p. 461)

The passage is important because it breaks through Lawrence's habitual tendency to represent internal chaos in terms of dualism ('the man who could see things through the veils at once of two customs, two educations, two environments' (p. 30)). But just as significant is the self-reckoning he describes on his thirtieth birthday in Chapter CIII. As elsewhere, he confesses to feeling fraudulent, and he writes of his 'detached self always eyeing the performance from the wings in criticism' (p. 580). He then describes the notes out of which *Seven Pillars* was written: 'Instead of facts and figures, my note-books were full of states of mind, the reveries and self-questioning induced or educed by our situations'. He continues, 'always feelings and illusion were at war within me' (p. 581), and concludes 'the truth was I did not like the "myself" I could see and hear' (p. 584). What is apparent in the whole chapter is that on this his thirtieth year to heaven, or hell, Lawrence's 'myself' is wholly at issue. His 'citadel of integrity' is radically cracked and ahead now lie all the ambivalences of his advocacy of the Arab cause, his attempted self-immolation in the RAF as a corporal, and his bizarre, masochistic sexual practices of the later years. Lawrence's exotic desert war, just like the mechanised, mass war of the western front, acted not as an initiation into confirmed selfhood but as a rite-of-passage into self-brokenness.

Yet the desert campaign did spare Lawrence some of the more sociological contradictions of organised army life evidenced both in memoirs like Blunden's *Undertones of War* and works like *Parade's End* and *In Parenthesis*. In his book *No Man's Land* Eric J. Leed writes persuasively about the various self-disintegrative forces operating within the First World War armies. The unexpected scale of mechanisation, the gulf between home and front, the general 'proletarianisation'[22] of front-line labour, the long confinements under ground, the suppression of aggressive impulses in a war of defence – all these and similar factors acted to break down the idealistic men who came to fight. Leed writes: 'the war experience was nothing if not an experience of radical discontinuity on every level of consciousness' (p. 3); and again: 'there is abundant evidence . . . that the war imposed upon its inhabitants a restrictive and fragmented consciousness' (p. 117). Much of the evidence he uses to demonstrate such proposals is German. As we shall see, there are English literary texts which also bear out this notion that not only battle neurosis but also the whole process of self-incorporation into army life had a profoundly disruptive effect upon men. This was particularly so for middle-class men – the kind of combatants who were to write about the war. Brought up in a secure bourgeois individualism, they found themselves simultaneously homogenised into a vast fighting machine and subjected, on the front, to extreme fighting conditions which fragmented them internally. Battle anxiety crumbled them into disparate and grisly memories, phantasies, dreams. But, already, selfhood had been rent and dispersed into corporate tensions, beginning with the ego bombardment of parade-ground abuse and continuing as a daily self-alienation in nerve-testing complexities of function, labour and responsibility. Officers, most traumatically, found themselves in physical conditions which only miners and ditch-diggers were approximately familiar with:[23] they had to operate simultaneously as labourers and inspirers, companions and leaders, warriors and substitute parents, in conditions where the social tensions of civilian society were focused and intensified – and all in a narrow strip of trench-land which the first really industrialised and total war dictated as the arena of decision. Here, for instance, is Ford's officer-hero:

> Hundreds of thousands of men tossed here and there in that sordid and gigantic mud-brownness of mid-winter . . . By God, exactly as if they were nuts wilfully picked up and thrown over the shoulder by magpies . . . But men. Not just populations.

Men you worried over there. Each man a man with a backbone, knees, breeches, braces, a rifle, a home, passions, fornications, drunks, pals, some scheme of the universe, corns, inherited diseases, a greengrocer's business, a milk walk, a paper stall, brats, a slut of a wife . . . The Men: the Other Ranks! And the poor —— little officers. God help them. Vice-Chancellor's Latin Prize men . . .[24]

Such 'Latin Prize men' directly and personally experienced what Richard Aldington, in *Death of a Hero*, called 'the tremendous revolution in everything, of which the war was a cause or symptom' and like his hero, George Winterbourne, they lived with 'hallucinated memories where images and episodes met and collided like superimposed films'.[25] In addition, soldiers like Owen and Sassoon were emotionally split between conscience and responsibility – both loathing the war, both loyally returning to the front to be with their men. The Great War, then, enforced a twofold message on those who were to produce its literature: the final fragmentariness of the self under fire, and the socialism of the serving self as self-distribution into disparate army roles and functions. Both are expressed in war literature. And both have their legacy in post-war Modernism where the disjunctive self is simultaneously the socially dispersed self. The 'waste land' is the post-war version of No Man's Land, and the 'hollow men' are civilian versions of Aldington's 'lost souls . . . in a new Inferno'[26] or Owen's sad 'shadows'. The message is continuous:[27] 'I can connect/Nothing with nothing'.

'BROKEN AND MAD'

Critical accounts of Siegfried Sassoon's poetry tend, inevitably, to trace the change in his attitude to war and the development of a more Realist and ironic style. Jon Silkin, for instance, quotes Robert Graves to indicate 'how much Sassoon's earlier attitude to the war changed, and how dramatically, when seen in relation to a background that seemed unlikely to equip him to deal with war and to make a substantial protest against it'.[28] The change is indeed dramatic and based on first-hand battle experience. The aspect of that change which is relevant here is the way his war experiences radically modified his sense of the self and led him, in some quite unusual poems, to represent selfhood in terms of splitting, confusion and emotional inconsistency. Obviously many of the satiric poems, with their clear note of protest, are not very pertinent, for they are predicted on an integral attitude – disgust at the way the war was being perpetuated – which disguises the radical uncertainty he felt in himself. Yet, no doubt, the intensity of his anti-war conviction, and the effectiveness of some of his protest itself, sprang from the radical effects both front-line and hospital experience had in fragmenting his earlier *Fox Hunting Man* persona and searching out the conflicts within him. It is by paying attention to a few poems that express the brokenness of selfhood, then, that Sassoon's contribution can be better understood, and that his pioneering work in representing 'shell shock' neurosis can be placed within the general Modernist discourse about the mind.

Predictably, the earlier poems express a selfhood firmly in possession of itself: unitary, continuous, rational and at ease even under pressure:

> War is our scourge; yet war has made us wise,
> And, fighting for our freedom, we are free.
>
> ('Absolution', April–Sept., 1915)[29]

No ontological self-doubt here, and no neurotic disintegration. A year later he wrote to Graves:

> And I puff my pipe, calm-hearted,
> Thinking how the fighting started,
> Wondering when we'll ever end it,
> Back to Hell with Kaiser send it.
>
> ('A Letter Home')

A more thoughtful note here – but no fragmentation. In 'At Carnoy' he says 'And I'm content'; and 'A Letter Home' ends: 'War's a joke for me and you / While we know such dreams are true!' But it was also in 1916 that the presence of another version of selfhood is registered. In 'Died of Wounds' he writes of a soldier who 'raved' in the bed opposite his before dying:[30] 'And calling out for "Dickie". "Curse the Wood. / It's time to go. O Christ, and what's the good?"'

Dreams here are no longer a romantic ideal realm. They can take over the self, as here, in terms of lurid images and distracted cries. In 'A Night Attack' the youngster who laughs and toasts his companions is not taken at face value: '(Terror and ruin lurk behind his gaze)'. And 'Christ and the Soldier', later regarded by Sassoon as 'an ambitious failure', was written when he was 'altogether confused, and became increasingly disillusioned and rebellious'.[31] Sassoon was beginning to experience in himself the neurotic symptoms he had witnessed in others. His hospital poem 'Stretcher Case' expressed a desperate attempt to hold selfhood together:

> Feebly now he drags
> Exhausted ego back from glooms and quags
> And blasting tumult, terror, hurtling glare,
> To calm . . .

In 'The Road' only the dead are exempt from the 'reeling brain' mocked by dreams.

But 1917 was, of course, the year that constituted Sassoon's personal watershed and poetic *annus mirabilis*. His celebrated 'Statement Against the Continuation of the War' marked his courageous act of personal rebellion and protest. The resulting compromise, his stay at Craiglockhart War Hospital, was even more important for this study, for there he met the psychologist[32] Dr W. R. H. Rivers. This meeting was crucial in revealing Sassoon's inner feelings to his conscious self and freeing him to write out of his own sense of self-disintegration. In *Sherston's Progress* Sassoon avows the importance of Rivers to him: 'My definite approach to mental maturity began with contact with the mind of Rivers'.[33] But although he writes of himself as Rivers' 'patient', he terms the therapy sessions 'these friendly confabulations every evening' (p. 518). The emphasis is on their differing views of the war, on the advice to practise golf, and on Rivers' indirect 'arguments'. The autobiography is written from a position of rebuilt selfhood, and it is only through hints in the text, along with certain poems written at the time of their meeting, that it becomes clear how strong a transference situation had been built up in the sessions. This is clearest in the near-schizoid 'Letter to Robert Graves' (24 July 1918):

> O Rivers please take me. And make me
> Go back to the war till it break me.
> Some day my brain will go BANG.

At that time Rivers was acting as both (unconscious) father and mother substitute for the 'orphaned' Sassoon: on the one hand a screen onto which male admiration could be projected ('that intense survival of his human integrity', p. 534); on the other a fountain from which sympathy and comfort could be drawn: 'his name had obvious free associations with pleasant landscapes and unruffled estuaries' (p. 517);[34] 'he understood me better than I understood myself' (p. 518). During his stay in this 'museum of war neuroses' Sassoon was, doubtless, right in deciding 'I haven't broken down; I've only broken out' (p. 523): but his times with Rivers also revealed to him how uncertain is the front-line between self-possession and traumatic self-dispersal, and occasioned in him upsurges of strong feeling which were never wholly under control.

'Repression of War Experience' (July 1917) and 'Survivors' (October 1917) both speak quite directly of the fear of self-fragmentation. The second has distanced the experience (and thus given it powerful imagistic presentation) by using externalised characters – battle survivors – as objective correlative. The descriptions ('stammering, disconnected talk'; 'eyes that hate you') are reinforced by empathetic evocation of emotional states – 'haunted nights'; 'dreams that drip with murder'. The title suggests probable representation of physical disability and suffering – Owen's 'Disabled' with a larger cast. But the poem is more like his friend's 'Mental Cases' and its aim is to image what Ivor Gurney called 'strange Hells within the minds War made'. The pitiful condition of these men signifies essentially internal ravages. The 'old scared faces' are the outward and visible sign of 'haunted nights', tormented by the kinds of dream Sassoon later described in *The Complete Memoirs*.[35] Similarly, the 'disconnected talk' springs directly from the 'shattering' of the men's pride. Hence the disturbing ambiguity of 'learning to walk'. It is surely not that all have been crippled physically, but rather that the 'boys' have been traumatised back into infantile states so that even basic human physical functions must be relearnt. The pre-battle ego ('grim and glad') has been shattered. The survivors are now 'broken and mad'.

But the poetry is not in the pity and the poet is not concerned with it either, at least not in an Owenesque way. For where Owen's characteristic verse establishes a coherent and humane authorial position ('These are men whose minds the dead have ravished', 'Mental Cases'), Sassoon allows his writing position to be invaded and fragmented by the horrors he describes. The irony is unsettled and unsettling:

> Of course they're 'longing to go out again', –
> These boys with old, scared faces, learning to walk.
> They'll soon forget their haunted nights; their cowed
> Subjection to the ghosts of friends who died . . .

No wonder John Middleton Murry wrote 'Mr Sassoon's mind is a chaos'[36] and Winston Churchill was represented as commenting that the poems in *Counter-Attack* were 'cries of pain wrung from soldiers during a test to destruction'.[37] But if for Murry this did not generate the 'harmony and the calm of soul' he associated with the poetic, then so much the worse for his aesthetic. The intensity and integrity of such a poem lies precisely in the way anger, compassion, horror, scorn, lament and protest are mingled uncertainly in the tone. Sassoon (and like Owen in this) is less interested in 'the poetry' than in truth-telling. And neurotic changeability, emotional confusion, unstable irony is the essence of the truth he tells. So the poem effects a peculiar distantiation of its surface phrases: it foregrounds its own implications in inadequate verbal postures. '"Longing to go out again"' is given its ironic quotation marks, but in a sense these could be applied almost anywhere: 'soon "get well"' and '"proud / Of glorious war"'; but also '"shock" and "strain"', '"cowed/Subjection"', or even 'shattered all "their pride"'. The text is in danger of providing its own deconstruction kit, for words are shown to be finally inadequate to the intensities which inform the poem's writing. In *Sherston's Progress* Sassoon remarks 'one could easily imagine "anxiety neurosis" as a staple front-line witticism' (p. 524), and a similar uneasy discordance between jargon, emotional realities and the attempt to express the latter more truly is enacted throughout the poem. The final epigram only works because 'broken and mad' – an inadequate description in itself – has been evidenced in the uncertainties of the text.

'Repression of War Experience' writes out such torsions from the 'inside': the strategy might nowadays be called confessional. Like the later, more diffuse, 'Letter to Robert Graves' (see below, p. 115) the poem expresses its uncomfortable self-truths in terms of bizarre imagery and textual discontinuities. As Jon Silkin has noted,[38] the moth that 'bumps and flutters' suggests the poet's mental state – and indeed it also suggests the movement of the text itself. For, even more than in 'Survivors', the poem enacts its own contradictory impulses through foregrounded discordances. The use of anacoluthon is one means of achieving this: ' –/No. no, not that, –'; '. . ./Why won't it rain? . . .'; 'O yes, you would . . .' The text is constructed in terms of radical self-conflict: denial followed by sudden avowal, and all precariously articulated in a language which half-mocks its own articulations: 'What silly beggars they are'; 'look what a steady hand'; 'Books, what a jolly company they are': 'You'd never think there was a bloody war on'. This is not a poem which offers a coherent 'criticism' of the war. As Sassoon expostulated in 1965, when pestered by anthologists and critics, 'Why can't they realize that the war poems were improvised by an impulsive, intolerant, immature young creature, under extreme stress of experience?'[39] What he seemed not to realise, however, was that their power and experimental achievement sprang directly from this condition of their writing. The young Sassoon's 'improvising' enables the poetry to capitalise on its very denials and anarchic associations, and so achieve a novel and exemplary representation. The rationalisation of the 'crowds of ghosts among the trees' as 'old men with ugly souls' makes visible and eloquent the tensions attendant on 'repression'. He writes: 'Not people killed in battle – they're in France' and thereby precisely avows the psychic reality which is overtly refused – the war dead are not in France, but living presences in the room. At such a point we can sense the Oedipal intensity of Sassoon's scorn for the 'old men' he felt were manipulating the war for their own ends. His 'view' of the war is emotionally sited in the fear of self-destruction (and/or castration) at the hands of villainous father-figures – a fear physically justified because of his self-identification with dead companions. Such psychic material is allowed to disrupt the rhetorical coherence of the poem at various points and introduce irrational but emotionally charged connections: 'glory' imaged as 'liquid flame', 'right as rain' invoking a phantasy thunderstorm, guns which 'thud, thud, thud' and yet are described as 'whispering'.

Quite overtly, the poem articulates an argument between different parts of the mind: 'Come on: O *do* read something' or 'why, you can hear the guns'. The scenario establishes an external reality –

room, candle, moth, pipe, books etc. – but the development of the poem evidences the peripheral status of such in terms of the mental drama. So the room becomes a psychic space where soldiers jabber, rain sluices the dark, ghosts move among trees and guns mutter incessantly. At the same time, the poem generates a suspenseful imminence: 'The garden waits for something that delays'. As in Eliot's 'Gerontion' and, crucially, in *The Waste Land*,[40] this imminence is imaged in terms of waiting for rain. But Sassoon's rain is not a symbol of renewal through fertility, but of cleansing and even of judgement, expressed with almost psychotic intensity: 'bucketsful of water to sluice the dark, / And make the roses hang their dripping heads'. The title of the poem came from a lecture given by Rivers in 1917[41] and the poem itself was written at Sassoon's home at Weirleigh – hence at a time when he was separated from his psychological mentor. In view of Sassoon's play with the liquidity of Rivers' name (see above), we may well feel that more is involved here than a muggy night. The pent-up emotions in the poem demand a cleansing release – the kind of psychic freeing that only Rivers could guide him to at this time. Was 'right as rain' a phrase Rivers used perhaps? . . .Whether or no, the immediate collage splice to 'Why won't it rain?' transfers us to the vision of liquid cleansing which seems quite central. In the absence of such a release, the dead ghosts continue to plod across the poet's brain, the voices of arguing selves quarrel on and the poem ends in a kind of migraine of remembered explosions: 'I'm going stark, staring mad because of the guns'. In its own way this poem too is saying: 'O Rivers please take me'.

Craiglockhart War Hospital grounds also, perhaps, contribute to the imagery of the poem. The front line of battle was characterised by the devastation of plant life, so the haunting double image – 'jabber among the trees' and 'crowds of ghosts among the trees' – seems to embody Sassoon's terror at some of the sights he had seen among the 'anxiety neurosis' cases. Clearly at this time he felt that he was close to breakdown himself. The use of the trees here is canny[42] and powerful enough for Virginia Woolf – who had reviewed Sassoon's war poems[43] – to transplant the image quite directly, I believe, into her depiction of the shell-shocked Septimus Warren Smith in Regent's Park (*Mrs Dalloway*).[44] At the same time a degree of poignance is involved in the poem being set in Sassoon's room at home. The traumatic memories of the war are the more powerful because they co-exist with (and emotionally engulf) long familiar object companions – the candle, the pipe, Sassoon's books. Indeed, his war experience even transforms the loved books into a semblance of fighting men, a 'company', standing at ease on the shelves, 'dressed' in dim brown – before the poem clutches back to the realistic, with 'and black, and white, and green'. The self who sits among these objects and 'listens to the silence' is indeed a radically different self from that of the aristocratic youth who once went off to hounds from the same room. In fact, as the poem shows, he has become many different selves warring one with the other and speaking the different discourses of Weirleigh, Craglockhart, London and the Flanders front. 'I'm going crazy' is the poem's conclusion, 'stark, staring mad' – phrases whose army-slang banality emphasises the final impossibility of expressing the intensities and the dynamics of self-fragmentation in words.

Sassoon, then, is a 'war poet': but in being so, in combining in his verse a literary sensitivity with the dogged honesty to experience of a front-line soldier, he is able to cast a new light on the complexities of selfhood. He was no natural self-doubter and relativist, like Conrad or Eliot; hence what his work evidences is the cumulative bombardment of a tough and courageous ego until it begins to fragment into the contradictory impulses within. But the courage remained. We know from Graves how courageous he could be in battle; his statement against the war shows his political courage; but his final courage lay in publishing poems which acknowledge neurotic self-division by exploring 'shell shock' both from without and from within. In literary–historical terms, it is worth noting how innovatory this writing is in its awareness of modern psychological insights and terms, and how 'Modernist', in fact, it feels at times. By 'improvising' his verse in the pursuit of self-truth, Sassoon also helped to shift the dead weight of traditional treatments of selfhood and pioneer a new, more self-aware poetic discourse.

'"NO BRAIN COULD STAND MORE"'

Ford Madox Ford's *Parade's End* is a bizarre and magnificent sequence of three (or is it four?)[45] novels in which the 'condition of England' translates the metaphor of war into nightmare reality. The trilogy, in particular (*No More Parades, Some Do Not, A Man Could Stand Up*), is stylishly polished yet wayward in control, 'impressionistically' indirect to create powerful 'progression d'éffet': compelling, grotesque, hilarious, sentimental and sombre in implication. It is a work obsessed with the probability of madness and obsessional in its defensive insistence that the hero, Christopher Tietjens, does not succumb to the fragmenting pressures which beset him. Tietjens remains at the core – even in the fourth novel, *Last Post*, where he scarcely appears – as a model of the unitary self, egregiously sponsored by an authorial narration, which nevertheless contrives, almost in spite of itself, to reveal his repressive inadequacies. A man of exemplary 'brilliance', encyclopaedic in knowledge, Christ-like in patience and forbearance, militant only in defence of decency, he is assailed by twentieth-century forces which are constantly on the brink of breaking him into pieces. He remains whole and is able to rebuild his life and is thus vindicated: but not without a corresponding narrative implication that he is largely lacking in self-knowledge, absurd in many of his convictions, impulsive in small matters and negligent or impotent in large. Ford preserves his hero from the disintegrative forces that theaten him; but the price is a fragmentation of narrative purpose. The writing takes on itself the implications of self-fragmentation, which is its theme and whose symptom and symbol is war.

At its most overt, *Parade's End* represents its hero as a tradition-grounded man, an uncorrupted survivor from the seventeenth or eighteenth century (it is never quite clear which), whose views are as Tory-tough as his body is Yorkshire-solid. He is a superb statistician (initially his job), who is comprehensively informed on both historical and contemporary geopolitical matters, and who is an expert with animals, and in financial matters and niceties of the law. He is also a fine classicist, has a discerning knowledge of English literature, evidences (compassionate) ingenuity as an army administrator, and shows a cool and efficacious presence under shell-fire. Even more than Percival, in Virginia Woolf's *The Waves*,[46] he is a construction of the authentic English ego. His wife, Sylvia, finds him to be the only man in England worth loving. His eventual mistress, Valentine, believes him the one man she has met who is worth giving herself to, so saving him from the forces which have assailed him. At narrative face-value, Christopher Tietjens represents a British White Anglo-Saxon Protestant version of the Western self, spiced by a fanciful Christ comparison, sanctified by reactionary views.

From virtually the start of the sequence Tietjens' sanity comes under attack. Sylvia, in particular, is demonically intent on destroying her husband's mental balance. Having put the paternity of their child in doubt, she proceeds to cuckold him, 'kill' his mother by her return, spread malicious rumours about him, embarrass him at the war front, take over his inheritance, alienate his son from him and, finally, live with his godfather. Sylvia is represented as the bitch–whore for whom aggressive whim and random passion are the only realities, intent on making a gender war out of their relationship. Nor is her characterisation as harpy an exception in the novels. In France Tietjens comes into intimate contact with O Nine Morgan and the shell-shocked Captain McKechnie, both of whom are destroyed by their wives' infidelities, while his best friend MacMaster becomes corrupted (and alienated from Tietjens) by the machinations of his irrationally vindictive mistress and eventual wife, Edith Ethel Duchemin. The threat of fragmentation in the sequence, then, is situated at the battle front of the war between the sexes. And it is further extrapolated in terms of the whole shadowy 'family romance', with implicit intergenerational conflict. This post-war 'saddest story' involves loss of mother, rejection by the father, the triumph of a sibling (Mark, his brother), alienation from an only son, cuckolding by a godfather and a constant process of symbolic emasculation culminating at the point when Sylvia's tenant cuts down the Great Tree at Groby Hall, the patriarchal seat. The threat of mental disintegration is given full psychoanalytic resonance within a sexual conflict that finally speaks the hero's inner self-alienation.

But the threatening forces operating against Tietjens also include the whole new social order as given by Ford. Where our hero represents honesty, integrity and objectivity, the new men are given over to deception, inauthenticity and ruthless self-interest. Tietjens refuses to fake statistics and so is expelled from the Civil Service: MacMaster wins a knighthood by utilising Christopher's hypothetical wheeze to short-change the French (now war allies) by statistical sleight of hand. Such bureaucratic dishonesty seeps into every aspect of the developing war effort. As the home front is increasingly run by 'cynically care-free intriguers in long corridors', so the battleline is infected by 'endless muddles; endless follies: endless villainies' (*No More Parades*, IV, p. 15). In charge of transferring troop drafts to the front, Tietjens is harrassed by a nightmare of regulations, necessities, interruptions, explosions and incompetent superiors. Later, after he has been ordered to the front in semi-disgrace, he is nearly blown up by a shell-burst which symbolises the whole devastating disorder of contemporary reality:

> There was so much noise it seemed to grow dark. It was a mental darkness. You could not think. A Dark Age! The earth moved . . . Long dollops of liquid mud surrounded them in the air . . . The earth manoeuvred for an infinite time. He remained suspended in space . . . The noise was incredible.
> (*A Man Could Stand Up*, IV, pp. 424–5)

After this climactic moment, a crazy normality returns when Tietjens, having just heroically rescued a man, is demoted by a visiting general (his godfather) for incorrect dress and deportment. Bureaucratic madness has invaded the front, but its root is traced back to pre-war administrative muddle and malice. From the standpoint of the western front reality of perpetual high explosion, Ford inscribes disintegration and disorder as the Edwardian social fact. like Lawrence in *Women in Love*, Ford writes the Edwardian moment back-to-front, as it were, as the onset of lethal fragmentation.

Tietjens' first (narrative-suppressed) war wound boldly figures what is at issue. Through an earlier shell-blast he becomes almost entirely amnesiac:

> Something burst – or 'exploded' is probably the right word – near me, in the dark . . . The point about it is that I don't *know* what happened and I don't remember what I did. There are three weeks of my life dead . . . What I remember is being in a C.C.S. and not being able to remember my own name.
> (*Some Do Not*, III, pp. 211–12)

The very clumsiness of the words indicates the deterioration of Ford's hero from his one-time rational fluency. At this point in the saga, Tietjens, who used to be able to correct entries from sheer erudition, is forced to memorise his way painfully through the *Encyclopaedia Britannica* to restock his knowledge. Though somewhat outrageously symbolised, Ford's point is clear: through shell shock, his representative unitary mind has been blown apart and razed. However, the author is disinclined to let his hero succumb at this moment and Tietjens rebuilds himself to suffer the later shell. But the interim is also characterised by mounting pressure from without and within once he is back in France: 'Sylvia would tear the world to pieces to get at me . . . to disturb my equanimity' (*No More Parades*, IV, p. 78); 'it was plain . . . that Tietjens was in the middle of a full nervous breakdown' (p. 186) 'It might mean that there was a crack in his, Tietjens', brain' (p. 240); 'He said. "I am at the end of my tether"'; (p. 241) 'Panic came over Tietjens . . . No brain could stand more. Fragments of scenes of fighting, voices, names, went before his eyes and ears. Elaborate problems . . .' (p. 250); 'If you cannot hear your thoughts how the hell are you going to tell what your thoughts are doing' (p. 327); 'He imagined that his brain was going: he was mad and seeing himself go mad' (p. 336). At the same time Tietjens is accompanied by others who have succumbed; mad Captain McKechnie, the doctor's batman ('blown literally out of most of his senses', p. 71) and Cowley ('always . . . subject to small fits . . . But getting too near a H.E. shell . . . had brought them on, violent' (p. 103). The hero then represents almost the ghost of the Western ego, at bay among mad men and on the brink himself. Just as the armies lack a single 'unified command', so it appears that Tietjens will finally lose unified command of his own mental processes, which are at times expressed as disjointed stream-of-consciousness:

> It was remarkably quiet in that thick darkness. Down below, the picks continued their sinister confidences in each other's ears. . . . It was really like that. Like children in the corner of a schoolroom whispering nasty comments about their masters, one to the other. . . . Girls, for choice. . . . Chop, chop, chop, a pick whispered. Chop? another asked in an undertone. The first said Chopchopchop. Then Chup. . . . And a silence of irregular duration. . . . Like what happens when you listen to typewriting and the young woman has to stop to put in another page. . . .
> Nice young women with typewriters in Whitehall had very likely taken from dictation, on hot-pressed, square sheets with embossed royal arms, the plan for that very *strafe*. . . .
> (Dots as in the text, *A Man Could Stand Up*, IV, p. 335)

But the western front does get a unified command (if only to lose it in the wheeler-dealing of Versailles) and Tietjens, incredibly, stays together. Back at home the girl he loves, Valentine, is under the impression that he has cracked and so (due to adroit narrative manipulation) is the reader. 'It appears to be the war that has broken him down' (p. 303); 'She was going to pass her day beside a madman; her night too' (p. 437). But it is partly the memory of Valentine that has kept Tietjens sane in spite of all, and it is her presence at the Armistice Night reunion that gives him the will to live. Val, as the new Woman, is the key to the hero's recovery. If Sylvia embodies the Pre-Raphaelite, Edwardian *femme fatale*, Valentine expresses an ideal version of the Suffragette – independent, intelligent, down-to-earth, passionate and loyal. Indeed Val is written as comparable to Tietjens in brilliance, honesty and forthrightness. So their union provides a comedic resolution to the trilogy. But a price must be paid for their future happiness. Tietjens loses altogether his acknowledged place in respectable society. The brilliant Civil Servant becomes reduced to a rustic antiques dealer residing in illegitimate domesticity. The moral seems clear: the integral self survives only at the margins of contemporary society. The fragmented mind of post-war England is given over to the anarchic machinations of hysterical women and utterly hollow men.

Yet the sequence is not as schematic as all this suggests, and the narrative control yields, at times, to the pressure of disturbing insights. Overall, Ford writes Tietjens as unitary rationality under threat: but at key moments that rationality, that defensive integrity, is radically questioned. The second section of *Some Do Not* considers at some length the limitations of the English integral self, though, with typical perversity, Ford attributes the questioning to Tietjens himself:

> It has been remarked that the peculiarly English habit of self-suppression in matters of the emotion puts the Englishman at a great disadvantage in moments of unusual stresses. In the smaller matters of the general run of life he will be impeccable and not to be moved; but in sudden confrontations of anything but physical danger he is apt – he is, indeed, almost certain – to go to pieces very badly . . .
> In the face of death – except at sea, by fire, railway accident, or accidental drowning in rivers; in the faces of madness, passion, dishonour – and particularly – prolonged mental strain, you will have all the disadvantages of the beginner at any game and may come off very badly indeed.
> (*Some Do Not*, III, pp. 223–4)

Such an awareness, signalled deftly at other points of the text, threatens to unravel the overwhelmingly dominant weave of textual implication. The dominant meaning of the sequence appears as an elaboration of two key English (masculinist) aphorisms: 'Hell hath no fury like a woman scorned' and 'If you can keep your head . . . / You'll be a man, my son.' But other insights undermine such constructions. Once admit the post-Freudian point (and the books boast their share of psychoanalytic jargon) that 'the repressions of the passionate drive them mad' (*No More Parades*, IV, p. 15) and one views quite differently the early characterisation that 'the basis of Christopher Tietjens emotional existence was a complete taciturnity' (*Some Do Not*, III, p. 15). There seems to be an almost symmetrical balance between what assails the hero from without and what he denies within. And perhaps the forces which attack him are only intolerable because he cannot bear what he cannot wholly control, and he refuses to act instinctively to protect himself. This is clearest on the plane of sexual emotion, and one short tirade by Sylvia is enough to subvert Ford's apparent moral bias:

> If . . . you had once in our lives said to me: 'You whore! You bitch! You killed my mother. May you rot in hell for it . . .' If you'd only once said something like it . . . about the child! About Perowne! . . . you might have done something to bring us together . . .
>
> (*Some Do Not*, III, p. 216)

Read from this point, Sylvia's conduct throughout the series can be seen as an impassioned attempt to force her husband into an honestly expressive emotional relationship – the kind of relationship which his superego stubbornly (often clownishly) resists. And such a reading casts its own ironic light on Tietjens' eventual union with Valentine, since they both see its possibility as a matter of having long, intelligent 'talks' together.[47] From this standpoint, Tietjens appears pure anti-hero: hopelessly repressed; chronically passive. He allows his marriage to break down through his refusal to express feeling; he loses both parents and son through silence and inactivity; he abets MacMaster's corruption and his own poverty by refraining from claiming his debts; he alienates himself from his profession, bank and club by defensive rudeness; he loses his small command by not standing up to his godfather. All this,

his brother Mark sees as Yorkshire virtue – but the deeper structure of the text invites us to see it as grotesque stubbornness: the crazy hubris of an integrity which sacrifices marriage, career, family, inheritance and friends in defence of an absurd notion of ego.

Thus the subtlety of Ford's writing effects a weird torsion of implication that the overt narrative cannot control. We are unable to see Tietjens as both heroic integrity and self-deceived clown without feeling that the writing has walked away with the writer: in short, that the writing itself is fragmented. *Parade's End* itself lacks a 'single command', that central cohesion which obsesses both Christopher and Mark. Disturbing though this is, it makes the sequence more, rather than less, compelling as a literary site; for it sets the confusions, breakdowns and disorientations that are its subject into anarchic internal resonance, whose effect is variously perplexing, absorbing, horrific and often plainly funny. Tietjens as Christ-figure with bits of the dinner his wife has thrown at him sticking on his uniform – or Tietjens the Johnsonian genius solemnly lecturing his wife on the inevitability of war with France: such premonitory touches of Waugh flicker out of a Conradian portentousness, itself riven through by an anger comparable to Aldington's and impassioned inconsistencies that remind us of Lawrence. Fragmented itself, the writing has a fragmenting effect on its readers as discontinuities of time, place and viewpoint precipitate us into ontological insecurity and the *progressions d'éffet* detonate their culminating revelations like literary high explosive.

Are we to read *Parade's End* as another twenties version of the war, where vehement textual contradictions bespeak a sensibility itself in partial breakdown? . . . Certainly, one can guess what ravages battle experience would have had on a sensibility as nervous (and often hypochondriacal) as Ford's. Yet it is also a sequence which, while often amusing, seems to have a palpable intent on the reader: an intent to disorientate. Ford described the predominant feeling of the Great War troops as having been 'let down':[48] there is a sense in which his sequence, magnificent as it is, lets down the reader who tries to make overall sense of its insights. Ford's literary generalship seems to replicate the military generalship of the war so that the reader is immersed in a plethora of numbingly vivid evocations and special effects. The sequence, like the war, generates, within its crisis scenario, a host of profound issues without being able to provide a secure viewing point or establish any overall coherence. The constrictions of a patriarchal social system; the changing conflict between the sexes; the decay of Protestant individualism; the lethal nature of modern geopolitical struggle; the break-up of traditional English life; the fragility of man's mental make-up: these and many other themes inform the cleverly manipulated development of *Parade's End* without ever being brought into consistent intellectual perspective. At the heart of the sequence – for all its variations of mood – is an awareness rather than a conception, a terror rather than a truth: the terror of mental fragmentation. The unity of the trilogy lies in the way it conveys this possibility at its narrative core and circles compulsively around its implications. *Parade's End* expresses a mentality at the end of its tether, in a war-torn society where the best lack all direction and the worst are full of rumour and intrigue.

'ALL GONE TO PIECES'

David Jones's *In Parenthesis* was published in 1937,[49] over 20 years after the events it chronicles. Unlike most 'war poetry', it was not a 'spontaneous overflow of powerful feeling' about very recent experience, written either at the front or on leave, but constituted a carefully crafted, if uncertain,[50] aesthetic project. It was pondered and worked at over a long period of time during which Jones was subject to recurrent neurotic depressions,[51] closely related to his war experiences. Its aim is epic rather than lyric, although its form as a prose-poem collage is best regarded, I think, as a Modernist experiment. It is rooted in personal experience ('things I saw, felt, & was part of', 'Preface', p. ix), yet the text calls into question the very notion of the authorial subject. For, in Jones's aesthetic – part neo-mediaeval,[52] part Modernist – the writer is seen as a 'maker', primarily, and the aim is to create a 'shape in words' (p. x). At the same time the impact of army experience itself helps to problematise the nature of selfhood in the context of the close bonding of very disparate types of men within a complex social structure whose tongues, training goals and techniques are various. In some respects we might see the work as 'Repression of War Experience' writ large; in other ways it reminds us of the shifting emotions, inconsistent stances and narrative experimentalism of *Parade's End*; but in the end it remains totally unique. The very text itself exists

'In Parenthesis', as does the authorial 'self' who writes it: both are uneasily suspended 'in a kind of space between – I don't know between quite what' (p. xv).

The primary effect of the work is not to evidence the strains of battle as destructive of selfhood, although there are enough instances of this – the man (is it the hero?) who has 'all gone to pieces and not pulling himself together' (p. 153), or the Jew who 'offers . . ./walnut suites in his delirium' (p. 155), or the surrendering Germans, 'sleep-walkers whose bodies go unbidden of the mind' (p. 170). Jones is more concerned to show how the very training and organisation of the army machine disperses selfhood into an elaborate hierarchical behaviour, whose final meaning is set within a history of military actions and discourses. So Jones dramatises himself as the anti-heroic John Ball, a typical caricature of the clumsy foot-soldier, whom we discover, much to our surprise, reading mediaeval poetry in an idle moment. Ball does not succumb to breakdown, though he has traumatic moments: instead we follow him through the progressive dissipations of his personality in the slow progress up to the front line, and finally leave him wounded (as Jones was wounded) in Mametz Wood, while the reserves, other 'Kimmerii to bear up the war', tramp uncommunicatively past him. Critics have noted the historical allusion in the name John Ball.[53] However, it does not seem to me that the radical priest executed during the Peasants' Revolt is of primary importance. The name is surely a composite pun. It is very close to John Bull – humurously so, since Ball is nothing like the plump, self-confident figure so named. But the surname also draws on the lewd jokiness of army life (cf. Major Knacksbull).[54] Any soldier referred to as '0 1 Ball' (O, one ball!) inevitably appears as a comic butt. And the name has further resonance in terms of the 'balls-up' or 'bollocks' our hero is always liable to create. It also reminds us of ball (as in musket-ball or cannon-ball), of 'bawl', of anyone bounced around constantly, and of B— All, as in 'All quiet china? – bugger all to report?' (p. 55). Altogether, the 'Ball of your section' is a comically named Everyman-as-clown, created by a writer familiar both with Cockney rhyming slang and with Joyce's word-play in 'Work in Progress'.[55] More importantly, here, the name, with its multiple associations, suggests a character whose selfhood is already dispersed into the resonances of social mythology. Private Ball is, in fact, a very public Ball indeed.

Thus far has Jones distanced selfhood in terms of multi-level caricature, and made a point about any private 'self' in so communal a society as the army. But the chief contribution he makes to the modern discourse of self-fragmentation is the peculiar, sometimes grotesque, deployment of the writing self in the work. This is most easily evidenced with respect to the stylistic discontinuities which operate throughout. Briefly, the self has no 'voice' – or rather it represents itself as a heterogeneity of voices:

>Maiden of the digged places
>>let our cry come unto thee.
>
>*Mam*, moder, mother of me
>Mother of Christ under the tree
>reduce our dimensional vulnerability to the minimum –
>cover the spines of us
>let us creep back dark-bellied where he can't see
>don't let it.
>There, there, it can't, won't hurt – nothing
>shall harm my beautiful.
>   But on its screaming passage
>their numbers writ
>and stout canvas tatters drop as if they'd salvoed grape to the
>mizzen-sheets and the shaped ash grip rocket-sticks out of
>the evening sky right back by Bright Trench
>and clots and a twisted clout
>on the bowed back of the F.O.O. bent to his instrument.
>. . . theirs . . . H.E. . . . fairly, fifty yards to my front
>. . . he's bumping the Quadrangle . . . 2025 hours? . . .
>35 degrees left . . . he's definitely livening.
>   and then the next packet – and Major Knacksbull blames
>the unresponsive wire.

(p. 177)

Even after *Ulysses* and *The Waste Land*, such drifting and shifting between language usages is highly disconcerting. The liturgical opening leads straight into the poignantly personal '*Mam*', which instantly invokes a mediaeval *alter ego* – 'moder'. The ironical use of army technical jargon ('reduce our dimensional vulnerability') intervenes between prayerful petitions. 'Don't let it' stands out abruptly as a whole (grammatically disrupted) line. 'There, there . . .' interpolates the maternal voice, which switches on a half-line to high literary realism: 'But on its screaming passage . . .' This in turn modulates into the consciously poetic ('the shaped ash grip rocket-sticks') and back to the Imagistic banal ('the bowed back of the F.O.O.') before the terse jargon of the telephonist's report. Finally, the passage ends in prosy understatement: 'Major Knacksbull blames . . .'. The fear and confusion of the represented experience seems to have dissipated all authorial control. This is not the poetic self's 'true voice of feeling'. Rather, the poet's subject position has been invaded by a changing sequence of discourse deployments which make even the appealing '*Mam*' appear as one more communal term.

Such authorial self-dispersal into contrastive discourses is, I think, a more complicated matter than either Sassoon's representation of psychic conflict or Ford's narrative confusion of purpose. For all his 'neurosis', Jones's predicament here is ultimately a case of social and ideological disjunction. It is a matter of the conscious subject torn apart in terms of disparate ideological placements. *In Parenthesis* focuses (as, say, his *Anathemata* cannot) on Jones's anomalous position as educated aesthete playing Tommy among working-class Londoners and Welshmen. The predicament is early revealed on page 2 when 0 1 Ball's sense of 'ill-usage' at having his number taken resolves into a vision of Mr Jenkins 'like San Romano's foreground squire, unhelmeted'. But the ideological contradictions are more complex than even this bizarre contrast can evidence. For the work's placement of self is attempted within various incompatible discourses, each speaking its own specificity – army Cockney, liturgical Latin, the 'discipline of prose' (p. 103), Welsh and English vernacular, 'white-man talk' (pp. 54–5), modern technical jargon, high poetic style, Imagistic realism and so on and so forth. The writing self is dispersed into a plethora of language usages which speak contrastive social placements and render consciousness as radically fragmented. Ball, and even more 'Jones', becomes a site of desperate struggle between class, racial and cultural differences.

Of course the project of the work is to create a synthesis of these differences through such Modernist techniques as mask adoption, the patterning of allusions and montage. But few would claim that these methods wholly succeed here. Even in terms of genre, the work seems to precipitate out into contrastive entities: a vivid 'soldier's tale'; a study of men coping; a comic satire; an allusive tour-de-force; a modern epic; the Rise and Fall of the Volunteer

Army. And, of course, the writer's position varies in each case: Jones is simultaneously humble rifleman, social observer, ironic jester, literary traditionalist, epic bard and military historian – as well as many other things. Like Eliot in the footnotes to *The Waste Land*, Jones is unwilling to surrender the sense of an inclusive consciousness ('the man who was on the field . . . and who wrote the book', p. 187), but, as in Eliot's poem, that consciousness is manifested as a Babel of discourses, a 'heap of broken images', as 'fragments' shored against ruin. It is for this reason that a critic like Jon Silkin finds moral inconsistencies in the work. He writes: 'It is true . . . that those killed in this sector of the Somme get mourned, and thus, by implication, all those slain in war; but it is also true that the Boast "I was there" implies pride in service and a very different response to war than the elegiac conclusion'.[56] This is just, and helps differentiate Jones's work from Owen's poetic compassion or Sassoon's bitter irony. For Jones does not so much develop an attitude to war as render the experiences of war – including moral contradictions and emotional inconsistencies. Jones is precisely Modernist in his fidelity to 'presentation'. He would doubtless have agreed with Pound that 'art never asks anybody to do anything, or to think anything, or to be anything' and that 'clear presentation is of the noblest traditions of our craft'.[57] In Jones's case, 'bearing witness' through presentation entails the expression of the self's confusions and discontinuities in specific war situations – unreconstructed to fit any moral schema. This involves both the conflicting feelings of the soldier at war, as evidenced so strikingly in Richard Holmes's *Firing Line*,[58] and the complexities of social and ideological positioning already mentioned. In this sense the work has no perspective (but then it is a montage). What it attempts to offer instead is the sense of historical depth.

I use the word 'depth' because I don't believe 'continuity' is necessarily implied. Continuity is precisely at issue in *In Parenthesis*, just as it is in *Ulysses* and *The Waste Land*. If the notes to the poem are at times overprescriptive, Jones's 'Preface' seems more aware of the difficulties of the historical dimension: 'It would be interesting to know how we shall ennoble our new media as we have already ennobled and made significant our old – candlelight, fire-light, Cups, Wands and Swords . . .' (p. xiv). The poem does demonstrate 'continuities' – of army drill and discourse for instance: but, as in the case of Joyce's Homeric parallels, these also serve

Self at War

to highlight radical discontinuities – of situation, character and response. The spectacle of the wounded Ball abandoning his rifle under a tree 'for a Cook's tourist to the Devastated Areas' (p. 186) exemplifies how grotesquely different is the situation in Mametz Wood to that of the fabled Roland at Roncevaus or Malory's Arthur ordering the return of Excalibur to the Enchanted Lake. Most of the time, I would argue, the literary allusions serve to stress discontinuities within a vaguely felt continuum. Take, for example, the end of Dai Great-Coat's boast:

> I am the Single Horn thrusting
> by night-stream margin
> in Helyon.[N]
>   Cripes-a-mighty-strike-me-stone-cold – you don't say.
>   Where's that birth-mark, young'un.
>   Wot the Melchizzydix! – and still fading – jump to it
> Rotherhithe.
> > Never die never die
> > Never die never die
> > Old soljers never die
> > Never die never die
> > Old soljers never die they never die
> > Never die
> > Old soljers never die they
> > Simply fade away.
>
> (p. 84)

The reader is only on firm ground here with the marching song at the end. The note N is needed to make sense of the first lines. The action of a mythical unicorn to purify the waters of Marah, in Helyon, is pretty obscure matter (as is the source) and, even when we are enlightened, it is difficult to imagine how this is relevant to modern soldiers. So Dai, like Madame Sosostris in *The Waste Land*, must be regarded as a figure, simultaneously ironic and portentous, who mediates as signifier between the modern Welsh fusilier and arcane tradition of which, in a sense, he is deemed the heir. Similarly, the reference to Melchisedec – though more acceptable in the context of a chapel-going culture – is theologically freighted and distantiated from the surface. In both cases the chasm between tradition and modern Taffy is pointed up by stylistic contrast:

'night-stream margin' – 'Cripes-a-mighty . . .'; 'Where's that birthmark' – 'Wot the Melchizzydix'. And this is true of the running collage of allusion and vernacular throughout the work. Jones is claiming a kind of collective unconscious which the soldiers inherit, but their habits and speech stand out in comic contrast to it. So that even if we can accept the presupposition of a near-mystical cultural rooting, the text's surface ensures that we see this as bizarrely at variance with the fusiliers' actions and awareness. The army Taffy or Tommy is no more akin to his legendary forebears than is mild-mannered, kinky Leopold Bloom to valiant and wily Odysseus. *In Parenthesis* suggests 'heroic' antecedents only to exemplify the radical and inexorable discontinuities that Kronos enforces. Selfhood, then, becomes even more drastically fragmented. The modern Welsh fusilier is simultaneously (somehow) Fluellen, Arthurian knight, one of the Catraeth 300 – and yet not so. Ball–Jones is in a sense all the heroes and anti-heroes whose personae are evoked by allusion, as well as being many other contemporary selves. So the placement of awareness within a traditional dimension generates peculiar self-estrangements and incompatibilities. Selfhood becomes dispersed not only synchronically in psychic conflicts and social contradictions but also diachronically into a collectivity of diverse historical precedents. The common-sense self-defence of the ordinary Tommy or Taffy is understandable: 'Wot the Melchizzydix' or 'Who gives a bugger for/the Dolorous Stroke' (p. 162).

Such complexities of dissociation make the work difficult to read and suggest that, in conventional terms, it constitutes an incongruous failure. However, I suggest that the richness of *In Parenthesis*, and its fascination for those who can persist with it, also spring quite directly from these very qualities – as does its significance for Modernist ways of presenting selfhood. It is above all an experimental work – albeit one written as much out of trench mud and shell shock as from the mythical ivory tower. As such, it challenges both conventional modes of rendering battle experience and traditional ways of representing selfhood. Of course, the two go together; for the selfhood expressed in *In Parenthesis* is specifically a self at war (and in specifically modern army conditions), while the war represented here is not so much one against human counterparts as one of self-alienation and self-dispersal. So the collagistic form of the work is indispensible in conveying its content, and it can do so with considerable power:

> And a great untidiness breaching the
> neat line of bivvies; and unpiled arms by great violence with
> rove-off piling swivels.
> The Quarter's knocked-off S.R.D.
> is blown to buggery,
> diluted and far from home,
> what won't half get him shirty.
> Mules broke amuck across the open ground, where it said
> no traffic by daylight, just where his last salvo made dark
> corona for the hill.
> Echoes that make you sit up and take notice tumbled to and
> fro the hollow in emptied hard collapse, quite other than the
> sustained,
> boomed-out
> boom-oom, boom-oom
> and the felt recoil . . .
>
> (p. 141)

The broken style and oddities of detail vividly express the disorientation of such experience. Self-fragmentation is not so much Jones's theme as the very condition and affect of the writing. The 'maker' is in this sense an unmaker – or resembles a catalytic chamber where selfhood is unmade. The Great War was experienced by Jones as, finally, a crisis of self-meaning. The poem shows the self dispersed into contradictory roles and attitudes, split apart by contrastive emotions, dissipated among all the available historical precedents which might provide intelligibility. So the final meaning is in the discontinuities themselves, welded together by aesthetic montage. Selfhood in modern war is self-dispersal. 'The geste says this' (p. 187) – it is Jones's version, and the style authenticates it.

4
Fragmentary Self

'A Myriad Impressions'[1]

The decade 1914–24 represents the historic node of English literary Modernism. It also evidences a virtual paradigm shift in the presentation of self-experience – by consciously 'artistic' writers in particular. The 'men of 1914',[2] following the lead of James, Conrad and the French Symbolists, initiated a dissociation of integral selfhood and, as we have seen, the war writers provided vivid socio-psychological evidence that, *in extremis*, the familiar Western egoic self was, quite literally, a sham. It was during the war years that Yeats's exemplary career finally left behind the phantasies of fairyland and embraced the problems of radical self-deception and self-conflict. But the younger 'men of 1914' included some important women writers too: H.D., for example, May Sinclair, Dorothy Richardson and Virginia Woolf. Arguably, the new male emphasis on splitting, emotional confusion and anguished helplessness constituted a 'feminisation' of the masculinist ego: and it is fitting that much early Modernist experimentation was first published in the renamed *New Freewoman*.[3] Be that as it may, writers of both sexes began to explore inner space as never before, desperately trying to map the debris left by selfhood's disintegration. The race was on to find new forms and a new language which could fittingly represent the new, 'post-Copernican'[4] self.

The quest for new forms, though not the solution to the methodological problem, is expressed in Lawrence's well known letter to Edward Garnett of June 1914:

> In Turgenev, and in Tolstoy, and in Dostoevsky, the moral scheme into which all the characters fit – and it is nearly the same scheme – is, whatever the extraordinariness of the characters themselves, dull, old, dead. When Marinetti writes: 'it is the solidity of a blade of steel that is interesting by itself, that is, the incomprehending and inhuman alliance of its

molecules in resistance to, let us say, a bullet. The heat of a piece of wood or iron is in fact more passionate, for us, than the laughter or tears of a woman' – then I know what he means . . . Because what is interesting in the laugh of a woman is the same as the binding of the molecules of steel or their action in heat: it is the inhuman will, call it physiology, or like Marinetti, physiology of matter, that fascinates me. I don't so much care what the woman *feels* – in the ordinary usage of the word. That presumes an *ego* to feel with. I only care for what the woman is – what she is – inhumanly, physiologically, materially – according to the use of the word . . . You mustn't look in my novel for the old stable *ego* of the character. There is another *ego*, according to whose action the individual is unrecognizable, and passes through, as it were, allotropic states which it needs a deeper sense than any we've been used to exercise, to discover are states of the same single radically unchanged element. (Like as diamond and coal are the same pure single element of carbon. The ordinary novel would trace the history of the diamond – but I say, 'Diamond, what! This is carbon'. And my diamond might be coal or soot, and my theme is carbon.)[5]

This is both confused and confusing. No doubt the 'moral scheme' is relevant to the literary convention of a placed, integral self which Lawrence wished to abolish. But what are we to make of Marinetti's 'inhuman alliance' or Lawrence's vague 'inhuman will'? And what are these 'allotropic states'? And is the diamond–carbon analogy really illuminating with respect to the representation of psychic states as characterisation? The letter, in fact, exemplifies in its own discourse the problem it seeks to address – the difficulty of finding a means to convey the complexities of actual self-experience. Lawrence is successful in labelling what he wishes to transcend – 'the old stable ego' – but not so in suggesting what the new mode of self-representation might be.

The issue is not resolved in Lawrence's fiction, I believe, despite the brilliance of his insights. He does not create a radically new method, and his new wine is constantly threatening to burst the old bottles. Here, for instance, is Gerald's 'crisis' in the most innovative of his novels, *Women in Love* (published in 1921, though written during the war):

As the evening of the third day came on, his heart rang with fear. He could not bear another night. Another night was coming on, for another night he was to be suspended in chain of physical life, over the bottomless pit of nothingness. And he could not bear it. He could not bear it. He was frightened deeply, and coldly, frightened in his soul. He did not believe in his own strength any more. He could not fall into this infinite void and rise again. If he fell, he would be gone for ever. He must withdraw, he must seek reinforcements. He did not believe in his own single self any further than this.[6]

This is moving in its own way, and gives us an overall sense of Gerald's despair, but the language is somehow distanced and abstracted from actual self-experience: 'suspended in the chain of physical life'; 'he was frightened deeply, and coldly'; 'he could not fall into this infinite void and rise again'. It lacks any of the specificity of, say, the image of Stephen's dead mother in *Ulysses* or the 'bats with baby faces' in *The Waste Land*. It relies too much on archaic religious terms ('bottomless pit of nothingness') and not enough on Imagistic particulars or Symbolistic resonance. But even when Lawrence does use symbolism – as in Ursula's last vision in *The Rainbow* or when Birkin stones the moon in Willey Water, there is frequently an uneasy match between realist and psycho-symbolic planes ('"Cybele – curse her! The accursed Syria Dea! Does one begrudge it her! What else is there – ?"', p. 278). In fact, though his psychic subject matter is Modernist, Lawrence's discourse is fundamentally nineteenth century. This passage shows no advance on the rendering of Paul's breakdown in *Sons and Lovers* (see above, p. 19): it is also little different from Carlyle's representation of Teufelsdröckh's 'Everlasting No' in *Sartor Resartus* or Hawthorne's rendering of his hero's forest experience in *Young Goodman Brown*. Lawrence, then, was highly aware of the complexity and heterogeneity of self-experience, but he failed to find a consistent method by which to express it persuasively; indeed after *Women in Love* he returned to more conventional characterisation.

However, Lawrence had gone further in attempting to confront the issues than most other writers at the time. In *The New Machiavelli* (1912) H. G. Wells had shown an awareness of modern self-experience. His hero writes:

Fragmentary Self

> I am tremendously impressed now in the retrospect by the realization of how little that frontage represented me . . . Behind it, yet struggling to disorganize and alter it altogether, was a far more essential reality, a self less personal, less individualized, and broader in its references . . . It is just the existence and development of this more generalized self-behind-the-frontage that is making modern life so much more subtle and intricate to render.[7]

Again the problem is identified. From 'frontage' through 'less individualized' to 'subtle and intricate to render' the passage uncannily acts as a link between Lawrence's letter and Virginia Woolf's evocation of the 'myriad impressions' in 'Modern Fiction'. But Wells's writing neither attains, nor even seeks to develop, a new method and discourse to represent this 'self-behind-the-frontage'. Wyndham Lewis also showed awareness of the issue in *Tarr* (1918):

> A complicated image developed in his mind as he stood with her. He was remembering Schopenhauer: it was of a chinese puzzle of boxes within boxes, or of insects' discarded envelopes . . . He was a mummy-case, too. Only he contained nothing but innumerable other painted cases inside, smaller and smaller ones. The smallest was not a substantial astral baby, however, or live core, but a painting like the rest. – His kernel was a painting, in fact: that was as it should be! He was pleased that it was nothing more violent than that.[8]

Tarr perceives himself, then, as hollow at the core. But again, Lewis does not attempt to follow the insight up in terms of a new method of characterisation – indeed he would have regarded it as 'Bergsonian'[9] to do so. Lewis's experimental discourse does not represent experience from within but caricatures behaviour from without – a kind of neo-Futurist reduction of egoic energy to a collocation of mechanistic body functions.

The situation in poetry was not dissimilar. Experiments in 'dissolving' selfhood, whether in peacetime or at war, did not achieve any specific new method of representation until *The Waste Land* (1922). Pound's early attempts at a long poem manifest an unease about both the deployment of self in language and the heterogeneity of experience, without resolving the formal problem of method:

> Hang it all, there can be but one 'Sordello':
> But say I want to, say I take your whole bag of tricks,
> Let in your quirks and tweeks, and say the thing's an art-form,
> Your Sordello, and that the modern world
> Needs such a rag-bag to stuff all its thoughts in;
> Say that I dump my catch, slimy and silvery
> As fresh sardines slapping and slipping on the marginal cobbles?
> (I stand before the booth, the speech; but the truth
> Is inside this discourse – this booth is full of the marrow
>   of wisdom.)[10]

This 1917 draft of Canto I precisely acknowledges the problem of 'discourse' and the 'I' that is simultaneously inside and outside of it. But it was not until some years later that Pound resolved the problem in terms of an 'ideogrammic' shorthand that simultaneously expresses self and world:

> Hang it all, Robert Browning,
>   there can be but the one 'Sordello'.
> But Sordello, and my Sordello?
> Lo Sordels si fo di Mantovana.
> So-shu churned in the sea . . .
>
>   (Canto II)

However, as Pound's obsession with economics grew through the twenties and thirties, the *Cantos* became less concerned to express selfhood (though in fact they do so in a quite idiosyncratic way) than to recycle historical discourses as a 'light for the future'.[11] It was only after his arrest for treason at the end of the Second World War, and his incarceration at Pisa, that the 'tale of the tribe' developed into an anguished and spectacularly fragmentary Song of Myself (see below, pp. 165–73).

Back in the years of the Great War, Pound's friend Yeats was also experimenting with the deployment of self in poetry. At this time he relied mainly on a simple technique of self-splitting – *Hic* and *Ille*, Aherne and Robartes, Saint and Hunchback, He and She. But 'The Second Coming', his greatest single poem before publication of *The Tower*, develops a high rhetoric through which image and archetype resonate with a finally psychic intensity. Although the poem addresses universal change, it is also very much about the fragmentation of self-experience within an apocalyptic world disintegration:

> Turning and turning in the widening gyre
> The falcon cannot hear the falconer;
> Things fall apart; the centre cannot hold;
> Mere anarchy is loosed upon the world,
> The blood-dimmed tide is loosed, and everywhere
> The ceremony of innocence is drowned . . .[12]

If the 'centre' is, in one sense, integral selfhood, then 'anarchy' may be internal as well as external, presaging the emergence of the 'wild, old wicked man'.[13] So Yeats himself embodies both the 'best' and the 'worst'[14] and the 'revelation' concerns recognition of the 'savage god' within himself as well as in history. The last lines of the poem are characterised by darkness, nightmare and portentous visitation. The tone is fittingly one of appalled fascination: for the 'rough beast' which slouches towards birth and domination comes out of the cellarage of Yeats's deepest being. It is significant that after the collection in which this poem appears came the mature Yeatsian poetry of radical self-questioning and metamorphic self-assertion.

The years of the Great War produced another experimental text by one of Yeats's fellow countrymen. G. B. Shaw's *Heartbreak House*[15] develops a quite extraordinary representation of selfhood. The place of drama within Modernism is problematical and it has not so far contributed to this argument – partly because innovation in dramatic writing between 1900 and 1925 mainly concerned the introduction of Realism in which coherent characterisation is of the essence. (Had Expressionist drama had a greater representation in England than, for example, Wyndham Lewis's *Enemy of the Stars* (1914)[16] there might have been more to write about drama and self-fragmentation). But *Heartbreak House*, with its bizarre blend of the conventions of Realism, Farce, Expressionism and Problem Play, does much to unsettle notions of self-coherence and self-consistency. Its heroine is an ingénue who progresses in the course of one night, from naive idealism, via a half-minute 'heartbreak', into, first, hard-headed practicality, then spiritual 'marriage' and finally rhapsodic self-destructiveness. Throughout, she is surrounded by people who are not what they seem, partly because they are self-contradictory: for instance, the heroic braggart (Hector), the harpy with a heart of gold (Hesione) and the murderous 'Nurse'. This is not just a matter of Shavian paradoxicality, and the normal Shavian dramatic mechanism of recognition emerging out of disillusionment does not operate here. There is no final prognosis for the disease of contemporary England and we remain, at the end, shocked and disoriented. The Shaw who wrote the play seems as mysterious and enigmatic as the play's main character, Captain Shotover, who is both wise and whimsical, destructive and creative, devilish and puppy-doggish, portentous and ridiculous – a Lear, a Mikado, a Mad Hatter, an Ancient Mariner, a Captain Hook and a Prospero all in one. The play is dream-like and in the end it is best to construe it as a dream – starting from the initial stage directions where Ellie falls asleep over a copy of Shakespeare. In its affects the play invites us to consider its 'dreamwork' in a specifically modern sense.[17] Its comically paradoxical characters are, in the end, themselves self-parts, each overdetermined, and transformed by 'displacement'. So the young girl's dream of acceptance into an adult world of marital relationships and money is worked out in terms of sudden metamorphoses of interaction between disparate husband figures, father figures, mother figures and sisterly rivals (specific characters frequently symbolising at least two functions at different times), in a weird and wonderful 'family romance' which ends in an ecstasy which ought to be nightmare. In this, *Heartbreak House* is far closer to Strindberg than to Chekhov, for all the doom that hangs over its roof. Out of his own wartime ambivalences and anxieties, the normally most rational 'meliorist' has mused a 'fantasia' with a radically new method of representing self-experience. But, in this, it was a one-off in Shaw's long and individualistic career.

Dorothy Richardson's sequence of novels, *Pilgrimage*,[18] begun with *Pointed Roofs* in 1915, evidences one writer's exemplary persistence in advancing beyond representations of self-dissolution to develop the most successful literary method of expressing fragmentary selfhood – stream-of-consciousness. Like many modern writers, she moved towards more radical fragmentation through a heightened sense of opposites inside the self:

Within me . . . the third child, the longed-for son, the two natures, equally matched, mingle and fight. It is their struggle that keeps me adrift, so variously interested and strongly attracted, now here, now there. Which will win? . . . she could not imagine either of them set aside. Then her life *would* be the battleground of her two natures.

(III, p. 250)

Like other writers she was aware of psychoanalytical terms and practices and, like Woolf in particular, she was haunted by fear of a total collapse of self-meaning into madness. At such moments her 'shroud of consciousness' style can become as intense, lapidary and rhythmically powerful as the later Beckett's:

It's always the same. I always feel the same. It is sending me mad. One day it will be worse. If it gets any worse I shall be mad. Just here. Certainly. Something is wearing out of me. I am meant to go mad. If not, I should not always be coming along this piece without knowing it, whichever street I take. Other people would know the streets apart. I don't know where this bit is or how I get to it. I come every day because I am meant to go mad here.

(II, p. 136)

'Selfhood' is wholly in question here. Indeed, throughout the sequence Miriam uses the term 'I' in contrasting formulations: 'I suppose I'm a new woman'; 'I'm some sort of bad unsimple woman'; 'I wouldn't be a man for anything!'; 'I'm like a man'.[19] Indeed, the name Miriam itself is reminiscent of the word 'myriad'. If Richardson's work is necessarily less celebrated than Joyce's, it remains important and exemplifies in its development the new means of representing the multiplicity of selfhood.

I take it that *Ulysses*, *The Waste Land* and *Mrs Dalloway* exemplify the new discourse of self-fragmentation, and these works are discussed below. In Chapter 6, 'Discontinuous Self', I go on to discuss later representations of fragmented selfhood in *The Waves*, *Four Quartets* and the Pisan *Cantos*. However, this charting of the main lines of Modernist discourse about the self leaves out of account *Finnegans Wake*, that 'glory, jest and riddle' of the modern literary world. It is doubtful how far the *Wake* should be considered as a discourse about selfhood at all: it surely represents a communal rather than a personal dream. Further, a proper examination of its relevance to the project of self-fragmentation would require a book in itself. However, its puzzling presence should at least be acknowledged in this context. Leon Edel construes it as 'an entire litany of self-aggression and self-depreciation, in which Joyce suggests his schizoid nature',[20] and believes Joyce is pronouncing on himself when he writes: 'condemned fool, anarch, egoarch, heresiarch, you have reared your disunited kingdom on the vacuum of your own most intensely doubtful soul'.[21] This seems a rather reductive reading, even if it is on to something within the text. Clearly, whatever the book does tell us about selfhood has stretched the bounds of discursive intelligibility as far as it will go. The experimentality which began with James, Conrad and Ford has reached in the *Wake* its peculiar consummation. Fragmenting self can go no further than, for example, this:

> I have abwaited me in a water of Elin and I have placed my reeds intectis before the Registower of the perception of tribute in the hall of the city of Analbe. How concerns any merryaunt and hworsoever gravesobbers it is perensempry sex of fun to help a dazzle off the othour. What for Mucias and Gracias may the duvlin rape the handsomst! And the whole mad knightmayers' nest! Tunpother, prison and plotch! If Y shoulden somewhat, well, I am able to owe it, hearth and chemney easy. They seeker for vannflaum all worldins merkins. I'll eager make lyst turpidump undher arkens. Basast![22]

'LORD THE CRACKED THINGS COME INTO MY HEAD'[23]

Joyce's method of rendering selfhood in *Ulysses* constitutes a kind of fragmentation montage. It is atomistic, disjunctive and comically metamorphic. Slowly, elaborately, with infinite detailing, it builds up its main 'characters' out of a myriad contrasted perceptions and reflections, memories and phantasies, feelings and concealments. There are no centres or firm boundaries to the selves that are Stephen, Bloom and Molly – in the conventional sense they are not characters at all. Selfhood in the book consists in self-multiplicity: it is heterogeneous and yet slyly patterned – a bravura balancing act among the infinite variety of its component parts.

Joyce's stream-of-consciousness writing constructs self as utterly different from the 'old stable ego'. It is neither stable nor naively egoistic. Rather it is fluxive, dynamic, multiple, changeable and contradictory.

It has been remarked that Joyce's work has the most 'Freudian flavour'[24] of all stream-of-consciousness writing. At the same time we can see the predominant method in *Ulysses* as the fullest literary exemplification of William James's notion of consciousness as a theatre of simultaneities. As James wrote: 'the discovery that memories, thoughts, and feelings exist outside the primary consciousness is the most important step forward that has occurred in psychology since I have been a student of that science'.[25] Whether or not Joyce had any direct knowledge of James's writings, the method of *Ulysses* seems to exemplify a post-Freudian adaptation of James's 'stream' of awareness to represent selfhood as radical fragmentation through literary montage. Self is thus mapped as a patterned vortex of heterogeneities and discontinuities. The patterning results from Joyce's lovingly traced associative interconnections. But such associations are humorously revealed in terms of the mind's compulsive need to relate incompatibles; the drive to 'only connect' – even if the connections are as arbitrary as those in dreams. At the same time, the method is dramatically variable, unlike the comparatively uniform stream-of-consciousness of Richardson or Woolf. The three main characters in *Ulysses* can be seen to represent three different models of consciousness: say Bloom as Lockean, in that secondary associations tend to spring from primary perceptions; Stephen as Coleridgean, in that imaginative and intellectual power seems to govern even the nature of his perceptions; and Molly as Freudian since her thoughts and phantasies are shown as dancing attendance on her psychosomatic needs. Yet in each case the method of heterogeneous montage informs the entire representation: what changes is the quality of awareness and the style to convey it.

The consciousness of Leopold Bloom is at the core of *Ulysses* and Joyce's most typical means[26] of expressing it remains the crucial exemplification of his use of interior monologue to represent selfhood. In this 'Bloom-stream' we find Imagistic everyday impressions as well as coded subconscious feelings, trains of curious speculation alongside self-indulgent phantasies and sudden strategies of denial. It remains the most persuasive literary representation of the plenitude of selfhood ever written. To get the measure of it we need to consider a quite ample sample, inevitably intruding *in medias res*:

> Fool and his money. Dewdrop coming down again. Cold nose he'd have kissing a woman. Still they might like. Prickly beards they like. Dog's cold noses. Old Mrs Riordan with the rumbling stomach's Skye terrier in the City Arms hotel.
>   Molly fondling him in her lap. O the big doggybowwowsywowsy!
>   Wine soaked and softened rolled pith of bread mustard a moment mawkish cheese. Nice wine it is. Taste it better because I'm not thirsty. Bath of course does that. Just a bite or two. Then about six o'clock I can. Six, six. Time will be gone then. She . . .
>   Mild fire of wine kindled his veins. I wanted that badly. Felt so off colour. His eyes unhungrily saw shelves of tins, sardines, gaudy lobsters' claws. All the odd things people pick up for food. Out of shells, periwinkles with a pin, off trees, snails out of the ground the French eat, out of the sea with bait on a hook. Silly fish learn nothing in a thousand years. If you didn't know risky putting anything into your mouth. Poisonous berries. Johnny Magories. Roundness you think good. Gaudy colour warns you off. One fellow told another and so on. Try it on the dog first. Led on by the smell or the look. Tempting fruit. Ice cones. Cream. Instinct. Orangegroves for instance. Need artificial irrigation. Bleibtreustrasse. Yes but what about oysters? Unsightly like a clot of phlegm. Filthy shells. Devil to open them too. Who found them out? Garbage, sewage they feed on. Fizz and Red bank oysters. Effect on the sexual. Aphrodis. He was in the Red bank this morning. Was he oyster old fish at table. Perhaps he young flesh in bed. No. June has no ar no oysters. But there are people like tainted game.
>
> (p. 174)

We have here interrupted Mr Bloom's light meal in Davy Byrne's pub, breaking into his meditation on Nosey Flynn's gambling habits – uncharacteristically caustic because Flynn had brought up the subject of Molly's tour with Boylan. Bloom's thought-stream jumps from Flynn's nose, to kissing, to dogs' noses and so to Molly fondling Mrs Riordan's terrier. Then his attention is briefly occupied with his wine and sandwich. But after accounting for his lack of thirst, his resolve to eat sparingly leads by a conscious connection (eat again at six o'clock) to his subconscious anxiety – Molly's prospective adultery with Boylan. The repeated 'six' – suggestively close to 'sex' – mediates between the two psychic levels. But once the subconscious preoccupation begins to surface, it is abruptly edited out: 'She . . .'

Bloom concentrates his attention on the wine again, the phrase 'off colour' serving to rationalise his anxiety. Then he meditates on the shelves of tins he sees (food has been on his mind for much of the chapter). His curiosity ponders man's habit of miscellaneous food-gathering, but the first examples which spring to his mind – periwinkles, snails, fish – suggest a tangy viscosity, probably associated for him with Molly's sexuality. The sentence 'If you didn't know risky putting anything into your mouth' may well constitute a coded warning to Molly, who has not yielded to Boylan before this. 'Poisonous berries', 'roundness' and 'gaudy colour' are all similarly coded, while 'one fellow told another . . .' has an added implication on a day when Molly's reputation is frequently bandied about between leering males. 'Try it on the dog first' is partly quirky speculation (and typically Bloomian in this). But it also refers back to the dog he remembers Molly fondling, and in the larger context of the book has a further meaning. The Blooms' son Rudy was conceived after Molly was excited by two dogs copulating in the street and begged Leopold for 'a touch' (p. 90). Perhaps the deeper anxiety here is that Molly might conceive by Boylan at a time when (Rudy having died) Bloom badly feels the lack of any son and heir. With 'led on by the smell or the look' we have overt innuendo which continues through 'tempting fruit', 'cones', 'cream', 'instinct' and 'orangegroves'. The last thought takes Bloom's mind back to the advertisement he had seen earlier in the day (p. 62), evoking also 'immense melonfields'. The connection with Molly is strong since much later Bloom kisses 'the plump mellow yellow smellow melons of her rump' (p. 656). But the advertisement with its Bleibtreustrasse address is also associated with Bloom's ambivalent feelings about his Jewishness, since the fruitgroves are in Palestine. Defensively, his thought switches back to the general topic of food – only to be betrayed by his subconscious preoccupation. For 'oysters' leads him inevitably through associations of filth and viscosity (and the coded 'who found them out') to 'Red bank', 'sexual' and 'Aphrodis'. Bloom was earlier aware of Boylan outside the Red Bank (p. 94). He acknowledges the association, but unnames his rival as 'he'.

However, his masochistic streak allows a brief speculation on Boylan's sexual prowess before he effects a denial through the evasion 'June has no ar no oysters'. 'Tainted game' then provides the *double entendre* which allows him to continue his thoughts about food in a less anxious frame of mind.

This passage, if heightened by the onset of sexual jealousy, is typical of the main Joycean method of representation. Bloom's consciousness is rendered as layered, fluxive and heterogeneous. From 'dewdrop' to 'tainted game', from the City Arms Hotel to Bleibtreustrasse in Berlin, from 'off colour' to 'gaudy colours', from 'doggy-bowwowsywowsy' to 'all the odd things people pick up for food', Bloom's awareness constitutes the fragmentary self in its most representative form. As Robert Humphrey has noted, the term 'stream' (even though it is used by Joyce himself in the book)[27] 'is not fully descriptive'.[28] Indeed it is really quite deceptive, since it implies a continuity and consistency of material which is constantly denied by Joyce's method. The notion of 'free association' is useful, and doubtless the literary technique is partly informed by the psychoanalytic practice, but again it can be misleading since the interior monologue contains material (and adopts rhetorical ploys) which could never be voiced on the couch in this way. We are left, then, to juggle with finally inadequate terms – stream, montage, symbolism, patterning etc. – to express a technique which is both brilliantly original and complexly variable. At times, Joyce seems just as interested in the linguistic possibilities (and relativities) of representation itself as in the mental contents which are thus expressed. The rendering of Gerty MacDowell's selfhood is all novelettish pastiche in 'Nausicaa'; that of Stephen's in 'Ithaca' a satire on encyclopaedic sophistry; that of Bloom's in 'Circe' a dramatic Expressionistic extravaganza. But if we cannot theorise Joyce's method as a whole, we can observe that, whatever the stylistic pyrotechnics, the rendering of selfhood is always a matter of fragmentation. Indeed, it is specifically by undermining the discourse of coherence and continuity that Joyce reveals to us the spectacle of self's discontinuities and incoherence. The 'old stable ego' is revealed as a rhetorical fiction.

The quality of Stephen's selfhood is shown as very different from that of Bloom's. The whole timbre and ratio between self-parts is quite different in each case. This is demonstrated from without in 'Eumaeus' and 'Ithaca', but it is set up earlier, and in far greater depth, through the main stream-of-consciousness method. Here, for example, is a brief extract expressing Stephen's awareness, which contrasts strongly with the 'Bloomstream' quoted above:

> Under the upswelling tide he saw the writhing weeds lift languidly and sway reluctant arms, hising up their petticoats, in whispering water swaying and upturning coy silver fronds. Day by day: night by night: lifted, flooded and let fall. Lord, they are weary: and, whispered to, they sigh. Saint Ambrose heard it, sigh of leaves and waves, waiting, awaiting the fullness of their times, *diebus ac noctibus iniurias patiens ingemiscit*. To no end gathered: vainly then released, forth flowing, wending back: loom of the moon. Weary too in sight of lovers, lascivious men, a naked woman shining in her courts, she draws a toil of waters.
>
> Five fathoms out there. Full fathom five thy father lies. At one he said. Found drowned. High waters at Dublin bar. Driving before it a loose drift of rubble, fanshoals of fishes, silly shells. A corpse rising saltwhite from the undertow, bobbing landward, a pace a pace a porpoise. There he is. Hook it quick. Sunk though he be beneath the watery floor. We have him. Easy now.
>
> (p. 55)

This is typical of Stephen's intellectual imagination; both of his Protean[29] speculations and of his constant tendency to reorganise heterogeneities ('signatures of all things') into aesthetic patterns. It is a quite sustained meditation, inspired by the proximity of the sea as he rests on the strand. Even so, it focuses a whole spectrum of self-qualities in a kind of Cubist analysis – his appreciation of the feminine, his feel for the connotative texture of words, his scholastic training, his ambiguous emotions concerning his father, his love of Elizabethan and Romantic literature, his sense of the macabre, his sensuous appreciation of physical details and so on. Transformation is the operative process here – as it is in Ariel's song ('Full fathom five . . .') and in Eliot's response to this and other passages in *The Waste Land*.[30] This occurs even on the level of allusion: the Psalmist's 'day unto day' translated into Ambrose's 'diebus ac noctibus', Arnold's 'Sophocles heard it' into 'Saint Ambrose . . .', Ferdinand's sea-changed father into a ten-day-old contemporary corpse. But the chief transformation occurs on the plane of verbal connotation. Stephen's disparate awareness and associations are continually modified and synthesised in terms of the music of words: in particular by alliteration ('lifted, flooded and let fall'), rhythmic repetition ('Day by day: night by night') and internal rhyme ('loom of the moon'; 'found drowned'). Stephen's mind seems to occupy a crucial point of mediation between the multiplicity of experience and the aesthetic synthesis of art. The banal ('at one he said'), the epiphanic ('a corpse rising saltwhite'), the allusive ('full fathom five . . .') and the symbolically ineffable ('a naked woman shining in her courts') all coexist in the process of aesthetic transformation. Stephen's selfhood is a site of constant reorganisation of the real into the ideal. Its fragmentation is dynamic – a matter of constant rearrangement of self-parts within a charged aesthetic field.

The case of Molly Bloom is very different. She is fragmented in terms of conflicting surges of desire and the litter of disparate memories that make up her sleepy thought-stream:

> theyd die down dead off their feet if ever they got a chance of walking down the Alameda on an officers arm like me on the bandnight my eyes flash my bust that they havent passion God help their poor head I knew more about men and life when I was 15 than theyll all know at 50 they dont know how to sing a song like that Gardner said no man could look at my mouth and teeth smiling like that and not think of it I was afraid he mightnt like my accent first he so English all father left me in spite of his stamps Ive my mothers eyes and figure anyhow he always said theyre so snotty about themselves some of those cads he wasnt a bit like that he was dead gone on my lips let them get a husband first thats fit to be looked at and a daughter like mine or see if they can excite a swell with money that can pick and choose whoever he wants like Boylan to do it 4 or 5 times locked in each others arms or the voice either I could have been a prima donna only I married him comes looooves old deep down chin back not too much . . .
>
> (p. 684)

Sleepless, cut off from all but a few sensory impressions by the darkness, Molly's thoughts circle endlessly around her bodily functions, her desires, her life. In this short passage the word 'I' occurs six times, 'my' six and 'me' twice. Such self-preoccupation is predicated against contrastive 'they's (six occurrences, reinforced by 'their' and 'them') – in this case referring predominantly to

Kathleen Kearney's protegés ('her lot of squealers'), who are construed as both musical and sexual rivals. Molly's selfhood asserts itself in a world seen in terms of male demands and female rivalry. The world is full of 'they's, 'he's and 'she's who are inextricably bound up in her own conflicting impulses. Such impulses could conveniently be categorised in terms of the seven deadly sins. If gluttony does not loom large here, Molly certainly abounds in lust, pride, greed, sloth, anger (often disguised through scorn) and envy (though she would deny it). To an extent, this is a Jesuitical construction of woman as embodiment of all those weaknesses the flesh is heir to.

And yet this humanised Magdalene is given a Madonna's mystique. She triumphs in acknowledged self-plenitude, affirming that wayward multiplicity of self which the Catholic system would seek to repress and control. The whole of Molly's long spiel expresses, in a sense, 'looooves old deep down', famously starting and ending with 'Yes'. The comical heterogeneity of self is rendered through a language flow in which syntactical and punctuation rules are appropriated or ignored in the interests of infinite self-realisation. Complete sentences ('I knew more about men and life when I was 15 than theyll all know at 50') are seamlessly incorporated into the linguistic flux, while overt defiance of grammar ('my eyes flash my bust that they havent passion') is made expressive of the continual metamorphosis in awareness which typifies Molly's interior life. The slight, but continuous, abernations in syntactical discourse are central to the exposition and enable Joyce to represent the fragmentary nature of the self's life while remaining almost fully intelligible. At the same time, the adherence of much of the text to grammatical (if unpunctuated) discourse can also point up, without irritating streams of full-stops or dashes, the way Molly's attention can switch in an instant from one preoccupation to another: 'they dont know how to sing a song like that Gardner said no man could look at my mouth and teeth . . .'; or in the reverse direction: 'he was dead gone on my lips let them get a husband first . . .'. Gardner (later Boylan) can serve as signifier for the reinforcement of her self-esteem which, throughout the passage, is in nearly dialectical relationship to the threat she perceives in the younger women – expressed defensively as scornful dismissal of their charms. So there is a predominant psychic fluctuation: dismissal followed by self-reinforcement, followed by further dismissal, breaking again into further self-reinforcement. Throughout, Molly's disparate memories are used as a fund from which to pluck instances to justify her good opinion of herself. However, not all the material in the passage is subsumed into this tension between self-esteem and the threat of self-detraction: e.g. her father's stamps or 'chin back not too much'. There is more going on than simple self-division. Further, in other parts of the chapter Molly shows that she has a variety of strategies beyond dismissal/reinforcement to cope with her complex being-in-the-world. Ideally, as in the cases of Stephen and Bloom, we need far more material than a single passage can provide to demonstrate the cunning intricacy of Molly's self-fragmentation.

In each case, then, Joyce presents his main characters as fragmentary fields of awareness, and each character is fragmentary in a unique mode and style. What does this make of the final narrative 'self', who never overtly appears but remains 'invisible, refined out of existence, indifferent, paring his fingernails'?[31] Inescapably, *Ulysses* represents the authorial Joyce as himself radically split and wholly heterogeneous, a self-expressive balancing act between masculinity and femininity, youth and middle age, creativity and perceptual passivity rendered — without the interposition of any reconciling 'I' – in the fluxive and dramatically contrastive metamorphoses of discourse. If in 'Scylla and Charybdis' Shakespeare is shown as 'midway' between Hamlet and his father's ghost, then in *Ulysses* as a whole, Joyce is 'midway' between Stephen, Bloom and Molly – and indeed between Simon Dedalus, Gerty MacDowell, Rev. John Conmee S.J., the one-legged sailor and the whole host of minor characters down to the man in the mackintosh, Bloom's cat and Garryowen the dog. As Stephen says of Shakespeare:

> He found in the world without as actual what was in his world within as possible . . . Every life is many days, day after day. We walk through ourselves, meeting robbers, ghosts, giants, old men, young men, wives, widows, brothers-in-love. But always meeting ourselves.
>
> (p. 213)

Joyce, as writing self, reveals selfhood as an inexhaustible plethora; like Shakespeare he is 'all in all', and he can only be this by being infinitely fragmentary. If the dramatic writer, like the 'God of creation', is 'within or behind or beyond or above his handiwork',[32] it is because his selfhood includes everything, however incompatible, from the rival plenitudes of different characters right down to 'a shout in the street' (p. 40). Joyce's selfhood is expressed as an infinite simultaneity of parts and particles. And a stream-of-consciousness method, however adaptable from chapter to chapter, constitutes the literary discourse *par excellence* for representing the fragmentary self.

'THESE FRAGMENTS I HAVE SHORED'

The Waste Land (1922) bears the marks of Eliot's recent reading of Joyce's masterpiece.[33] Characteristics such as Imagistic urban realism, the incorporation of untranslated foreign phrases and evoked snatches of music, the diffused interest in sexuality (including bisexuality) – in the small, the symbolisation of the drowned man; in the large, the allusive mythic 'sub-structure': all these bear an influence from *Ulysses*. It is hard to doubt, too, that Joyce's varied versions of interior monologue helped the establishment of the dislocated discourses which speak the poem's complex awareness. Nevertheless, the strength of Eliot's 'esemplastic' power – his ability to assimilate and yet wholly transform – is evidenced by the striking originality of the lines, various as they are; and the self-fragmentation which the poem both evidences and enacts is wholly unique. Where Joyce's work is cool, dramatic, calculating, omniscient, Eliot's – for all the theory of 'impersonality'[34] – is anguished, associative, brokenly intuitive and finally personal. But the personality, expressed through a plethora of personae, is never in coherent possession of itself or its mental contents. In so far as the poem speaks the Western mind of the twenties, it expresses it as heterogeneity, contradiction and multi-layered multiplicity – in short, as a species of chaos. Selfhood here is at the end of its tether and desperate. Pound should never have vetoed Eliot's chosen epigraph: 'The horror! The horror!'

That Eliot's mini-epic – the 'justification' of the Modern movement according to Pound[35] – should have represented selfhood in this way is scarcely surprising, granted the situation out of which it was written. More powerfully than any of the current Dadaist stunts, it expressed both the ravages of the first total war and the political and economic anarchy which succeeded it. In addition, and in a way not finally dissociable from that situation, it expresses the mind of a brilliant and learned young man in a state of breakdown. This is most particularly so of parts III and V. It was in a shelter at Margate, while convalescing from nervous exhaustion, that the poet wrote those lines connecting nothing with nothing which could have come from *King Lear*. And it was from a clinic in Switzerland, still in therapy, that he wrote the whole of 'What the Thunder Said', virtually 'automatically',[36] and invoked the tears of Babylonian exile by the waters of Lake Leman. But the whole poem is, in fact, an articulation of a breakdown in selfhood, and all of it is written *de profundis*. The sections proceed, disjunctively, like some fearful dream, while the fractured syntax and collage of 'found-sounds' articulate the modern Babel as Bedlam. At the same time the constant disruption of quotations and allusions expresses less the mythic control sought for by two generations of scholars than the chronic unravelling, under stress, of a broad-based Harvard education.

The pressure of anxiety within the structure is as evident here as in the war literature we have considered. And, imaginatively, it is almost of the same order. Eliot, who – once America had entered the struggle – made varied and rather desperate attempts to join the armed services, seems to have appropriated the fragmentary implications of the Great War more fully than many soldier–writers. *The Waste Land* is permeated by war anxiety if not battle neurosis, and Robert Fussell's reading in *The Great War and Modern Memory*[37] remains persuasive. In addition to the 'rat's alley' lines, there are many elements in the poem which speak the legacy of the years 1914–18, for instance: the presence of an arch-duke, a buried corpse, the returning soldier Albert, the ear-to-ear 'chuckle' of teeth in its bone-rattling context, the soldier's song about Mrs Porter, the drowned sailor, the 'hooded hordes', bursting city and falling towers, the tumbled graves and the late, nursery-rhyme evocation of Bertrand Russell's vision of a disintegrated London Bridge. There is here, perhaps, dispersed guilt as well as imaginative involvement and a strained intellectual detachment. But what matters most is the effect as a representation. Through disruption of familiar conventions and self-immolation into grotesque masks and nightmare images, Eliot provides a mode of discourse for expressing war fragmentation which, as we have seen, a veteran like David Jones could adapt to represent his own army experience. If *The Waste Land* (according to its author's disclaimer) came to express a generation's 'illusion of being disillusioned', it could do so partly because it enacted a dissolution beyond any prospect of illusion – even that of authorial consistency and cohesion.

When the poem was first published, it startled its readers with its radical disconnections – so much so that some thought it rather a loose grouping of poems. Such disconnections can be seen within individual personae, however briefly introduced, and thus continuously represent self-fragmentation. Tiresias is simultaneously male and female while that other central persona, the Fisher King, is a type of mentally dismembered Osiris, finally taking refuge in his own 'fragments'. Other personae are similarly disjunctive: Marie, of split nationality, frightened or free and routinely bored; the nostalgist of the Hyacinth Garden, caught in a nothingness between life and death; Belladonna, dispersed into contrastive literary types; the neurotic woman, a rhythmic insistence of unanswered questions; the Thames maidens, heart beneath feet, who expect nothing and cannot connect; Phlebas, subsumed into both age and youth as he enters the whirlpool; the 'broken Coriolanus' who resolves into the Fisher King and peters out as a diaspora of uprooted quotations. The waste land is the broken land, and its hollow inhabitants lurk in their Bradleian 'prisons' of selfhood, split apart into fragments of memory and desire. So insubstantial are they, so self-dispersed, that they can indeed 'melt' into each other; never 'wholly distinct' because their identities are never centred.

Eliot's well known footnote ascribes to Tiresias the role of uniting all the characters.[38] This seems rather wishful – a metaphysical hankering after some final 'point of view'. If Tiresias is deemed to 'see' the whole of the poem, one can only remark that in the text itself there is one point, alone, where he is seen to be seeing anything. Indeed, the Fisher King would seem to have a better claim to operate as comprehensive persona in terms of the whole mythic sub-structure. But in fact the poem is not overtly unified by any of its fragmentary personae and its whole project is expressive of relativistic self-dispersal, both before and after Pound's editing job. And yet, of course, in some sense the whole must be the product of some self, some performer of 'the police in different voices'[39] – and that self is the poet behind the poem. But this selfhood represents itself as more rent, more dispersed, more radically discontinuous than any previous writing self in English poetry. The effect of *The Waste Land* is to demonstrate fragmentation at every level and the writing subject appears, in defiance of two thousand years of literary convention, as a congeries of split-off self-parts.

If there is a consistent method in the poem to express this fragmented selfhood, it must surely be based upon dream, which is the 'logic of the imagination' *par excellence*. Conrad's *Heart of Darkness* insists upon the dream-like nature of the experience it represents; the 'nightmare' nature of the 'horror' itself. In the twenty-odd years since its publication there had been much investigation and discussion of the dynamic and meaning of dreams, and it is likely that Eliot was familiar with the substance of this.[40] In particular, there was a general agreement among psychoanalysts about the nature of dream-work and the function of its two main aspects – condensation and displacement. Freud described the way 'latent' dreams or 'dream-thoughts' were transformed into 'manifest' dreams thus:

> By the process of *displacement* one idea may surrender to another its whole quota of cathexis; by the process of *condensation* it may appropriate the whole cathexis of several other ideas.[41]

The notion of condensation is perhaps the simpler: a part stands for a much greater whole (as the garden corpse in *The Waste Land* represents, at once, the Great War dead, spiritual negation, fertility-cult burials and so forth). Some 'latent' elements may be omitted in the part; but it typically fuses many such elements and so is overdetermined. At the same time, by condensation, one element of the 'latent' dream may be represented by several images (rather in the way that the feminine principle in *The Waste Land* is distributed among a variety of personae and symbols). Displacement, on the other hand, transforms or distorts the emotional importance of the 'latent' cathexis with respect to the manifest part (as in *The Waste Land* the 'Emmaeus' encounter – via Shackleton's Antarctic experience – is transformed from comradeship and expectation into uncanny dread). By displacement, too, minor things appear major (the pub scene) and major ones minor ('To Carthage then I came'). Freud writes of displacement: 'no other part of the dream-work is so much responsible for making the dream strange or incomprehensible to the dreamer'.[42]

The Waste Land has often been described, loosely, as dream-like – especially such proto-Surrealist passages as the one beginning 'A woman drew her long black hair out tight'. However, to my knowledge, no one has yet considered its 'kaleidoscopic' technique, its allusive method and its emotional transformations in terms of the two key processes of dream-work. My suggestion is that it makes sense to compare Freud's 'latent' dream-thoughts with the complex emotions, ideas and cultural echoes whirling about in the poet's mind at the critical time of writing; and that the employment of a kind of literary dream-work has resulted in a bizarre poem very comparable to a 'manifest' dream, characterised throughout by radical shrinkages and overdetermination, and by strange emotional transformations. This literary dream-work, then, has resulted in a compelling textual representation of the fragmented self. The usual rational connectives, whereby integral selfhood is constructed, are almost entirely missing: in their place, a disintegrated self is represented – as in a dream – by a collocation of personae which melt into and out of each other, and by a congeries of 'broken images'. Thus is explained a whole range of new poetic devices: the Imagistic condensation (roots, hair, rock, towers, bones); the plurality of Symbolistic representations for each primal motif (Marie, Belladonna, Lil, nymphs, typist, Thames maidens etc. for the feminine; or Buddha, Augustine, Phlebas, Christ, Osiris for life-in-death); the overdetermination of individual scenarios or figures (desert, water, city or Sosostris, Belladonna, Tiresias, Fisher King with all their allusive implications); and the extraordinary emotional weirdness of the poem (the cruelty of Spring, fear in dust, the 'nothingness' of sexual ecstasy in the Garden or, at the end, the 'crouching' jungle, the hypothetical gaiety of response to 'controlling hands', the terrible threat in the child's nursery rhyme 'London Bridge is falling down'). I do not suggest that the whole poem should be yielded up to Freudian interpretation (as Eliot remarked 'interpretation is the other fellow's description'),[43] nor are all its symbols to be construed in vulgar Freudian terms (a falling tower also represents the crisis of war). However, I do suggest that the best single way to theorise the experimental technique in the poem is to see it as a literary kind of dream-work. Whether this was a result of a thought-out programme or of yielding to the processes of 'trance' does not seem to matter much. But it is more than mere analogy to suggest that it is by condensation and displacement that Eliot here achieves his representation of radically fragmented selfhood. And the success of the method is not surprising, since it is in our dreams that we experience, most directly, a selfhood that is neither integral nor consistent.

However, the dreamer of selfhood expressed through the poem as a whole is multi-lingual and formidably dispersed into the discourses of others. In a sense, we might say that the dreaming mind is the 'mind of Europe'[44] speaking through the 'self' behind the arras of the text. Or, to continue the dream suggestion, we might say that much of the content of the 'latent' dream-thoughts has been supplied by Eliot's immersion in cultural discourses, at both conscious and pre-conscious levels, prior to writing. At times such material may be 'lifted . . . into the manifest content of the dream [text] as a ready-made structure' (Nagera, *Basic Psychoanalytic Concepts*, p. 38). In *The Waste Land* the Tarot-pack description or the Phlebas epiphany may be examples of this. However, it is noticeable that much cultural material appears in the poem modified by the 'dream-work'. So the whole resonant corpus and authority of Dante (which in one sense places the waste-landers) is shrunk by condensation to a line fragment or two, while Jacobean tragic morbidity suffers a sea change by displacement into the figure of the friendly 'Dog' – so different in affect to Webster's wolf. Indeed, one can say that most of the mythological material appears in the poem radically modified from its possible 'latent' meanings by the operation of literary 'dream-work'. This is what has made literary exposition of the poem's intent so complicated, for:

> Not only are the elements of a dream determined by the dream-thoughts many times over, but the individual dream-thoughts are represented in the dream by several elements. Associative paths lead from one element of the dream to several dream-thoughts, and from one dream-thought to several elements of the dream.
>
> (Nagera, *Basic Psychoanalytic Concepts*, p. 37)

By Eliot's notion of interpretation, the mind of Europe 'behind' the poem can never be reached objectively. Hence we must stick with that which is presented as a continuous disjunction of quotations, allusions, style changes, snatches of song and evoked myths. The European dreamer, like the private dreamer (Eliot), is only there in the dream itself. We must cleave to the one clear meaning which is abundantly evident – that selfhood is a fragmentary dream. This, I take it, is what Eliot meant in saying that the critic should not *interpret*, but through comparison and analysis bear witness to the specific 'entelechy' of a work.[45]

The break-up of selfhood is enforced in *The Waste Land* (as in *Ulysses*) by the most drastic means a writer can use – the surrender of personal style to the discourses of others. This does not mean that the poem has no style at all: but it does mean that its distinctive virtú is achieved only through a collage of assimilated styles. The poem foregrounds its own radical intertextuality. This is spectacularly so at the very end. But the creation of a multi-voiced textuality to express modern selfhood is effected, with varying density, from the evocation of Chaucer and Whitman at the beginning right through to the last borrowed 'shantih'. Just as the poem evolves through the melting of one persona into another, so it develops as a constant metamorphosis of one style into another, often interpenetrated by quotation and allusion: 'Son of man / You cannot say . . . "Jug Jug" to dirty ears . . . "What shall I do now?" . . . asked me in demotic French . . . Highbury bore me . . . O you who turn the wheel . . . And voices singing out of empty cisterns and exhausted wells . . .' The voice of the poem's self is dramatic, allusive, variable, multi-lingual, disjunctive, many-layered and metamorphic. Though, at any one point, it offers a complexity of meanings, the overall effect is of a kind of dream babble: the 'mind of Europe' crying out from its nightmare sleep in disparate tongues: 'Oed' und leer das Meer . . . hypocrite lecteur . . . Ta ta. Goodnight . . . O ces voix d'enfants . . . O Lord Thou pluckest . . . *Datta* . . . Quando fiam uti chelidon.'

The notes to the poem add a further dimension which we might liken to 'secondary revision' in dreaming. In addition to the dramatic 'I's of the poem we find another disconcerting 'I' which offers remarks such as: 'a phenomenon I have often noticed' or 'the ballad . . . was reported to me from Sydney, Australia' or 'one of the Antarctic expeditions (I forget which but I think one of Shackleton's)'. Whatever the occasion for adding the notes, Eliot uses them partially to help explicate and normalise the disturbing vision of the poem. Actually, they merely complicate matters, adding to the dream voices a rationalising censorship masquerading as the 'real' self. In spite of Eliot's warning that the poet commenting on his own poem becomes merely another reader, without special privileges,[46] many critics have tended to take the notes as a sure guide – hence the insistence, on Eliot's say-so, that Tiresias does indeed unite the whole. Freud's comment on the deceptive coherence suggested by secondary revision is cautionary:

> It is our normal thinking that is the psychical agency which approaches the content of dreams with a demand that it must be intelligible, which subjects it to a first interpretation and which consequently produces a complete misunderstanding of it . . . It remains an essential rule invariably to leave out of account the ostensible continuity of a dream as being of suspect origin . . .
>
> (Nagera, *Basic Psychoanalytic Concepts*, p. 90)

Suggestions in the Tiresias footnote that the poem is somehow united in spite of its 'entelechy' seem to me to be of this order; as does the hint borrowed from Eliot's review of *Ulysses* that the fertility myth allusions somehow provide a means of 'ordering and controlling' the anarchic panorama that is the dream-scape of the poem.[47] The 'primary process' dream-speech serves to chant such notions out of court: 'O, O, O, O, . . . Twit twit twit . . . Weialala leia . . . Co co rico . . . Da . . . Da . . . Da . . .' So too do the ghost voices of the literary father figures whose poly-vocal presence stands always behind the text. There is no coherence or rational continuity here: that is the truth of the poem. Self in *The Waste Land* is of such stuff as dreams are made on, and in its enchanted realm 'this music' resolves into 'the isle is full of noises'. *Pace* the notes, it is only after the miracle of creation that the tired Prospero threatens to drown his own book.[48]

The Waste Land, then, is a major document in the Modernist establishment of a new discourse of selfhood. It succeeds in transcending the 'old stable ego' by founding an experimental language and method which is most fittingly theorisable in terms of the processes of dream formation. Through a literary mode of condensation and displacement it expresses a wholly diffused and dispersed selfhood in terms of personified self-parts which melt into each other and separate again, and a collocation of quotations, allusions and style postures which speak the dreaming mind of Europe. If the poem constitutes 'rhythmical grumbling', then it is a polyglot and near-cosmic grumbling which resonates in the echo chamber of the writing subject. Everything here is converted into something 'rich and strange', and such transformation, operating always in terms of energised fragments, offers a wholly new paradigm of experience. For this reason, it is fruitless to look for

Fragmentary Self

an allegorical coherence behind the poem – in the latent dream-thoughts, as it were: that is to fall into the trap of interpretation. The message is in the mode, and the dream-work speaks the new version of selfhood. The 'hypocrite lecteur' who looks for meanings of the old kind is neither 'semblable' nor 'frère' to the Eliotic vision: he has had the experience but missed the meaning. The 'shantih' of understanding and acceptance can only come when we recognise the poem's radical restatement of selfhood. After the post-Cartesian interval of Western ego centrality, the poem reasserts the complexity of selfhood in heightened dream-logic. The sombre aspect of its vision can be summed up: 'Hieronymo's mad againe'.

'"I – I –" HE STAMMERED . . . "I – I –"'[49]

Virginia Woolf's *Mrs Dalloway* (1925) pitches the fragmentary self between ecstasy and madness. Its style is nervous, lyrical, elegiac, atomistic, sometimes scornfully ironic – expressive of a selfhood characteristically 'scattered and various'.[50] In its emphasis on symbolic death and the dissipated social effects of the Great War, it perhaps reflects Woolf's immersion in *The Waste Land* (which she had set laboriously into print) and sombrely anticipates that later conjunction of Ophelia's 'Goodnight sweet ladies' and 'Fear death by water' in her own demise in the river Ouse. And yet it is one of her most optimistic books. It celebrates the rich plenitude of moment-by-moment interiority; it hymns the collective consciousness of shared memories; it rejoices in the heterogeneity of the self's overall awareness – 'life; London; this moment of June'. Joycean in its exploitation of the date-line of a single day and its space–time montage, it perhaps expresses, in its lyrical acceptance of the common world, more of the spirit of *Ulysses* than she consciously knew.[51] And like the last chapter of *Ulysses* – a work she had read and discussed with Eliot between 1920 and 1922[52] – it energises, in strangely suggestive imagery, a specifically feminine life affirmation in the midst of transience and separation:

> still, though it issued from so rude a mouth, a mere hole in the earth, muddy too, matted with root fibres and tangled grasses, still the old bubbling burbling song, soaking through the knotted roots of infinite ages . . . fertilising, leaving a damp stain . . .
> ee um fah um so
> foo swee too eem oo.
> (pp. 91–2)

Mrs Dalloway was the first book in which Virginia Woolf fully established her 'method' – the 'new form for a new novel'.[53] It fulfils her proposition of 1919 in 'Modern Fiction':

> Examine for a moment, an ordinary mind on an ordinary day. The mind receives a myriad impressions – trivial, fantastic, evanescent, or engraved with the sharpness of steel. From all sides they come, an incessant shower of innumerable atoms. . . Life is not a series of gig lamps symmetrically arranged; life is a luminous halo, a semi-transparent envelope surrounding us from the beginning to the end. Is it not the task of the novelist to convey this varying, this unknown and uncircumscribed spirit, whatever aberration or complexity it may display, with as little mixture of the alien and external as possible?[54]

Like Joyce and Dorothy Richardson, Virginia Woolf chose the vehicle of interior monologue to represent the 'stream of consciousness'. But, where Joyce is variably dramatic, Woolf is stylistically consistent, and where Richardson suggests subjective solipsism, Woolf evokes a shared intersubjectivity. Clarissa, Peter Walsh and Sally Seton, in particular, are characterised as much by shared memories as by individualist perceptions. And the self-life of all the main characters is rendered in a similar way as fragmentary, caught in the continuum of subjective time and voiced as a single stylistic flow:

> She sat on the floor – that was her first impression of Sally – she sat on the floor with her arms round her knees, smoking a cigarette. Where could it have been? The Mannings'? The Kinloch-Jones's? At some party (where she could not be certain), for she had a distinct recollection of saying that to the man she was with, 'Who is *that*?'
>
> (p. 37)

This meditation of Clarissa Dalloway's does not differ in stylistic substance from, say, a similar reflection by Peter Walsh:

It is Clarissa herself, he thought, with a deep emotion, and an extraordinarily clear, yet puzzling, recollection of her, as if this bell had come into the room years ago, where they sat at some moment of great intimacy, and had gone from one to the other and had left, like a bee with honey, laden with the moment. But what room? What moment?

(p. 56)

The author mediates and interprets each character's self-experience through the same subtly contrived, intuitive discourse. It is a specifically Woolfean style, attained only after much thought and practice with words. As she wrote in 1922: 'I have found out how to begin (at 40) to say something in my own voice'.[55]

The novel is, above all, a celebration of one day in the life of Clarissa Dalloway. Her self-experience is at the centre of the book. Clarissa constitutes a unique instance of selfhood which appears as perpetual self-conflict, alternating between self-confidence and self-doubt, enthusiasm and coldness, impulse and calculation, expectation and dread, love and scornful dislike. Socially, she reacts with feline instinct: 'if you put her in a room with someone, up went her back like a cat's; or she purred' (p. 11). But although she aspires to be a successful hostess, and her day is full of social encounters culminating in her party, it is in her solitary self-life that we meet her most directly and here that she is most characteristically fragmentary, fluid and contradictory. Her mood, and her construction of her life, varies considerably during the course of the day. In the morning she is all bounce and excitement ('What a lark! What a plunge!', p. 5). But by midday, when she goes up to her room, loneliness and a sense of failure govern her meditations: 'narrower and narrower would her bed be', (p. 35). The visit of Peter Walsh, shortly afterwards, puts her in a different frame of mind again which reaches a sudden consummation: 'and then, next moment, it was as if the five acts of the play . . . were now over and she had lived a lifetime in them and had run away, had lived with Peter, and it was now over' (p. 53). However, we are not to see Clarissa as aberrant or absurd. It is those characters in the novel who construe themselves as unified and self-consistent – Hugh Whitbread or Dr Holmes, for instance – who are satirised as absurd self-deceivers. Virginia Woolf has focused her fiction on Clarissa's volatility in order to make a point about the reality of all self-experience. Selfhood is variable and moments of synthesis occur only out of its heterogeneity: 'that was herself when some effort, some call on her to be herself, drew the parts together, she alone knew how different, how incompatible. . .' (p. 42). Such moments represent self-wholeness not as rational consistency but as a (finally aesthetic) balancing act among contrarieties. Further, the drawing of the 'parts together' does not conform to a single static model, found and then lost and then found again, but will vary in nature from occasion to occasion. What matters is not the constituency or arrangement of the self-parts but simply the sense of balance between such fragments as are experienced at any one time. It is the ability to harmonise, to draw together, to accept heterogeneity positively, which prevents Clarissa from disintegrating and succumbing to the terror of nothingness. So her last epiphany in the book is not a repetition of earlier moments of self-integration but constitutes a radical readjustment to cope with the news of Septimus Warren Smith's suicide. She imaginatively assimilates his desperate death leap into her own awareness and is then able to construe it as an act of defiance at the relativity of experience and the impossibility of maintaining continuous self-wholeness:

> Death was an attempt to communicate, people feeling the impossibility of reaching the centre which, mystically, evaded them; closeness drew apart; rapture faded; one was alone.
> (p. 204)

She, too, feels she has 'lost herself in the process of living' (p. 205), but it does not destroy her. Having faced the terror of losing her balance, she prepares to face the party again. And just as the party enacts a social balancing act among incompatible people so it symbolises the personal balancing act between rival self-parts. As Clarissa realises, just prior to finding Sally and Peter, 'she must assemble' (p. 206). In mature Woolf the ability to achieve experiential wholeness is very much a matter of active *assemblage*.[56]

Clarissa's volatile and fragmentary selfhood is the norm in *Mrs Dalloway* rather than the exception. It is something she shares, for instance, with Peter Walsh. Within a few pages of Peter's entry into the narrative, we find a conspicuous example of Peter's Protean selfhood:

but I'll show Clarissa – and then to his utter surprise, suddenly thrown by those uncontrollable forces, thrown through the air, he burst into tears; wept; wept without the least shame, sitting on the sofa, the tears running down his cheeks.

(p. 52)

Peter's sensations, thoughts and memories are very similar to Clarissa's as he walks the streets of London. The difference between them is, perhaps, that while Clarissa looks for an inward perception of self-reconciliation, Peter is more inclined to act out his impulses. He is the existential 'romantic buccaneer' (p. 60), who performs what Clarissa would only phantasise, risking his life sense in love as in work. Because of this, he has the reputation of not amounting to anything; and yet his refusal of a socially acceptable egoic role is shown sympathetically – in contrast to the hollow conformity of, say, Professor Brierly, 'the Professor on moderation' (p. 195). Peter's adult life is comparable to Sally Seton's youthful flings. We scarcely get inside Sally in the book, but her unannounced eruption into the party parallels Peter's sudden invasion of Clarissa's sewing room. She, too, is a bolder type of volatility and her legend signifies the same as Peter's formulation of selfhood:

For this is the truth about our soul, he thought, our self, who fish-like inhabits deep seas and plies among obscurities threading her way between the boles of giant weeds, over sun-flickered spaces and on and on into the gloom, cold, deep, inscrutable; suddenly she shoots to the surface and sports on the wind-wrinkled waves.

(p. 178)

Clarissa's daughter, Elizabeth, who for most of the book has appeared immersed 'fish-like' in Miss Kilman's religiosity, also has her own eruption into impulsive freedom. On top of a London bus she rehearses her possibilities: 'she would become a doctor, a farmer, possibly go into Parliament, if she found it necessary' (p. 151). Even Richard Dalloway, a foil to Peter for much of the book, is given his moment of uncharacteristic impetuosity when he buys flowers for his wife. What the novel seems to be saying is that self-authenticity depends on the ability to acknowledge, if not always to act upon, the contradictory and fluid reality of self-experience. In this sense it is a properly existential text.

The villains in *Mrs Dalloway* tend to be 'other-directed'[57] – typically pompous (and male) individuals who are content to live out (and are adept at coercing others to conform to) the fiction of self-integration and self-consistency. If Dr Holmes is the melodramatic exemplum of this, then Sir William Bradshaw is the satiric Aunt Sally:

> Sir William . . . made a fine figurehead at ceremonies and spoke well – all of which had by the time he was knighted given him a heavy look, a weary look . . . which weariness, together with his grey hairs, increased the extraordinary distinction of his presence and gave him the reputation (of the utmost importance in dealing with nerve cases) not merely of lightning skill and almost infallible accuracy in diagnosis, but of sympathy; tact; understanding of the human soul.
>
> (pp. 105–6)

The hollow man, then, is to be located in Harley Street, masquerading as a specialist in the nature of selfhood. His doctrine of Proportion is merely a middle-class version of the myth of the integral self, where all aspects of experience are subordinated to the imperial ego. Virginia Woolf insists that the issue at stake is between self-honesty and humbug; and, even more, between empathy and the lust for power. The fragmentary self does not ruthlessly repress its heterogeneity – and so can reach out to the reality of others' experience ('what does the brain matter . . . compared to the heart?', p. 215). But the conformist self denies its own authentic reality and so refuses the reality of others. It can only demand of others that they deny themselves and submit to the integral myth about selfhood. Hence the connection, in the text, between Proportion and Conversion:

> But Proportion has a sister, less smiling, more formidable, a Goddess . . . even now engaged in dashing down shrines, smashing idols, and setting up in their place her own stern countenance. Conversion is her name and she feasts on the wills of the weakly, loving to impress, to impose, adoring her own features stamped on the face of the populace . . . she . . . offers help, but desires power.
>
> (pp. 110–11)

The paragraph on Conversion, together with the descriptions of Bradshaw bullying his patients, constitutes the most vehement satiric writing in the novel: so much so that these passages threaten to undermine the book's overall message concerning the importance of intuitive empathy. But Woolf is surely right in her underlying awareness that the 'Robinson Crusoe' self is inherently imperialistic and subversive of authentic relationships: and that the fragmentary or fluid self, if kept in a state of balance, is conducive to authentic relationships as well as to self-honesty.

However, Woolf had personal reasons to fear the possible implications of fragmentation, if self-balance could not hold. *Mrs Dalloway* is threaded through with the terror of personal breakdown. And it is peculiarly fitting for my overall argument that the author should have embodied her own very personal (and feminine) fear of self-disintegration in the person of a Great War veteran – Septimus Warren Smith. Smith, who is represented in terms of the poet–combatant, expresses 'the horror' of losing firm self-definition. Like the simplistic versions of Rupert Brooke or Wilfred Owen, he is likened to Keats and 'went to France to save an England which consisted almost entirely of Shakespeare's plays' plus the image of a British woman 'in a green dress walking in a square' (p. 95). The shock of battle, and in particular the death of his friend Evans, sets him 'jabbering among the trees' (and indeed about the trees) as graphically as in Sassoon's nightmare vision in 'Repression of War Experience'. In the novel's narrative present, Smith's reality is rendered as typically fragmentary and frequently on the brink of terror:

> He lay on the sofa and made her hold his hand to prevent him from falling down, down, he cried, into the flames! and saw faces laughing at him, calling him horrible disgusting names, from the walls and hands pointing round the screen . . . he began to talk aloud, answering people, arguing, laughing, crying, getting very excited and making her write things down.
>
> (p. 75)

The result is closer to Dadaism or Surrealism than any contemporary English veteran's poetry:

> Diagrams, designs, little men and women brandishing sticks for arms, with wings – were they? – on their backs; circles traced

round shillings and sixpences – the suns and stars; zigzagging precipices with mountaineers ascending roped together, exactly like knives and forks; sea pieces with little faces laughing out of what might perhaps be waves: the map of the world . . . Now for his writings; how the dead sing behind rhododendron bushes; odes to Time; conversations with Shakespeare; Evans, Evans, Evans – his messages from the dead; do not cut down trees; tell the Prime Minister. Universal love: the meaning of the world.

(p. 163)

The writing suggests that, *in extremis*, self-disintegration expresses itself as bizarre montage. This is not so in the case of Woolf herself: when she was in mental institutions her diary entries simply stop.[58] But in *Mrs Dalloway*, which contains her most sustained study of mental breakdown, the one-time 'poet' is reduced to wild jottings which appear, from the outside, to be merely schizoid. So the crisis of the fragmentary self is construed as a crisis in discourse too, which leads to the writer's social marginalisation. The 'death of the soul' becomes a death of writing. Smith's eventual suicide constitutes self-disintegration as, simultaneously, literary demise – the extinction of all communication which is not deemed 'sane'. Perhaps Ivor Gurney is the true prototype of Septimus Warren Smith.[59]

But Woolf's own project is to mediate between 'consciousness disjunct' and its 'final exclusion from the world of letters'.[60] It develops a discourse whereby both the ecstasy and the terror of fragmentariness can be accommodated as experimental narrative and eventually recouped as literature. It does this by montagistic methods which never lose all relation to conventional development. Hence her 'poetic' style:

It was fascinating to watch her, moving about, that old lady, crossing the room, coming to the window. Could she see her? It was fascinating, with people still laughing and shouting in the drawing-room, to watch that old woman, quite quietly, going to bed alone. She pulled the blind now. The clock began striking. The young man had killed himself; but she did not pity him; with the clock striking the hour, one, two, three, she did not pity him, with all this going on. There! the old lady had put out her light! the whole house was dark now with this going on, she repeated, and the words came back to her, Fear no more the heat of the sun. She must go back to them. But what an extraordinary night!

(pp. 205–6)

The style is itself fragmentary – and yet insistent, repetitive, pulsating with an onward flow. It relies on specific Imagistic details – the blind, the clock, the 'young man' – which piece by piece construct the (patterned) heterogeneity of the mind's awareness. It also relies frequently on present participles to create the effect of ongoing process. It is, too, prodigal of commas, colons and semicolons, question marks and exclamation marks. It combines the sudden short sentence ('Could she see her?') with more leisurely sentences which are nevertheless fragmented by disjunctive commas, or more radical punctuation: 'The young man had killed himself; but she did not pity him; with the clock striking the hour, one, two, three, she did not pity him, with all this going on.' Although Woolf frequently uses conventional syntax, the overall effect is paratactical – this and this and this and then this . . . . Everything seems to be atomised, reduced to shimmering particles on an equalising plane where hierarchical notions, such as 'profound', 'trivial', 'important' etc. no longer pertain. The fragmentary self is rendered as selfhood where all parts and aspects are of the same interest; where everything is equally valid. And yet everything flows, too, in a forward-moving current of rhythmical energy where repetition also provides a sense of almost musical patterning. So the very discourse of *Mrs Dalloway* exemplifies its message concerning authentic selfhood. Selfhood is not unitary, but multiple, changeable, heterogeneous. And this truth is conveyed by a language which has released itself from the normal tyranny of 'rational' narrative progression and exploits the possibility of quasi-poetic effects to express that 'incessant shower of innumerable atoms' which is the self's life.

5
Self-deception and Self-conflict

'No . . . Yes . . . I won't lie . . . there'[1]

Self-deception and self-conflict have always been major themes in literature – some might say *the* major themes. Oedipus and Don Quixote, Lear, Arsinoé, Philip Pirrip and Willie Loman – all are, in important senses, self-deceivers whose inauthenticity generates conflict within. But the Modernist project of fragmenting selfhood enormously complicates the issues involved in these themes. If selfhood is fragmentary rather than coherent, we are beyond the mere paradoxicality of the lie in the self, and the question of the relationship between self-parts and the possibility of self-acknowledgement becomes acutely problematic. In the first place, Modernism writes self-deception as the banal norm rather than the spectacular (and heroic) exception. If fragmentation is a reality of experience then self-deception can never be finally evaded. Thus there is no instance when, for instance, Prufrock or Mauberley or Bloom or Gerald Critch see themselves quite clearly – as Oedipus or Dickens's Pip are represented as doing. Further, because awareness of fragmentariness is bound up with the relativities of language, there is no final formulation that might articulate full self-recognition. Where Oedipus can claim 'Everything has come to light' and spell out, in anguish, what he has been, the Modernist protagonist (or subject) is prone to testify, in bewilderment, the mismatch between experience and words: 'It is impossible to say just what I mean!'

In this, Modernist literature has gone further than most twentieth-century philosophical discussions about self-deception. Literary Modernism, we might say, was the major intellectual discourse to take on board the final implications of the 'death of God'. If human consciousness is all – arbiter not only of values and beliefs but also of the nature of reason and reality itself – then the possibility of human self-deception puts all in doubt. And again, since human language is not divinely guaranteed, and can be shown as inadequate to express accurately what is beyond it, quite what can be said to be the case about anything? As Nietzsche noted, we have scarcely abolished God if we still believe in grammar. Modernist writers tended not to believe in the surface value of language, and so what they tell us about deception and conflict within selfhood is most typically expressed by *anacoluthon*, slippages, evasions or ironic denials: Sassoon's 'No, no, not that', Prufrock's 'I should have been a pair of ragged claws', Bloom's 'June has no ar no oysters', or Lord Jim's satirised 'Eh? What? I am not excited, he remonstrated . . . and with a convulsive jerk . . . knocked over the cognac bottle'.[2]

The Modernist discourse about selfhood owed considerably to the psychoanalytic movement, as has already been evidenced. With respect to the problems of self-deception and self-conflict, the new perceptions of psychoanalysis were highly relevant. Whatever the developing struggles of emphasis within the Freudian group, their theory and practice clung tenaciously to the key notions of the Unconscious, repression and the work of censorship. Phantasy, projection, introjection and all manner of defence mechanisms were accepted as basic functions of the self. Man, the neurotic animal, was thus seen as condemned to self-conflict at the very heart of his intentions and motives – a confused state which only extended therapy could begin to unravel. Whether or not writers such as Eliot, Pound, Joyce, Yeats, Lawrence and Woolf were directly influenced by Freudian ideas (and some were) is scarcely the issue; they wrote out of an intellectual climate in which psychoanalytic notions had common currency. In this sense they were all 'jung and easily freudened', as Joyce put it. Psychic self-deception was no longer the infirmity of the exceptionally fated; it was the means by which Everyman came to terms with the contradictory drives within him as they impacted on the prison walls of reality.

The phenomenon of self-deception has become something of an issue in philosophy since the Modernist 'moment'. Sartre's description in *Being and Nothingness* remains one of the most authoritative:

Bad faith then has in appearance the structure of falsehood. Only what changes everything is the fact that in bad faith it is from myself that I am hiding the truth. Thus the duality of the deceiver and the deceived does not exist here. Bad faith on the contrary implies in essence the unity of a *single* consciousness ... It follows ... that the one to whom the lie is told and the one who lies are one and the same person, which means that I must know in my capacity as deceiver the truth which is hidden from me in my capacity as the one deceived. Better yet I must know the truth very exactly *in order* to conceal it more carefully – and this not at two different moments, which at a pinch would allow us to re-establish a semblance of duality – but in the unitary structure of a single project.[3]

In his book *Self-Deception*,[4] Herbert Fingarette makes the same point: 'What, then, shall we make of the self-deceiver, the one who is both the doer and the sufferer? Our fundamental categories are placed squarely at odds with one another' (p. 1). The tendency of Modernist literature, of course, is to explore the dynamics of this paradox rather than to resolve it rationally, stressing both the absurdity and the poignancy of the inauthentic man. At the same time, its discourse, which stresses the fragmentary nature of selfhood, dissipates the notion of 'the unity of a *single* consciousness' which informs Sartre's neo-Cartesian approach. It is closer to Lacan's formulation: 'I think where I am not, therefore I am not where I think.'[5] A recent English philosophical consideration of experiments on the bicameral nature of the mind also recommends dismantling the notion of a unitary self. In *Reasons and Persons*[6] Derek Parfit writes:

On the Cartesian view, a particular mental event occurs within a particular life solely in virtue of its ascription to a particular Ego. We can deny that the topography of 'Mental Space' is given by the existence of such persisting Egos. We can claim that a particular mental event occurs within some life in virtue of its relations to the many other mental and physical events which, by being interrelated, constitute this life.

(p. 252)

He compares Descartes's concept with Newtonian Space and Time and proposes a neo-Einsteinian correction so that 'the carrier of psychological continuity is *not* indivisible' (p. 259). His idea of 'successive selves' and the slogan 'a person is like a Nation' is very much the way writers like Eliot, Joyce or Woolf deal with the issues – and, as in Modernist writing – transfers interest from the paradox of the divided self to the complexity of interrelations between many 'selves'. Self-deception merges into radical self-conflict and the whole problematic nature of the fragmentary self.

Herbert Fingarette also inclines to the idea of 'the self as community' (p. 85), and stresses self-experience as an ongoing discovering and balancing act. He sees self-deception as less a problem of knowing than of being, engagement in the world and utterance ('spelling-out'). Knowing oneself is not a passive activity but a specific skill which can be tellingly withheld:

> Rather than a paradox of knowing ignorance, I have treated as central the capacity of a person to identify himself to himself as a particular person engaged in the world in specific ways, the capacity of a person to reject such identification, and the supposition that an individual can continue to be engaged in the world in a certain way even though he does not acknowledge it as his personal engagement and therefore displays none of the evidences of such acknowledgement.
>
> (p. 91)

Modernist writers are also concerned with the relationship between engagement and avowal (none more so than D. H. Lawrence), and they too see it as far more than a question of intellectual paradox. However, many twentieth-century writers are more sceptical about the possibility of 'authentic' avowal, the making of an 'integrated' self and the adequacy of language (hence knowledge?) to register the truth of engagements (what Fingarette calls 'spelling-out'). Starting from a sense of the self's fragmentariness and acute scepticism about the games language plays, the Modernists find the problem to be less what self-deception is than what any *truth* about self might be. They are less interested in the nature of disavowal than the status of avowal – i.e. its status beyond rationalisation, simplification or surrender to social cliché. Thus although Fingarette can be illuminating about classical examples of self-deception, his method of approach and some of his terms are rather called into question by Modernist writings. There is little in his account which could accommodate Conrad's perception of 'the convention that lurks in all truth and . . . the essential sincerity of falsehood' (*Lord Jim*, p. 75).

Yet Modernism's very scepticism about the adequacy of language to spell out the truth of self-experience implies that there is a reality beyond the tropes of discourse – that there are issues worth working towards, and that some kind of self-experience must be at the core of literary concern. However, because selfhood is given as fragmentary rather than whole and single, self-deception is often rendered as a form of self-conflict – different awarenesses and aspects of the self striving to attain a balance. Modern characters tend to shift from formulation to formulation, from story to story, from assertion to question to plea, as they endlessly debate with themselves whether anything they can say or believe about themselves is really true. 'I can connect/Nothing with nothing' is the common predicament of the twentieth-century anti-hero as he struggles to find out what, if any, 'self' he might have to be true to. Perhaps the real paradox here is that to be honest the hero must acknowledge that he is, at least partially, self-deceived. Which has, of course, its Socratic precedent – to know that one knows nothing.

There are many instances of this Modernist, radically self-doubting hero – from, say, James's Lambert Strether onwards. Eliot's Prufrock is one of the most exemplary. As we have seen, his selfhood is represented as uncertainly heterogeneous, and problems of self-recognition and honest self-articulation are at the core of his predicament: 'time yet for a hundred indecisions, / And for a hundred visions and revisions, / Before the taking of a toast and tea'. And, as I have suggested, the 'overwhelming question' could well be 'Who am I?' However, Prufrock is in no position to answer this (or even ask it) because of his super-sensitive awareness of the possibilities of self-deception: 'But though I have wept and fasted, wept and prayed, / Though I have seen my head (grown slightly bald) / brought in upon a platter, / I am no prophet – and here's no great matter.' Yet, in spite of his caution, it is arguable that the last part of the poem moves beyond relativistic uncertainty towards a formulation which represents a surrender to self-deception. Dismissing the analogy with Hamlet, Prufrock commits himself tentatively to his description of 'an attendant lord' – which we sense he is not at all. Then the last faintly absurd questions ('Shall I part my hair behind? Do I dare to eat a peach?') lead to a vision of mermaids which, despite possible disclaimers, represents mental relaxation into the self-indulgence of phantasy: 'We have lingered in the chambers of the sea / By sea-girls wreathed with

Self-deception and Self-conflict 113

seaweed red and brown'. As Eliot was to write later, 'human kind/Cannot bear very much reality'. Most of the poem shows Prufrock struggling, as honestly as he can, to express the realities of his self-conflict. But the ending enacts a cessation of that struggle, where phantasy is finally interrupted by the discourse of others ('human voices') which itself precipitates the ultimate phantasy – of drowning, silence, final peace.

Representative fiction of the Modernist period is also centrally concerned with self-deception. The whole movement of *Portrait of the Artist*, for instance, is a negotiation of various states of inauthenticity, brought on by pressures from without, towards a final declaration of the creative plenitude of self. One such state of self-deception occurs when Stephen repents and resolves to become a priest:

> Every part of his day, divided by what he regarded now as the duties of his station in life, circled about its own centre of spiritual energy. His life seemed to have drawn near to eternity; every thought, word, and deed, every instance of consciousness could be made to revibrate radiantly in heaven.
>
> (p. 148)

An authorial perspective on such inauthenticity is retained by phrases such as 'what he regarded now as' or 'seemed to have draw', and yet the measured, rhythmic, neo-Newmanesque discourse can induce in the reader himself a near-hypnosis of self-deception which persuades him that this is indeed the hero's authentic destiny. It is typical of Joyce that when he wishes to represent an escape from self-deception the discourse is broken and only semi-grammatical: 'And mine? Is it not too? Then into Nile mud with it!' (p. 250) The quest of Paul Morel in *Sons and Lovers* is also a search for authenticity which involves sloughing off the pressures of others to make him what he is not. It is only when his mother dies that he can fully face, in anguish, the authentic confusions within him. The last temptation is the possibility of escaping from himself into Miriam, but he senses that 'she could not take him and relieve him of the responsibility of himself' (p. 511). As I have mentioned before, the book ends uncertainly: 'He would not take that direction, to the darkness, to follow her. He walked towards the faintly humming, glowing town, quickly'. However, the Prufrockian phantasy of self-evasion through death is disavowed and the road towards self-recognition is begun. The book is itself biographically rooted in Lawrence's own self-deceptions and phantasies concerning his parents (hence the ambivalent treatment of both the father and the mother in the book). But what the ending signals is Lawrence's determination to write his way through to his own form of self-truth (like Stephen) – a process which by *Women in Love* he could feel was achieved.

A darker and more ironic fictional portrayal of self-deception is contained in May Sinclair's *Life and Death of Harriett Frean*[7] (1922). Here, inauthenticity is psychologically placed in terms of an inability to shake off parental pressure. In the key action of the book, Harriett relinquishes her lover Robin to her friend Priscilla under the influence of her parents' sense of propriety (Robin had come to their house as Priscilla's young man). The consequences of her self-denial bring misery to all three of them. Yet Harriett, again introjecting her parents' apparent values, constructs what she has done as virtuous – while in fact indulging in absurd spiritual pride:

> She esteemed herself justly. She knew she was superior to the Hancocks and the Pennefathers and to Lizzie Pierce and Sarah Barmby; even to Priscilla. When she thought of Robin and how she had given him up she felt a thrill of pleasure in her beautiful behaviour, and a thrill of pride in remembering that he had loved her more than Priscilla. Her mind refused to think of Robin married.
>
> (p. 67)

Sinclair's delicate irony chronicles the development of Harriett into an old maid whose typical self-placement is: 'You forget that I'm Hilton Frean's daughter' (p. 116). Harriett is eventually abandoned by the servant she had previously treated cruelly (and deceitfully), and the last we see of her she is recovering from an operation in hospital and greeting her friend Connie, with a smile of 'sudden ecstatic wonder and recognition', as 'Mamma – '. Harriett has failed to apply to her inner self the kind of risking honesty that her father, in fact, had applied to the physical universe: 'The fascination of truth might be just that – the risk that after all it mayn't be true, that you may have to go farther and farther, perhaps never come back' (p. 41).

But May Sinclair's study is not distinctively Modernist, because it is so distanced, smoothly ironic and secure in its own writing-position. It addresses a psychoanalytically modern problem, but in largely conventional terms. Siegfried Sassoon, by contrast, can, as we have seen, explore self-conflict from within, and raise important issues about the adequacy of normal language to express extreme experience. This is the case in 'Letter to Robert Graves'[8] as in 'Repression of War Experience'. The 'Letter' is a very uneasy poem where the subject position is always at issue, as the writing varies between banter and pleading, bluster and piquancy. The poem achieves no firm perspective on the situation expressed. Rather, it exists to articulate the very postures, ironies, language games and contradictions involved in the attempt to spell out an anguished self-experience:

> No visitors allowed
> Since Friends arrived in crowd –
> Jabber – Gesture – Jabber – Gesture – Nerves went phut and failed
> After the first afternoon when MarshMoonStreetMeiklejohn Ardours and enduranSitwellitis prevailed,
> Caused complications and set my brain a-hop;
> Sleeplessexasperuicide, O Jesu make it stop!
> But yesterday afternoon my reasoning Rivers ran solemnly in,
> With peace in the pools of his spectacled eyes and a wisely omnipotent grin;
> And I fished in that steady grey stream and decided that I
> After all am no longer the Worm that refuses to die.
> But a gallant and glorious lyrical soldjer;
>   Bolder and bolder; as he gets older;
> Shouting 'Back to the Front
> For a scrimmaging Stunt.'
> (I wish the weather wouldn't keep on getting colder.)

This type of broken confessional poetry is brought to artistic perfection in Pound's Pisan *Cantos*, at the end of another bitter European war. But the last complete canto, CXVI,[9] is perhaps the most telling, with respect to self-deception, because it calls into question its own expressive method and, indeed, the entire life project of the poem. It confesses guilt and weakness; but it also asserts purity of motive and the commitment to beauty. It is by no means a straight admission of failure as some have seen it;[10] rather it represents one of the most complex expositions of the search for self-honesty ever written. The viability of the *Cantos* themselves, for instance, is expressed as a contrast of disparate utterances which must all be collated together, and which overtly enlist the reader's own involvement:

> I have brought the great ball of crystal;
> who can lift it?
> Can you enter the great acorn of light? . . .
>
> And I am not a demigod,
> I cannot make it cohere . . .
>
> a nice quiet paradise
> over the shambles . . .
>
> i.e. it coheres all right
> even if my notes do not cohere . . .
>
> And as to who will copy this palimpsest? . . .
>
> But to affirm the gold thread in the pattern
> (Torcello) . . .
>
> I cannot make it flow thru.
> A little light, like a rushlight
> to lead back to splendour.

Images of patterning vie with ascriptions of chaos. Three key statements unsettle each other: 'I cannot make it cohere . . . it coheres all right . . . I cannot make it flow thru.' Is this straight affirmation versus denial, or is a distinction being made between *making* cohere and actual coherence? Or is there to be seen 'coherence' as opposed to 'flow'? The images also offset each other: 'great ball of crystal' versus 'a little light'; or 'acorn' in relation to 'palimpsest' or 'gold thread'. The viability of the *Cantos* is neither affirmed nor denied – it is opened out into the whole question of the writer's own ambivalences and confusions. So too, lines that speak of Pound's personal conduct represent neither straight admission nor pure apologia, but constitute a profound and complex examination of the relativities of what might be said:

Self-deception and Self-conflict 117

> Tho' my errors and wrecks lie about me . . .
> If love be not in the house there is nothing . . .
>
> To be saved by squirrels and bluejays?
>   "plus j'aime le chien" . . .
>
> Many errors,
>   a little rightness . . .
>
> And as to why they go wrong,
>   thinking of rightness . . .
>
> To confess wrong without losing rightness:
> Charity I have had sometimes.

This is the ultimate 'Puritan' poetry of self-examination; a wrestling with the internalised angel of God. Guilt is admitted, yet the desire for right(eous)ness is affirmed. Here, self-fragmentation appears as a surrender to the inevitability of self-deception and self-conflict, and a final reliance on something beyond the writer (perhaps the reader) to see a final meaning that he cannot. Beside this canto, Milton's poem of unitary selfhood 'When I consider' appears smugly self-justificatory.[11] Pound's lines, wrung out of self-condemnation, confusion and the yearning for forgiveness are far closer to the exemplary 'God be merciful to me a sinner'. And, as always, the relativistic status of language is a key issue. Hence the disruptions, the contrasting verbal gestures, the style changes, the question forms, quotations and allusions – the very stuff out of which literary selfhood is made. Fragmentariness here resides in the cluster of rhetorical ploys which seek to own to, as exactly as possible, a whole experiential field of different desires, influences, memories and mental connections. The *Cantos*, which at times trumpet a marble order against the 'ooze' of chaos, ends as an exposition of the means towards self-awareness which is honest to its broken lights but is finally unresolvable. As in other Modernist works, the fragmentary structure speaks the truth of the fragmentary self; but whether this resolves as mosaic or mere mess is left open.

'INSCRUTABLE AT HEART'

Conrad's *Lord Jim* may be seen as a study of inauthenticity which stretches the Victorian fear of the divided self toward the modern horror of fragmentation, where multiple self-deception is the order of the day. That Conrad's fiction should be preoccupied with this topic is scarcely surprising, since his own biography exemplifies many of the 'artful dodges to escape from the grim shadow of self-knowledge' (*Lord Jim*, p. 65) which his writing probes so acutely. His earlier seafaring life seems as ruled by phantasy, self-idealisation and sudden *Angst* as Jim's, while the married Conrad reveals himself in terms of psychosomatic illnesses, childish narcissism and compulsive pettiness.[12] Conrad himself is the primal Conradian anti-hero and writing for him was both an obsessive and a painful form of self-therapy. At the core of his life, as of his work, is a sense of the inscrutability – indeed the unreality – of self: 'Life knows us not and we do not know life, – we don't know even our own thoughts';[13] 'My nervous malady torments me, depresses me, and paralyzes all action and all thought. I ask myself, why do I exist?';[14] 'in our activity alone do we find the sustaining illusion of an independent existence'.[15] Based on such existential anguish, Conrad's dark scepticism sees all descriptions as partial versions: Kurtz's fulsome report, Jim's differing rationalisations of the portentous 'jump', the varying discourses of *Nostromo* which write the history of Costaguana as meaningless anarchy.

And yet Conrad, like Jim, is condemned to try to understand, to utter, to write. Words are the medium whereby partial meanings are produced, set into relativistic opposition and methodically undercut. Hence the obsessive quality of Conrad's writing at its most intense – repetitive, portentous, incantatory. At such moments the 'shape and ring of sentences' enact a frantic dialect of loss and recovery and loss again: the linguistic *Fort-Da*[16] of the stylist whose 'unremitting care' for the texture and ordering of words constitutes a desperate effort to control and contain chaos. So too the plethora of portentous adjectives to which F. R. Leavis took exception[17] – 'implacable', 'inscrutable', 'unspeakable', and so forth. This is not a question of a lapse in the technique of 'concreteness', since the literary self-deception involved in the search for a purely denotative language is precisely what Conrad's scepticism sees through. The implication behind Conrad's 'wall of words'[18] is that literature can give only indirect and biased insight into our nature because it, too, is implicated in deception, rationalisation and the phantasy of exact 'spelling-out'. So Conrad's meanings, like Marlow's, are 'not inside like a kernel but outside, enveloping the tale': the stylistic excesses signal the doubtful status of even this limited project.

'Inscrutable at heart' are the novel's last words on the subject of Jim: he thus remains so after all enquiries into his behaviour – not only to Marlow, but also to author and reader. But the urge to understand the 'case' is central to the text and of intense concern to its chief narrator. And this desire is given its firm, if ironic, model in the processes of social judgement described – the version and verdict of the Court of Enquiry. The function of the Court's process is to determine what happened, not underlying motives or lack of them. Given the established series of events, the judgement is automatic: 'certificate cancelled'. This ruling suffices to keep the mariners' code viable, but the implicit assumptions about Jim's cowardice become a key issue in the book. Nevertheless, the Court's version remains as an exemplum of simple 'spelling-out' which those interested in Jim would like to establish on the psychological plane. It serves also as a norm against which the hapless hero tries to assert his own tortuous versions. Self-deception, in Jim's case, is revealed not so much in that he refuses the Court's version as in his inability to come up with another coherent version as alternative. Of course, in a profounder sense this could be viewed as a form of unconscious honesty. Jim has a variety of convictions about what happened, but in the end he simply doesn't quite know what to think.

It is when Jim feels he does know what to think that he is liable to be in most error. This is demonstrated early in the conclusion he draws from his first missed opportunity. When there is a chance to rescue survivors of a collision, Jim appears paralysed by the storm and fails to join other training-ship boys in the rescue cutter. As soon as the cutter returns, successful, his whole attitude changes: 'The tumult and the menace of wind and sea now appeared very contemptible'.[19] The reconstitution of Jim's sense of his romantic heroism is ironically accompanied by descriptions of his ontological recovery: 'Now he knew what to think of it . . . He had enlarged his knowledge . . . He knew what to think of it . . . he exulted with fresh certitude'.[20] Knowing 'what to think of it' is in Conrad the mark of a self-deceived simpleton: the 'Intended' in *Heart of Darkness* ('I knew it!'), Mitchell in *Nostromo*, Verloc in *The Secret Agent* who is convinced he is loved 'for himself'. In minor characters, Conrad may show a grudging respect if such self-ignorance is matched by a useful practicality, but, as in *Lord Jim*, his interest is all in those whose sense of certitude becomes disrupted. Only these, like Kurtz, have a 'choice of nightmares'. The others are figures in moral bad faith, like Jim's father who 'possessed such certain knowledge of the Unknowable as made for the righteousness of people in cottages without disturbing the ease of mind of those whom an unerring Providence enables to live in mansions'.[21] It is Jim's fate to develop out of such culpable simplicity into the authentic, but horrific, self-conflict of ontological insecurity.

Jim's second chance sets the seal on his destiny. The 'facts' of the matter are clear. When his ship, the *Patna* appears on the verge of sinking, he escapes into a lifeboat along with the rascally captain and two other crewmen, leaving the cargo of Moslem pilgrims to their fate. As it happens, the *Patna* does not sink, and the true nature of the incident comes to light in a Court of Enquiry. Jim does not dispute the facts; indeed, he 'wanted to go on talking for truth's sake',[22] even more fully that the Court wishes. What Jim rejects is the picture of his conduct and character which the official version represents. He insists that he is not like this, and the most crucial action of the book shows Jim desperately trying to find a version of himself which corresponds both with his sense of honour and his action on the *Patna* – the fatal 'jump' into the lifeboat. Nor is Jim alone in his preoccupation with the subjective complexities of the case. Although the Enquiry can cast no light upon it, the packed audience there has an 'interest that . . . was purely psychological . . . the expectation of some essential disclosure as to the strength, the power, the horror, of human emotions'.[23] Among the listeners is Marlow, himself an old mariner, who befriends Jim and narrates the story; his interest is also 'purely psychological' – in his attempts not only to understand (and help exorcise) Jim's experience, but also to come to terms with his own self-doubt through their relationship.

Jim's confessions to Marlow smack of straightforward self-deception in that he appears to want to know himself and exonerate himself at one and the same time. He wishes to salvage his self-respect if only to be prepared for some future 'opportunity'. But the problem is more complex than this, for in seeking out the meaning of what happened, in attempting to both know and clear himself, he is faced with complexities of human motivation which cannot be reduced to any simple formulations. He fails to light upon any single cause, any central truth, any complete version of

Self-deception and Self-conflict

why he acted as he did. So his notorious phrase, 'I had jumped – it seems', expresses at once evasive inauthenticity and honest bewilderment. The cardinal act of his career is not something he can give meaning to and so own as his. Hence the contrasting emphases of his attempts at self-defence: 'he was not one of them' (p. 65); 'he was not afraid' (p. 71); 'Everything had betrayed him' (p. 73); 'The lights were gone. No mistake' (p. 91); 'It seems to me that I must jump out of that accursed boat and swim back to see' (p. 90); 'It was their doing as plainly as if they had reached up with a boat-hook and pulled me over' (p. 97); 'There was not the thickness of a sheet of paper between the right and wrong of this affair' (p. 102). These are, as Marlow notes, 'contradictory indiscretions'. There is a grim comedy involved which can easily lead the reader to Albert J. Guerard's kind of negative judgement on Jim.[24] However, the ontological appeal of the narrative has a force beyond any partiality in Marlow's presentation of Jim and a seriousness beyond easy irony. Jim's case is given as an instance of a complex universal predicament: 'those struggles of an individual trying to save from the fire his idea of what his moral identity should be' (p. 66); 'I was made to look at the convention which lurks in all truth and on the essential sincerity of falsehood' (p. 75). Hence we read the book not as an instance of special pleading for a culpable oddity but as an examination of a representative modern self-conflict: 'as if the truth involved were momentous enough to effect mankind's conception of itself' (p. 75).

Jim's attempts to explain his conduct to Marlow emerge out of a live behavioural context which further complicates any interpretation. The reader, like Marlow and like any psychotherapist, is forced to take note of a variety of non-discursive phenomena. Jim's account is given in specific person-to-person confrontation and the underlying conflicts and deceptions are revealed in actions as well as words. Jim alternately appeals, bullies, despairs and rallies, queries, asserts and demands. The interpersonal dynamics are at times stressed:

> He wanted an ally, a helper, an accomplice. I felt the risk I ran of being circumvented, blinded, decoyed, bullied, perhaps, into taking a definite part in a dispute impossible of decision . . . He appealed to all sides at once.
>
> (p. 75)

In addition there are telling details of body language: 'Eh? What? I am not excited, he remonstrated awfully hurt, and with a convulsive jerk of his elbow knocked over the cognac bottle' (p. 94). But then, Jim can be aware of his own inconsistencies and charmingly open at times: 'You've got to believe that too. I did not want this talk . . . No . . . Yes . . . I won't lie . . . I wanted it: it is the very thing I wanted – there' (p. 103). We are given then a full and detailed picture of a man in a specific situation trying to make sense of himself to a kind of father confessor. The whole situation must be taken into account. At the same time we are given no authorially guaranteed means of discrimination. The reader is put in the position of ultimate interpreter, but the interpretation he/she arrives at will be necessarily subjective. So *Lord Jim* constitutes an exposition, not an *exposé*, of the subtleties of self-deception.

Involved here is the problem of how we 'read' the narrator himself. He too appeals, asserts, queries and invites agreement: 'Hey, what do you think of it? . . . Wasn't he true to himself, wasn't he?' (p. 91). Well – no, or maybe, or sort of . . . it depends on the reader's response to the whole. Early on, Marlow indicates his own probable partiality: 'Was it for my own sake that I wished to find some shadow of an excuse for that young fellow whom I had never seen before, but whose appearance alone added a touch of personal concern to the thoughts suggested by the knowledge of his weakness – made it a thing of mystery and terror – like a hint of destructive fate ready for us all whose youth – in its day – had resembled his youth?' (p. 44). Jim acts as *Doppelgänger*, or 'shadow' to Marlow's 'persona', a projection of the fear, the uncertainty, the self-conflict within his own character, and that much of him, like Captain Brierly, would like to deny. So Marlow may himself be self-deceived and instrumental in deceiving us about Jim's case. But, although at times he may rig the narrative in Jim's favour (and Guerard is persuasive about this),[25] there is, again, no objective version of the case against which we could measure Marlow's bad faith. Rather, Conrad is insisting that in matters of such experience truth is always subjective and dependent on the individual's self-awareness. In addition, language is always relative to situation and intention, and subject to its own laws: 'The power of sentences has nothing to do with their sense or the logic of their construction' (p. 127). So there are only subjective 'versions' – and the reader's will be a further one. Jim and Marlow may both be self-deceivers, but in this they are like us. What distinguishes them is the dedication with which they attempt to transcend their partiality and their willingness to admit their limitations. 'Was I so very wrong after all?' Marlow queries at the end of the book. And then answers 'who knows?'.[26] Who indeed?

But there are characters in the book who on the surface appear undeceived. These tend to be villains like Chester:

> You must see things exactly as they are – if you don't you may just as well give in at once. You will never do anything in this world. Look at me. I made it a practice never to take anything to heart.
>
> (p. 125)

The giveaway is in the last sentence. Gentleman Brown and the German captain are also like this. Such characters may have a degree of animal cunning and are quite unashamably egotistical, but they do not see things 'as they are'. Indeed, Chester is so mistaken about his own self-interests that he cannot get any one of account to subsidise his wild projects. Such characters adhere to a type of villainy as naive as Jim's fictional heroism. They see neither the complexities of their own motivations nor the ambiguities in those of others. Like Jim after the training ship incident, they are the more totally self-deceived because they 'know what to think'. For this reason Conrad does not characterise them as existential entities but is content to sketch them as grotesques.

Lord Jim, then, is about the honesty of acknowledging self-deception and the deception involved in 'knowing' that one knows. In this it also concerns the reality of idealism as well as the phantasy life of cynical realism. In the Patusan episode the book goes on to consider the degree to which one can realise one's ideals – and the price that might have to be paid for this form of self-making. Marlow asserts that Jim did in large measure find himself in Patusan: 'Jim . . . had at last mastered his fate' (p. 244): 'Ah he was romantic, romantic . . . He was romantic, but none the less true' (p. 252). One might argue that he lapses into self-deception at the instigation of Brown. However, in facing death bravely he lives out the 'heroism' which had eluded him before, and in a sense overturns the verdict of the Court. Of course, the price for this 'exalted egotism' is paid largely by his girl Jewel, which raises different moral issues. But it is not that Jim denies the claims of love in his new life: he has to make a choice – and he chooses that aspect of his self-project which has been with him longest. However, the *Patna* incident remains the heart of the book in what it reveals about the fallibility of the self and 'that doubt which is the inseparable part of our knowledge' (p. 169). It is a book which dramatises the final impossibility of attaining that which 'by inward pain makes [man] know himself' (p. 165) – and yet the human obligation to understand as far as possible. As Marlow says: 'the last word is not said – probably shall never be said. Are not our lives too short for that full utterance which through all our stammerings is of course our only abiding intention?' (p. 171).

'THE CENTRE CANNOT HOLD'

Where Conrad in *Lord Jim* uses 'objective' dramatisation to explore the intricacies of self-deception and self-conflict, Yeats, in his later poetry, employs subjective theatricality. The poems collectively establish a site where the contradictory drives of selfhood struggle with each other in rhetorical display. To say which is not necessarily to indict the poet with personal self-deception, since to pit 'self' against 'soul', to rehearse 'vacillations' and to advertise the competing wares of the 'rag-and-bone shop of the heart' are overt and practised strategies of Yeats. At the same time, there are moments when the rhetoric seems to have convinced itself of the finality of some provisional posture – which other moments of passionate rhetoric as persuasively deny. There are fine moments of Heideggerian 'uncovering' – 'Man is in love and loves what vanishes' ('Nineteen Hundred and Nineteen'); 'seek those images / That constitute the wild' ('Those Images'); 'Cast a cold eye / On death, on life' ('Under Ben Bulben'); '. . . for we / Traffic in mockery' ('Nineteen Hundred and Nineteen'); 'All things fall and are built again, / And those that build them again are gay' ('Lapis Lazuli') – but these do not add up to a whole; rather, they clash argumentatively with each other. So in any attempted evaluation of Yeats's mature position there arises the spectre of an ultimate either/or: Yeats the pilgrim of authenticity, or Yeats the master poseur. I shall argue that these are, in a sense, the same thing, and that Yeats's greatness partly lies in his persuasive demonstration that authenticity lies in self-aware relativity.

An underlying sense of relativity had been with Yeats from the beginning of his career. As he recorded in *Autobiographies*; 'A

Self-deception and Self-conflict 125

conviction that the world was nothing but a bundle of fragments possessed me without ceasing'.[27] From early on, he felt the modern world to be 'Hodos Chameliontos', where 'common secular thought began to break and disperse'.[28] The results were appalling to a 'subjective' poet, one of the 'last Romantics': 'synthesis for its own sake, organisation where there is no masterful director, books where the author has disappeared'.[29] Yeats, as author, was never to disappear from his poems: rather he was to emerge from the decorative masks of the Celtic (and Indian) Twilight to split into Self and Anti-Self, and then multiply into a dazzling variety of personae. Such a near-schizophrenic project was always immanent in the early belief that 'the borders of our minds are ever shifting, and . . . many minds can flow into one another'.[30] The hope of a resultant 'single mind, a single energy' appears largely as a conventional piety, except in so far as all the poems are informed by the variable Yeatsian *virtú*. The pivotal decision to discard his 'coat / Of old mythologies' and walk 'naked'[31] entailed confrontation with the 'responsibilities' of selfhood in all their complexity. The subjectivity of the mature poems is grounded not in a unitary 'self' but in the self-experience that 'things fall apart'.

Yeats's career demonstrates a curious and passionate sensibility transcending its provisional intellectual frameworks by constant deconstruction. His pursuit of Alchemy, Magic and Mysticism signals less the attainment of a lost order of truth than dissatisfaction with the modes of explanation culturally given in the late nineteenth and early twentieth centuries. From early on, 'scientific' and empirical–philosophical discourses were rejected as inadequate to express the complexities of his experienced self-world. From Blake, and through him Boehme and others, he exploited the provisional, time-honoured strategy of projecting the *Ding und Sich* as binary opposition. 'Without contraries is no progression' became inscribed in his verse and prose alike as a mode of liberation which nearly proved an ultimate constriction. Hence the endless catalogue of contrasts to break with 'single vision and Newton's sleep': *Hic* and *Ille*, Body and Soul, Self and Anti-self, saint and swordsman, Robartes and Aherne, scholar and lover . . . . He wrote in *Per Amica Silentia Lunae*: 'If we cannot imagine ourselves as different from what we are, and try to assume that second self, we cannot impose a discipline upon ourselves though we may accept one from others.'[32] But the question here is all in what we think (or can write) of 'what we are' – and the nature of the antithetical self will be wholly determined by this. He continues: 'active virtue, as distinguished from the passive acceptance of a code, is therefore theatrical, consciously dramatic, the wearing of a mask . . .'.[33] Yeats, as Director of the Abbey Theatre, must have known that a dramatic mask is not the 'opposite' of an actor's 'self', and that theatricality involves the provisionality of all personal positions. He knew it, and his later verse demonstrates it continually, but as essayist he never completely overcame the binary bias.

A Vision, although still cross-weaved with antinomies, is large-scale enough to bear witness to his underlying perception of fragmentation. It is a bizarre document, whose existential purpose, I take it, was to fling a bone to occupy the dogs of 'intellectual' censorship while his poetic imagination proceeded to raid the rich larder of experience, to utter the 'unspeakable'. Hence I do not think the work 'explains' the complexities of the later verse. For the poetry foregrounds the very necessity of complexity to evade the deceptions of expository discourse. It is in the verse that the key Yeatsian problems are authentically expressed and exemplified: what is the meaning of desire – changeable and self-contradictory as it is? How does the experience of aging modify one's sense of selfhood? In what ways, if any, can selfhood be written, without falling into dishonesty or incoherence?

A case poem which expresses such issues intensely, if quite simply, is the celebrated 'Sailing to Byzantium'. With its echoes of Blake, Shelley and Keats the poem overtly bears witness to the intertextual nature of the writing 'self' – an 'I' as much written by the discourses of others as a source of personal utterances. The success of the poem is not so much of rational control as of a combination of ordering and release, where the voices of wayward desire and repressive defence argue among themselves. Thus, I take as crucial not the more usually favoured lines which 'load every rift with ore', but the simple half-line characterising the 'heart': 'it knows not what it is'. From this Socratic point of humility, the rhetorical posturing, the elaboration of an 'argument', the paradoxes and 'unconscious' slippages attain a focus and a meaning.

'Sailing to Byzantium' represents a self-aware expression of the inevitability of a self-conflict implicated in self-deception. The self asserts a desire to transcend for ever the realities that obsess it – thus confirming the strength of those obsessions. It proclaims the superiority of the art world because of its autonomy from nature, only to depict it as finally expressive of nature ('Of what is past, or passing, or to come'). It banishes the distractions of youth in favour of the 'intellectual' aloofness of purified old age and then constitutes the reborn 'golden' self as infantile longing – the threatening father's 'natural thing' displaced as source of generation by magical goldsmiths, and the new self shrunk to bird-size yet invulnerable: 'set' protectively on a golden bough for the phantasy approval of a weakened ('drowsy') father figure and the 'lords and ladies' of an idealised adult frieze. Overtly and awarely the argument subverts itself: turns statement into paradox, bends linearity into circularity, progresses through images and connotations which speak an uncontrolled desire. The poem starts in the land of the young, but Yeats's term surely suggests 'country matters' too. Rhetorically, this realm is dismissed as shallow, yet in such glowing words ('The salmon-falls, the mackerel-crowded seas') that, in fact, it is commended to our senses. The generations die, but, as in older poetry, 'dying' has a sexual meaning and reveals itself as the source of generation. There is, I suggest, simultaneous fascination and disgust. To be 'sick with desire' – whether old or young – is to combine longing with revulsion. As in 'Crazy Jane Talks with the Bishop', 'fair is foul' and 'love has pitched his mansion / In the place of excrement'. The sensual music is disturbing not just because old age is denied it, but also because the child inside the man cannot think of it without horror. The adult Yeats both loves and fears, even loathes, the female's 'dark declivities'.

The mechanism for saving the heart caught in such confusions is enacted at a number of levels – intellectual, spiritual, aesthetic. It also speaks itself somewhat 'under' the text, in terms usually yielded to psychoanalytic interpretation. There is the self-reduction and self-loathing implicit in the scarecrow image, the urge to self-castration and transcendence through the power of voice ('louder sing'), the escape journey across the maternal seas, and the phantasy of resurrection into impermeability through a fiery death written as ancestral cannibalism ('consume my heart away'). And thence to the fictive re-creation – a self as golden artefact, an aesthetic bird (not 'fowl' now), and the rooted roost on the golden bough. This is 'honest' precisely because of its status as defence, as dream of release, as imagined invulnerability. We do not read it as a final, integrated position – and if we do the end position of companion poems should easily disabuse us. The poem's plot succeeds because it carries its disclaimers with it to the last disturbing line. Thus it succeeds by letting us into deep-seated confusions, deceptions and contradictions within the human heart, inscribing them in a highly mannered discourse whose disruptions and paradoxes invite us to look below and through the rhetoric. That the self 'knows not what it is' is expressed by a text which *un*weaves its meanings in the very process of accumulating them.

The last section of 'The Tower' is perhaps a somewhat different case. The overt summoning-up of fictive idealisations – Rousseauan youth, mythic Ireland – combined with the assertive tone may appear to the reader as a kind of arrogant blarney. And yet the aggressive–defensive rhetoric always unravels itself into mellow elegy. On the one hand the assertive ego: 'It is time that I wrote my will'; 'And I declare my faith'; on the other, ravaged melancholy: 'Upon a fading gleam'; 'Or a bird's sleepy cry / Among the deepening shades'. The cynical reader may wish to dismiss such verse as an exercise in balancing humbug and self-pity – the swansong of a pseudo-aristocrat. But, at the very least, the modulations in the verse are self-knowing and there is a kind of desperate integrity in the way Yeats exposes his contradictory excesses to the point of self-caricature. The movement of the section is directed towards the declaration 'Now shall I make my soul, / Compelling it . . .'. This is a moment of existential challenge which is absurd in its implications: the exalted posture is doomed to collapse inwards into fragmentation. And it does. The self-educational programme is only just announced when it becomes dissipated into the 'wreck of body', 'death / of every brilliant eye' and the 'bird's sleepy cry'. The overt control of the syntax belies this to an extent. But, as often in Yeats, rhetorical argument constitutes the conscious pose which image, ambiguity and tone subvert. This is a poem not of self-making but of unmaking – the dissolution of aging consciousness into a plethora of memories, urges, denials, anguishes and lacks. Both the exalted tone and the self-pity enact, and even satirise, the pretensions of the ego as it strives to found itself as integral unit, only to fall apart again. The verse declares what the aging property owner might have denied: that a 'tower' is only an agglomeration of fragile materials, ready at the least movement of the earth beneath it to disintegrate into fragments. The 'deepening shades' at the end indicate not self-deception but a poignant renunciation of the urge to pretension.

But, as I have suggested, the ending of any individual poem

cannot be cited as evidence of some final Yeatsian position. Rather, different poems work out differing aspects of self-conflict to the point of varying provisional formulations. The poems must be read as a whole to get the full sense of the poet's relativistic method. In his fine book in the Modern Masters series, Denis Donoghue contrasts Yeats's method with Eliot's, in that the latter always gives the sense of a journey to some end point. Donoghue writes: 'Yeats's poetry . . . deploys itself in process, along the way of conflict, action incites reaction, statement calls forth counterstatement, each voice is given its due but a rival voice is always heard. No end to such a poetry is required'.[34] This is well observed, but I think his conclusion overaffirmative – 'Excess is the degree of energy which turns pathos into passion, pity into pride: it converts passion into power'. Well, yes – power in the sense of the creation of remarkable verse. But, within that verse, passion is, in turn, converted back into pathos, pride into pity, power into impotence. The Yeatsian poetic discourse is constantly turning realities inside-out, undercutting its own terms: causing strength to flow out of weakness, weakness out of the crumbling of strength. Donoghue quotes Yeats thus: 'My instructors identify consciousness with conflict, not with knowledge, substitute for subject object and their attendant logic a struggle towards harmony, towards Unity of Being'.[35] But the 'conflict' generated in the verse is very much a matter of the self striving for a 'knowledge' of itself, and so contrasting various versions of the self. At the same time, the struggle towards 'harmony . . . Unity of Being' is simultaneously a struggle *against* the familiar Western conventions of coherence and the myth of Cartesian self-unity. So the verse is characterised by dissonances rather than harmony, fragmentation rather than wholeness of being. Yeats's 'kind of power'[36] is simultaneously a demonstration of weakness, inability, unappeased lack. If a man makes poetry out of the 'quarrel with himself', it is because poetry expresses most directly the quarrel that *is* the self: at once a source of energy and a site of ultimate impotence.

I agree, then, with Richard Ellmann that we should emphasise the 'disconnections' between Blake and Yeats. 'When we think of Blake', he writes, 'we think of a mind of almost unprecedented assertiveness. When we think of Yeats, we think of a force of almost unprecedented modulation'.[37] Quite so. For all his subtleties and cultivated 'contraries' Blake asserts a version of the unitary self; for all his searching after unity, Yeats variously balances self-relativities. In short, Yeats is finally more Modernist than Romantic. When he questions whether the word 'belief' belongs to our age at all, one can include traditional belief in the coherence of the self. In Yeats's verse, an assertion about the self is always a discursive try-out, a pose, a bid. And this is exemplified by the characteristic personae of the late poems: the wild, old wicked man, the late-night scholar, the Swiftian denouncer, the Nietzschean vitalist, the connoisseur of memory, Crazy Jane in one or another mood, the sage, the sensualist, the stoic, the mystic and so forth. Each is a position in conflict with other positions, and all these positions change from poem to poem. 'Players and painted stage/Took all my love' he wrote in 'The Circus Animals' Desertion', and that is surely because the 'emblems' are all that can be circulated, perhaps even thought. The 'foul rag-and-bone shop of the heart' is itself only a metaphor for the fluxive reality that is beyond words.

So Yeats's verse, like so much twentieth-century writing, is never more truly itself than when it asks questions where we expect answers: 'Did she put on his knowledge with his power?' ('Leda and the Swan'); 'What else have I to spur me into song?' ('The Spur'); Are you the leaf, the blossom or the bole?' ('Among Schoolchildren'). The technique both admits the inadequacy of any 'spelling-out' and invites the collaboration of the reader in a project of understanding that must ultimately fail – at least in discursive terms. So in the koan-like double question at the end of 'Among Schoolchildren' there is a decisive break with the prevailing Western modes of discourse – 'scientific' writing or thinking that is always 'inside the covers of a book'.[38] Paradoxically, Yeats shows that self and language can only be 'sole and whole' when they themselves are 'rent'; when the 'philosophical' language of dissociated sensibility is broken down into meaning. So too, in Yeats, questions breed not answers but more questions. At the end of 'Among Schoolchildren' such a process reaches towards mystery, contemplation, silence. The self cannot finally be 'known' in terms of conventional discourse, for that discourse is itself implicated in self-deception. Wisdom can only lie in paradox, symbol, riddles. Thus Yeats's poetry uses words to reach beyond words, and reasserts being as a variable self-in-action. The dancer can never be finally separated from the ever-changing dance.

'NO ONE IS ANYTHING'[39]

If *Lord Jim* is a brooding exposure of self-deception, and Yeats's later poetry an agonised enactment of self-conflict, then Joyce's *Ulysses* appears, by contrast, as a comic celebration of both. Of course, the novel has its darker side, and there is satiric mockery and perhaps some disgust along with the ebullient good humour. But where the older writers found the relativities of twentieth-century experience disturbing and disorienting, Joyce seems to revel in them. He takes for granted that human beings are inconsistent, self-contradictory creatures and so does not need to agonise over the lost integrity of the Western ego. The only character who does show radical discomfiture over the schisms in the self is the intellectual Stephen, and his experiences on Bloomsday seem to indicate that his future fulfilment must lie in simply accepting the contradictions of selfhood without any 'irritable reaching after fact and reason'.[40] Bloom, the central hero as Everyman, is largely at ease with his many 'selves' – an existential balancing act rather than a cognitive resolution – and his stream-of-consciousness renders introspection as comedic repartee rather than tragic anguish:

> I was happier then. Or was that I? Or am I now I? Twentyeight I was. She twentythree when we left Lombard street west something changed. Could never like it again after Rudy. Can't bring back time. Like holding water in your hand. Would you go back to then? Just beginning then. Would you? Are you not happy in your home, you poor little naughty boy? Wants to sew on buttons for me. I must answer. Write it in the library.
> (p. 167)

The minor characters of *Ulysses* exemplify the simple model of self-deception. Mr Deasy in 'Nestor', for instance, glibly fictionalises history and avows a smug, suburban persona we know to be inauthentic. Similarly, Simon Dedalus (a praiser of his own past, according to Stephen) combines a prickly self-esteem with the lifestyle of an alcoholic ne'er-do-well, thus condemning his younger children to poverty and misery. The 'Citizen' in 'Cyclops' represents another form of bad faith, rationalising his drunken aggressiveness as patriotism. And then there is Father Conmee, a religious hypocrite for whom self-satisfied inauthenticity has become a way of life: he blesses a beggar, without offering any money, and then reflects on 'the providence of the Creator who had made turf to be in bogs where men might dig it out and bring it to town and hamlet to make fires in the houses of the poor'. (p. 221). All such are like Richie who 'believes his own lies'. (p. 271). But the most extended minor study of self-deception is given in the figure of Gerty MacDowell ('Nausicaa'), who experiences her every moment in terms of novelettish stereotype:

> And yet and yet! That strained look on her face! A gnawing sorrow is there all the time. Her very soul is in her eyes and she would give worlds to be in the privacy of her own familiar chamber where, giving way to tears, she could have a good cry and relieve her pentup feelings. Though not too much because she knew how to cry nicely before the mirror. You are lovely, Gerty, it said.
>
> (p. 349)

Gerty appears to live entirely in a world of wish fulfilment, projection, introjection and general phantasy. Her sexuality is rendered in terms of avoidance ('that thing' or 'the other thing') and yet in her actions she is knowing, flirtatious and masturbatory. Similarly, her vanity, envy and emotional greed are apparent to the reader, although almost wholly concealed from herself. She not only believes her own lies, she lives her entire life, it seems, as fictional phantasy.

However, it is through the three main characters that Joyce's vision of self-deception and self-conflict is most complexly expressed. Stephen's self-conflict, for instance, has both philosophical and psychological dimensions. On the one hand he finds major epistemological problems in the attempt to understand himself – or indeed, anything else. If the real is a matter of 'signatures of all things I am here to read' (p. 42), how, in a post-supernatural world, can they be accurately read? How, indeed, can he even read the 'book of himself' without falling into the subjective biases of self-deception? In a solipsistic world ('the soul is all'), relativity is the order of the day and his project of understanding collapses into paradox ('God . . . a shout in the street'). In fact, as Marilyn French points out, Stephen's attitude is frequently self-contradictory:

Self-deception and Self-conflict 133

Mulligan is to him a usurper, but also a hero . . . Scandinavian invaders of Ireland assailed Stephen's people, but Ireland is a 'paradise of pretenders then and now' . . . Stephen is a victim of the usurpers Mulligan and Haines, but is a pretender-usurper himself . . .
Stephen's ambivalence causes paralysis . . .[41]

There is no clear suggestion in the book that this paralysis, founded on the inability to resolve his intellectual conflicts, is about to be broken through. It is largely his intellectual subtlety that prevents him coming to terms with himself.

On the other hand, Stephen's predicament is portrayed also as psychological self-conflict. He has sought to establish an identity as artist–intellectual, but he cannot come to terms with the isolation and alienation this entails. He feels apart from his father, guilty towards his mother and ill at ease among his peers. He is appalled by the physical act of his engendering ('the couplers' will') – and yet has to own to his origin there. At the same time he wants to create himself – as Shakespeare in *Hamlet*: fulfil, through his art, the original Oedipal sin of usurping the father, possessing the mother and so, in a sense, begetting himself in words. As artist, he coverts the position of final self-source which would make him equal with God. But, so far, he has barely begun his literary career (which itself could only amount to a *symbolic* conquest of desire) and he remains paralysed in a world of self-possibilities with all their attendant *Angst*. His meeting with Bloom is notoriously anticlimactic, and he drifts out of the novel into a night of loneliness. Indeed, the most dramatic moment of his day does little but repeat the celebrated assertion at the end of *Portrait*. Drunk, beset by the vision of his dead mother in Bella Cohen's brothel, he strikes an attitude of defiance, rather than attempting to accept the deeper psychic elements of his life:

Ah non, par exemple! The intellectual imagination! With me all or not at all. Non serviam! . . .
No! No! No! Break my spirit all of you if you can! I'll bring you all to heel!

(p. 517)

Stephen's intellectual pride pits ego against both world and the unconscious parts of himself. So the psychological tension between the various parts of himself, and the different versions of desire he articulates in different parts of the book never achieve even hypothetical balance. Self-deception and self-conflict remain to be lived through again and again: only perhaps in the act of future artistic creation can Stephen, like Joyce in the novel, find a form of resolution through humble, if amused, acceptance.

Molly's self-world is the polar opposite of Stephen's. Where he is all anguished intellectuality, she represents exuberant physicality – as much symbolic Earth Mother as realistic woman. In addition she represents a swirling and eddying psychic energy. She is hilariously inconsistent and self-contradictory, but appears almost wholly unaware of this. Her long digressive spiel effects an avowal of everything she feels and thinks without any attempt to organise it into a coherent whole. The notion of a unitary 'self' would have as little meaning for Molly as the word 'metempsychosis' ('met something with hoses in it', p. 675). Her reiterated 'Yes' embraces everything that she is. So, from the outside she appears both amusing and ultimately disturbing. She represents Bad Faith without tears. Hence after the intense ravelled-up antinomies of Stephen's and Bloom's rather frantic juggling act with their different selves, she provides a kind of anarchic moral holiday for the reader. At the same time, since no authorial narrator provides any judgemental discrimination about her inconsistencies, the reader is forced to fall back on his/her own faculties of judgement. Molly has won both fans and detractors and both groups display differences of interpretation in what they have to say. Since such differences will themselves depend on the reader's own sense of being-in-the-world, with attendant self-deception, Molly becomes a sort of *Rorschach* test of the reader's self-knowledge.

Marilyn French has noted several aspects of self-contradiction in Molly:

> Molly's complete disregard for contradictions shows up in her ideas on the fairly simple subject of keeping a servant . . . Molly can praise and belittle Bloom in one breath and for the same set of actions . . . Molly gets furious with Milly's behavior, then immediately turns around to say she understands it, she acted the same way herself at Milly's age, it is all Bloom's fault after all. She is mean-minded one moment and generous-minded the next . . . Molly is so unaware of contradictions that even after her thoughts about the disconcerting Mrs. Fleming, she can

imagine a picnic with Boylan and seizes on Mrs. Fleming as a partner for Bloom.

(pp. 246–8)

This is accurately observed. However, I find Ms French's defence of Molly rather unpersuasive:

> Molly finally represents the nonrational sense of being which supports us all, which impels us to stay alive even when life seems a blight.
> Molly's attitude, illogical on the surface, has total integrity with the needs of the self. There is no gap in her between self and not-self, because everything in the universe exists for her, the sun shines for her, she believes that. She is emotionally self-sufficient, a quality often ascribed to the Eternal Feminine.
>
> (p. 250)

This is surely a case of special pleading. Molly only achieves 'emotional self-sufficiency' by totally ignoring the incompatibility of the claims she makes for herself. Normally the 'needs of the self' include some sense of authenticity. And Molly, indeed, claims just that: 'I hate that pretending of all things' (pp. 672–3); 'he cant say I pretend things can he Im too honest'. (p. 687). But Molly does pretend – to *herself*: both in the sense of acting as if untrue things were true, and by claiming a consistency she does not have. She is the apotheosis of the 'unexamined life' in that she permits no possibility that she might be self-deceived – scarcely a basis on which to sustain an adult relationship. But, in fact, Molly does not really represent a full 'self' as such. Rather, she is part of a self – a part that sometimes we should all like to be fully: i.e. invulnerable in our self-deception. But, in reality, that part always co-exists with the urge towards self-truth, and so the realisation that we are not always and entirely what we like to claim to be.

Molly's monologue, I suggest then, represents simply the human propensity for inconsistency and hence self-deception. Atypically, Molly does not feel or own her fallibility; she expresses an archetypal form of self-deception which does not include self-conflict. If Stephen is the extreme self-sceptic then Molly is the supreme (and mythical) self-believer; hence, perversely, we are attracted to her where we are somewhat repulsed by Stephen. She lets us forget for a moment our fragmented finitude: sustains, awhile, the phantasy of primitive 'naturalness' untouched by the *Angst* of the moral order. And yet, at the same time, she exhibits that fragmented reality: her spiel demonstrates the wanton self spiralling and backtracking and stalling and recovering again in the windy currents of discourse – intent only on staying smugly above the ground of reality.[42] She is portrayed as a dream of the flying self – consciousness without self-consciousness. It remains to Bloom – midway between Stephen's scepticism and Molly's self-confidence – to provide a model of down-to-earth self-reality, which can acknowledge and accept the self's fallibility without anguished paralysis.

Bloom's diurnal 'self' is surely the most fully representative consciousness in literature – a fitting modern Odysseus in Joyce's own terms.[43] His inner world is registered with minute fidelity – most particularly in the earlier 'stream-of-consciousness' chapters. And, for all his humble status and nature (perhaps because of it), he emerges as the twentieth-century man of good faith. Where Lawrence's Rupert Birkin – cast by some critics for the same role – preaches, argues and strives for the integrity of absolute freedom, Leopold Bloom (Poldy, Henry Flower, Papli, Sir Leopold, jewman, L. Boom, Ben Bloom, Elijah, etc.) is content to live the contrarieties that are himself with tolerance, compassion and good humour. And although there are aspects of his behaviour that might strike us as self-deceiving – his correspondence with Martha or his pursuit of Stephen – Bloom is the least finally self-deceived of characters because he is constantly checking and revising his awareness and actions, and is always aware that his view is not final: 'Bitten off more than he can chew. Am I like that? See ourselves as others see us' (p. 169). One of his least attractive features is the way, at times, he attributes to himself motives that are unworthy of his kindly impulses: 'Still better tell him. Does no harm. Free ad'. (p. 172). But this is the 'worldly' rationalisation of a man humble enough to mistrust his own possible virtue – almost a saintly quality. Usually his instantaneous self-checks and revisions are founded upon kindliness and the unwillingness to pontificate to others: 'Tell him if he smokes he won't grow. O let him! His life isn't such a bed of roses' (p. 72). At the same time, his moments of self-censorship or denial – for instance ellipses concerning his cuckolder ('Effect of the sexual. Aphrodis. He was in the Red bank this morning . . . Perhaps he young flesh in bed' (see above, p. 84)) – are not total avoidances, for he faces the

Self-deception and Self-conflict 137

issues at other moments. Rather, he is aware that one cannot fully acknowledge realities all the time: as he concludes after remembering his father's suicide (on page 78): 'no use thinking of it any more' – but he does, of course, later. Bloom seems aware too that one can never exactly spell out what self-reality is. As an advertising canvasser, he is quite aware of the approximations of rhetoric: 'Born with a silver knife in his mouth. That's witty, I think. Or no. Silver means born rich. Born with a knife. But then the allusion is lost' (p. 169). Without being an intellectual or claiming religious virtue, Bloom has a canny sense of the treachery of words, the complexities of selfhood and the individual's final littleness in the scheme of things. In this – perhaps only in this – 'There's a touch of the artist about old Bloom' (p. 234).

Given the intensity of focus on Bloom's actions and impressions, it is remarkable how self-honest he appears most of the time: especially if we compare with him figures like Father Conmee or Simon Dedalus or Gerty MacDowell, who appear self-deceived almost all of the time. It is not only that Bloom is common-sensically honest about himself and rarely indulges in projection (even when he loses his temper, as in 'Cyclops'); he also owns to and acts on those aspects of himself which appear furthest from 'common sense' – his voyeurism, fetishism and masochism, for instance. Bloom can be furtive in trying to hide these from others (as when he pretends to have dropped something when inspecting the statue's anus in the library), but he does not habitually hide them from himself: rather he consciously engineers ways of expressing them, as in his correspondence with Martha: 'Go further next time. Naughty boy: punish; afraid of words, of course. Brutal, why not? Try it anyhow. A bit at a time' (p. 80). Bloom is one of the first 'psychoanalytic' characters, not only in terms of his sexual oddities, but in his self-acknowledgement of them, and conscious indulgence in them in so far as they do not hurt others. He is a connoisseur of psychically charged trivia – petticoats, gloves, soap, word lapses, 'talismans' like the potato. And, at times, there is a libidinous blatancy to his actions: if he breaks wind surreptitiously, he masturbates semi-publicly, and can even get a charge out of the very sordidity of the act: 'What a brute he had been! At it again? A fair unsullied soul had called to him and, wretch that he was, how had he answered? An utter cad he had been . . .' (p. 364). Even Molly, the Goddess of polymorphous eroticism, can marvel at the overtness and perversity of her husband's sexual behaviour.

In this, one suspects from certain of Joyce's letters to Nora, the character merely effects the author's own perverse pleasures. What Yeats normally wrote under the text is advertised in *Ulysses* as behavioural compulsion, in terms of masochism, anality, exhibitionism, hermaphroditism and the fetishistic sacralisation of dirty linen of all kinds. No wonder Virginia Woolf did not like the hero or the book.

But Bloomsday is not, of course, the pornographic romp through perversity the English Customs and Excise Service was out to keep from potential readers. The point about Bloom is that he acknowledges the 'forbidden' as part of himself along with other quite ordinary aspects. He avows (and sometimes acts upon) the various parts of himself, always finding some sort of balance between them. So on the one occasion when the quarrel between his various 'selves' threatens to overthrow him, he is able to keep his head, while the less balanced Stephen breaks down when reconfronted by his 'agenbite of inwit'. 'Circe' or 'Nighttown' where this occurs, is an extended Expressionistic psychodrama in which the main facets of Bloom's consciousness are given bizarre personification. Since dramatised consciousness is all, here, (governing stage directions too) there is no authorially given reality against which to gauge possible self-deception. But because Bloom is consciously aware of this gallimaufry of selves, the real issue concerns self-conflict and the possibility of his self-balance being destroyed. The characters do not represent unconscious (and unowned) forces, nor are they phantasies as such; rather they are self-possibilities which have got out of hand. For instance, the New Bloomusalem scenario represents the political views of Bloom which are given argumentative expression in various parts of the novel. According to Molly, 'all the Doyles said he was going to stand for a member of Parliament' (p. 692), and, although she discounts this, we can read the scene as a caricature of the Citizen Len Bloom might have become, given some slight alteration in circumstances or choice. Similarly, Bloom's unsolicited letter, as described by The Honourable Mrs Mervyn Talboys, demonstrates the kind of reprehensible scoundrel he might become, if ever his particular erotic component got out of hand: 'He urged me . . . to misbehave, to sin with officers of the garrison. He implored me to soil his letter in an unspeakable manner, to chastise him as he richly deserves, to bestride and ride him, to give him a most vicious horsewhipping' (p. 449). Each character, then, is not a phantasm

Self-deception and Self-conflict 139

born of self-deception, but an exaggeration of self-acknowledged aspects of Bloom. In the dramatic melée, each one threatens to take over as sole, integral self, and so destroy Bloom's balance as a 'nation' of selves. The temptations of St Leopold represent attempts by a variety of swollen pretenders to destroy the liberal democracy of his selfhood and set up the dictatorship of a single unitary ego. For most of the chapter, in this Circean Walpurgis-Night, Bloom's balance has temporarily dissolved into a grotesque gallery of partial self-portraits.

Bloom's entry into the red-light district is Expressionistically significant: he passes two mirrors, one concave, one convex. The figure of Gladstone appraises the 'real' man – 'Bloom for Bloom' (p. 428); but our hero sees only two distortions: 'lovelorn longlost lugubru Booloohoom' and 'Jollypoldy the rixdix doldy'. Once inside the forbidden place (and especially after he enters Bella Cohen's brothel), Bloom is to be split further into a progressively changing variety of self-caricatures. For example, these images of Bloom as given in the stage directions:

> *Barefoot, pigeon-breasted, in lascar's vest and trousers, apologetic toes turned in . . .*
> (p. 446)

> *In workman's corduroy overalls, black gansy with red floating tie and apache cap*
> (p. 455)

> *Under an arch of triumph Bloom appears bare-headed, in a crimson velvet mantle trimmed with ermine, bearing Saint Edward's staff, the orb and sceptre . . .*
> (p. 457)

> *In Svengali's fur overcoat, with folded arms and Napoleonic forelock . . .*
> (p. 485)

> *With a piercing epileptic cry she sinks on all fours, grunting, snuffling, rooting . . .*
> (p. 488)

Not only do the images change serially, but at any dramatic

moment – most especially the trial scene – Bloom is simultaneously fragmented into a cast of selves all in dispute with each other. But, in spite of the spectacular splittings and metamorphoses he is subjected to, Bloom does not finally lose balance, and as soon as his stable normality is required – when Stephen smashes the lamp – he is instantaneously his old realistic, helpful self. Bloom is a character who is the less self-deceived because he owns to his fallibilities, and who can balance self-conflict even in semi-hallucinated *extremis*. He passes his most dramatic testing time in the book with proverbial flying colours. Having maintained his modest balance throughout the day, he is able finally to incorporate his new self-role as *mari complaisant* with respect to Blazes Boylan, the cuckolder; and to assimilate this new self-order with respect to his wife, by ordering breakfast in bed as a mode of self-reassertion.

Bloom, then, constitutes the most complete and satisfying study of self-deception and self-conflict in Modernist literature. He incorporates almost all main aspects of the issues within the space of his Dublin day, and by maintaining a balance when most self-assailed, he asserts a humanistic optimism about the possibilities of selfhood within the general Modernist consensus of near-despair. Of course, Joyce gives us the leeway to disapprove of Bloom – as of Molly. Further, the stylistic relativities of the later chapters not only distance the characters but put in doubt all forms of interpretation and discourse. *Ulysses*, more than any other contemporary work, strands the reader in his own subjectivity and calls into question the very self-bases from which he/she judges. Hence the evaluative aspect, at least, of my reading of Bloom and his world speaks my own biases: and my hunch that Joyce would have seen his hero in this, rather favourable, light is perhaps not to the point. *Ulysses* is the key work of Modernism in this as in other respects: that in denying authorial 'perspective' it probes the reader's own self-awareness. 'With me or not at all' is the challenge of all the main characters to the reader's ontological core: and each must answer in his own way. *Ulysses* locates the issues of self-deception and self-conflict as intrinsic to the whole writing–reading relationship. We must find our own balance in a world where 'everything speaks in its own way' (p. 123).

6

Discontinuous Self

'Me – and Me Now'

'All things give way, nothing remains' – so Walter Pater translated Heraclitus in one of the seminal texts for Modernist aesthetics.[1] In claiming a sense of flux as 'the tendency of modern thought', Pater anticipated both the preoccupations of writers such as Proust, Eliot and Woolf, and the new interest in pre-Socratic philosophy of such thinkers as Nietzsche, Bergson and Heidegger. As the normative Western categories of time began to disintegrate under scrutiny, writers became involved in tracing 'that strange, perpetual weaving and unweaving of ourselves' that Pater had described. Wyndham Lewis's perceptive, if cantankerous, book *Time and Western Man* registered with dismay, in the twenties, the modern rejection of 'rational' models of change and the literary experimentation with new techniques for representing time that went with it. The placement of the self in change was crucial to the new perceptions, for 'subjective' time could be characterised as common experience which belied the linear bias of cumulative, digital sequence. Bergson wrote:

> There is at least one reality which we all seize from within, by intuition and not by simple analysis. It is our own personality in its flowing through time, the self which endures.[2]

However, the appeal to a subjective flux also called into question the notion of an enduring self. Modernist writers tended to register the endurance of experience as something chaotic rather than coherent – subjective time as a cabaret of disjunctive self-roles; as Bloom feels it poignantly: 'Me – and me now'.[3] Hence, the traditional model of a unitary developing self was tested in terms of dissolution, metamorphosis, self-estrangement and self-renewal. Modernism moves towards Derek Parfit's notion of 'series-persons'[4] where interest is transferred from continuing identity to the 'Relation R' between experience and world.

As one might expect, the anguish and comedy of the discontinuous self is a theme more elaborated in later Modernist writing. We have seen that earlier texts – *Heart of Darkness*, *Lord Jim*, 'Prufrock', 'Hugh Selwyn Mauberley', *The Waste Land* – tend to focus on fragmentation within the frozen moment. At any given instant, the self reveals itself as a collage of disparities, conflicts, self-deceptions. But later (and frequently more mature) work registers the writer's own experience of aging – the deaths, transformations and rebirths of disparate selves within the flux of change. *Ulysses*, *Mrs Dalloway* and *The Waves*, *The Four Quartets*, Yeats's late poetry and the *Cantos* of Pound all represent the brokenness of the self's experience through time. Instead of a Cubistic patterning of the frozen moment's heterogeneities, we have 'consciousness disjunct' stretched across a lifetime's disparities. Selves are both made and unmade in time – they do not 'contain' it. So Pound's late desperation: 'I cannot make it flow thru'.[5]

But, of course, the sense of time's fragmentary agency is inherent in the frozen epiphany itself. Modernism typically represents the felt present as an anarchic continuum where memory, perception and possibility are co-equal generators of atomistic awareness. Bloomsday provides a typical example:

> No. She did not want anything. He heard then a warm heavy sigh, softer, as she turned over and the loose brass quoits of the bedstead jingled. Must get those settled really. Pity. All the way from Gibraltar. Forgotten any little Spanish she knew. Wonder what her father gave for it. Old style. Ah yes, of course. Bought it at the governor's auction. Got a short knock. Hard as nails at a bargain, old Tweedy. Yes, sir. At Plevna that was. I rose from the ranks, sir, and I'm proud of it. Still he had brains enough to make that corner in stamps. Now that was farseeing.
> (*Ulysses*, p. 58)

Sectioned off from within active time – between Bloom's question to Molly and his removal of his hat from its peg – this brief mental moment combines present perception (Molly turning over) with future potentiality (fixing the springs) and a plethora of memory associations sprung from the fact that their bed was bought by Molly's father. Recollections from the past and the promptings of the future here, as elsewhere, erupt randomly into the fabric of the present, effecting a complex experience continuum which belies the sequential self.

But such a model of interior time does not simply abolish or replace the more traditional time conventions; rather it co-exists with them in a kind of frictional complementarity. The clocks of Mrs Dalloway's London echo the chimes of St Mary Woolnoth in *The Waste Land*, and both offer acoustic realisation to the exacting hour schema of *Ulysses*. However, representation of the lived continuum does tend to marginalise the relevance of 'objective' time within modern literature. Clock time implies a linear model of self-definition which presupposes simplistic causality, irreversible transition and coherent development: subjective time demonstrates rather the experiential reality of causal overdetermination, fluxive change (with memory always retaining alive the previous reality) and anarchic succession of self after self. History itself appears to the modern writer as arbitrary and anarchic – a nightmare from which Stephen Dedalus is trying to awake, or, in the neo-Bradleian section of Eliot's 'Gerontion', a kind of treacherous adversary:

> Think now
> History has many cunning passages, contrived corridors
> And issues, deceives with whispering ambitions,
> Guides us by vanities . . .
>
> . . . Think
> Neither fear nor courage saves us. Unnatural vices
> Are fathered by our heroism. Virtues
> Are forced upon us by our impudent crimes.[6]

Such a vision of historical change is close to the flux of recorded event in early cantos of Pound, where the 'discontinuous gods' are implicated in the discontinuities of process: 'a wall / Here stripped, here made to stand'; 'One year floods rose / One year they fought in the snows, one year hail fell . . .'.[8] The *'virtù'* of an El Cid or Sigismundo Malatesta is a flexible energy, not a rational self-consistency, which confronts the nightmare of unpredictable events and struggles to overcome it. At the same time, the discourse of the poem bears witness to the fluxive anarchy of time. The writer is not a historian trying to demonstrate rational progression, but a chronicler marking down the discontinuities of change. Hence the later Confucian exemplum: 'when the historians left blanks in their writings'[9] – the witness of history as collage.

Characteristic dramatic 'selves' of Modernist literature are depicted as trapped within process, surveying the discontinuities of their life histories as reluctant connoisseurs of time's chaos: Gerontion, his life thread woven by 'vacant shuttles', aware of unaccountable loss; Crazy Jane, haunted by the passions that made and unmade her; Clarissa Dalloway continually reassessing the meaning of past loves and decisions. The lives of such seem to consist only of an endless mixing of memory and desire in which completed acts remain oddly provisional; while the present is dominated by a past that was always predicated in terms of a hypothesised future. Sequence here has dissolved into endless revisions and repetitions within the mental continuum.

Such self-discontinuities are typically represented in terms of loss – the characters are *condemned* to flux. Modernism is, on the whole, profoundly unhappy with the randomness it perceives in and writes into contemporary life. Just as nostalgia for a unitary self informs the frozen moment of self-fragmentation, so a yearning for the fiction of development underlies the rueful construction of self as flux. Pound, for instance, clings stubbornly to the organic metaphor acorn-to-oak to typify poetic development, even while his personal (and poetic) 'errors and wrecks' mount up to form a broken life. Stephen in *Ulysses* searches continually (and hopelessly) for the lost link between father and son that could give him a sense of continuity and identity. Eliot, too, in *Four Quartets* tries to transcend words and meanings in order to achieve mystical reconciliation between his past and present. The notion of ordered development – as of the coherence of selfhood – is one of mankind's most powerful myths, and one given masterful expression in the literature of the previous century. To lose the sense of the 'growth of a poet's mind',[10] to dispute the necessary consequences of 'great expectations', constitutes a dire fall from the Eden of rationality. So the Moderns speak back to their forebears from a point of radical deprivation; Prufrock and Mauberley are drained of the triumphant self-possession of Lippo Lippi, Blougram or the Duke of Ferrara; Bloom is a ludicrous foil to Odysseus; *The Waste Land* laments the lost selfhood of the Classical, Mediaeval and Renaissance periods and anticipates the characterisation of contemporaries as 'the lost men, the hollow men'.

As I have already suggested, *Portrait of the Artist* is a key transitional work between the neo-Romantic and Modernist versions of the self. It both plays out and unmakes the mythos of *Bildungsroman*, because its end point represents not a consolidation of development but a rejection of all the developmental building-blocks, coupled with a promise to remake family, country and religion out of the 'smithy' of a new, self-chosen self. It thus contrasts most strongly with the key nineteenth-century fable of self-development, *The Prelude*. For Wordsworth, the child is father of the man and the links between the 'seedtime' of the soul and the 'calm existence' of the grown man are organically direct:

> Dust as we are, the immortal spirit grows
> Like harmony in music; there is a dark
> Inscrutable workmanship that reconciles
> Discordant elements, makes them cling together
> In one society.[11]

For Joyce, the man is rather the assassin of the child – destroying his own previous development as he struggles with the Oedipal father and the 'Bad Mother' simultaneously. So in *Portrait* the new self is existentially chosen in opposition to all the influences on the old self, and those influences themselves are written not in terms of continuous development, but as discrete, stylistically autonomous stages of manipulation, all of which must be rejected in the diary discourse (voice of the emergent *new* self) at the end.

In 'disremembering' his past (as Maud Ellmann puts it),[12] Stephen unravels the logic of development and breaks the myth of 'growth'. In this he is closer to the father of autobiography, Augustine, than he is to Wordsworth. And indeed, Augustine's notion of time is closer to the Moderns than the Romantics, both because it stresses the subjective nature of the temporal and because it allows for the eruption of the Eternal into sequential time. There is nothing 'organic' or 'developmental' (in the ordinary sense) in Augustine's conversion. The *Confessions* depict rather a case of radical unmaking of development, a metamorphosis wrought by non-temporal Grace.[13] In this it is close to Stephen's act of existential assertion. In Augustine's case, it is the gleam of the Eternal which melts the time links of process and replaces the earthly father with a Heavenly Father as source. In Stephen's case, it is the artistic 'smithy' of the soul which melts the developmental links and enables him to own as father the legendary artificer of the Cretan maze. From this point – where aesthetic Eternity breaks into the mundane – he can (it is claimed) fly free of the influences of family, nation and religion to invent, *ex nihilo*, the 'conscience' of his race. The model is not evolution but revolution or paradigm shift, in a fully experiential sense. Stephen's act of rebellious self-remaking opens the way for the more specifically Modernist studies of life-time in *Ulysses* – Bloom who saunters wistfully along the Dublin streets in the company of all his past and present selves, and Molly lying sleepily in bed construing all her past, present and future as a giddy and repetitive dance of desire.

In *Women in Love* D. H. Lawrence gives subjective time in terms of a vivid polarity between freedom and determination, authenticity and bad faith, life and death. We are not constrained by our histories, is his message; we can be whatever we like, and the self can change and renew itself phoenix-like – but most people have not the courage to do so, and this is the modern disease. Where it comes to human nature, Lawrence is not a Romantic organicist but an existentialist–Modernist. He is not interested in the 'old stable ego' and the notions of development and causality as self-determinants. Continually and stridently he preaches free spontaneity, creative self-renewal from moment to moment. One must never allow oneself to be '7 . . . Somerset Drive' (p. 422). Thus he construes the traditional model of the continuous self as a matter of cowardice and inauthenticity. Gerald, for instance, is doomed because he refuses to acknowledge the self as flux. He clings ontologically to a sense of predetermination – himself as rich heir, soldier, explorer, captain of industry and the brother killer who inherits a family doom. Unlike Stephen Dedalus (and Birkin), he sees himself in terms of socialisation: he can only be what he has been made (the linear unitary self both his defence and the enemy within). So, when his father dies, he loses all sense of his own reality and flounders into the death-dealing relationship with Gudrun. He is 'hollow at the core' precisely because he lives by an illusion of solidity and developing continuity. Birkin, on the other hand, is given as modern hero because he denies the power of the past and refuses the rigidity of the fixed self. He is given over and over (often in overwrought prose) as free, spontaneous, a changer. We are told almost nothing of his past – family, education, relationships, etc. – and it is significant that we do not need to be: for Birkin does not conduct himself in terms of established reference points; he is continually exploring the future through the present, in terms of what to be and do. There can surely be no other character in fiction whose past background is less relevant to his represented personality. He lives almost wholly in the present flux – like a ball in a fountain jet – and that may be why some readers find him an unbelievable character. In some senses, indeed, he does seem to be more a symbol than a man – and yet what he stands for is an emphasis inherent in much of Modernism from Conrad to Woolf. Characters who see themselves and behave as socially determined beings, and nothing else, are represented in terms of inauthenticity, mechanism, hollowness; while characters who acknowledge their indeterminacy in flux (whether in anguish or ecstasy) are shown to be in good faith. Birkin stands out spectacularly in this company because of the millennarian optimism which his words and way of life imply.

Most Modernist selves-in-flux are in fact anti-hero(in)es. This may be partly due to the almost congenital pessimism of writers such as Conrad, Eliot and, to a degree, Woolf. But it is due also to the Moderns' preoccupation with urban isolation and alienation, with the new psychoanalytic construction of man as the neurotic animal, and with the phenomenon of the Great War. It was, I suspect, the eruption of war into European life and culture that most gave authority to representations of time as chaos and the self as discontinuity. It was this that lent weight to the Yeatsian rhetoric of 'Man is in love and loves what vanishes/What more is there to say?' or the Poundian pathos in: 'As a lone ant from a broken ant-hill/from the wreckage of Europe, ego scriptor . . .'.[14] Nothing else could destroy that popular linear fiction of the Edwardian era – the facile social Darwinism of ape-to-angel – as suddenly and effectively as the European reversion to barbarity in the Great War and its successor. So it is fitting that one of the most vivid and elaborated examples of the broken self should have been given in Ford's war sequence *Parade's End*.

As we have seen, Ford's Christopher Tietjens is represented as an essentially traditional figure – the integral self as independent Tory. In the course of the book he is assailed by representative disruptive forces – an obsessive woman, the madness of war, administrative chaos and treacherous acquaintances. He collapses in stages. Tietjens loses his inheritance, his brother, his son, his wife, his command and virtually his mind. A quite literal shell shock destroys his memory so that he has to reassemble an awareness from scratch, memorising his way through the encyclopaedia. Ford's admiring focus is on the way Tietjens maintains a degree of balance and dignity through all these adversities. Nevertheless, to all intents and purposes, his selfhood is broken and the gentle antiques dealer of *Last Post* is quite different from the brilliant intellectual aristocrat of *Some Do Not*. The death-in-life of the war experience – symbolic of all that Ford saw wrong in contemporary England – has shattered the tradition-nurtured personality of the representative good man.

The disruptive reality of the war and the key battle metaphor of explosion or 'fragmentation', become inscribed in a variety of ways in post-war writing. In *To the Lighthouse*, for instance, the Entr'acte section registers the temporal gap through the closed house awaiting the return of the changed characters in Section 3. Septimus Warren Smith in *Mrs Dalloway* relives shell shock when the London car backfires and leaps down to a parody bayonet-death on the area railings, in order to escape the hectoring generalship of peacetime – 'the coward', as the doctor says.[15] In the post-war poetry of Yeats and Eliot, change is seen in terms of the destruction and carnage of a universalised No Man's Land – with attendant buried corpses, rats, bones, broken statues, falling towers and a drunken soldiery who preside over the 'blood-dimmed tide'.[16] The figure of the impotent male – Lord Chatterley or Fisher King – symbolises the war-torn rent in succession and selfhood. As war had accelerated change in general, so the dark chasm between Edwardian twilight and bleak post-war dawn separated people from their past and provided a vocabulary of disintegration with which to characterise self-time. The early Modernist 'blasting and bombardiering'[17] had resolved into militaristic literalness. As in Yeats's Ireland, all was 'changed utterly'; and within and out of this change the main Modernist representations of change were born.

Through the agency of the war, we might say then, the Paterian awareness of flux became transformed into a Modernist registration of self-discontinuity. Though there are existentially positive models of this – Stephen Dedalus and Rupert Birkin – the main emphasis of the writers is on self-dismemberment. *Ulysses*, *The Waste Land*, Yeats's later poems, *Mrs Dalloway*, *To the Lighthouse*, *The Waves*, *Parade's End*, *Four Quartets* and the *Cantos* of Pound all write selfhood as progressive disruption, set against the lost myth of continuity. Key memories and passions endure in the mind as reference points, but their quasi-eternal status only throws into sharper relief the experiences of self-loss, metamorphosis and role change which time inflicts. Modernism constructs self-time as another aspect of self-fragmentariness; but of course different writers effect this in rather different ways.

'FALLS THE SHADOW'

The nature of time is a theme amounting to an obsession in Eliot's writing: a theme which finds expression in a variety of formulations which typically end in near-paradox. There is, for example, historical time which may be given as a matter of 'contrived corridors' and 'vanities' ('Gerontion'), or as a 'pattern of timeless moments' ('Little Gidding') or – especially with respect to the present – as an 'immense panorama of futility and anarchy'.[18] There is, too, 'tradition', a collocation of 'monuments' produced within time, and yet forming an 'ideal order' outside of it – which can, nevertheless, be disrupted and shaken into a different order by the intervention of the 'really new' work.[19] There is 'unredeemed' time, which largely consists of a variable continuum of perceptions, memories, anticipations etc., threaded meaninglessly by the phenomenon of sequence, and at best made endurable in terms of the repetition compulsion of habit ('short square fingers stuffing pipes'). And then there is the Eternal (especially in the later work), which is wholly outside time, and yet can break into it in moments of 'intersection', thus transforming subjective time or possibly – as in the Incarnation – historical time. But for all these formulations the underlying and informing concept is not development but discontinuity. And this is particularly so in respect of 'subjective' time – whether unredeemed or Eternally transformed. So we have the oddity that while, from the outside, we tend to see Eliot's poetic 'development' in terms of a slow, step-by-step pilgrimage to the Absolute, the poetry itself tells us that this apparent journey is only possible because causal sequence and personal maturation of the usual kind have been totally rejected. The beginning can be found in the end only when 'normal' time is disowned and denied, and the light of the Eternal remakes each instant with 'no before and after'. The self can be meaningfully shaped in time only by what is not in time – God. Hence, sequence is always a matter of constant disruption in Eliot: time is fragmented either by 'the shadow' or 'the shaft'. And so the self, too, is constantly being broken in time – either as dissolution into 'fractured atoms' or as continuous self-death and transforming resurrection.

Eliot's scepticism about the reality of 'normal' time began early in his life. The second poem in 'Poems Written in Early Youth' states that 'time is time, and runs away / Though sages disagree'. During his university years, Eliot had plenty of opportunity to study what 'sages' and others had to say about time. His philosophy course included reading Heraclitus and other pre-Socratics, as well as later theoreticians of time; his study of anthropology and Eastern religions introduced him to radically non-Western notions about it; and his preoccupation with literature immersed him in the 'subjective' complexities of experienced time, as recorded in different cultures. Later, his postgraduate research on F. H. Bradley focused his mind on a modern sceptical Idealist who totally denied the validity of Western causal time:

> say that the present state of the world is the cause of that total state which follows next on it. Here, again, is . . . self-contradiction. For how can one state a become a different state b? It must either do this without a reason, and that seems absurd; or else the reason, being additional, forthwith constitutes a new a, and so on for ever. We have the differences of cause and effect, with their relation of time, and we have no way in which it is possible to hold these together. Thus we are drawn to the view that causation is but partial, and that we have but changes of mere elements within a complex whole.[20]

Eliot completed his thesis on Bradley, in spite of various vicissitudes, and maintained his respect for the philosopher at least until 1927, when he wrote an essay on him ending: 'the tendency of his labours is to bring British philosophy closer to the Greek tradition'.[21] Bradley's distinctions between 'immediate experience' of time, time as inadequate relational concept, and time and the absolute surely help inform Eliot's notions of the subjective flux, the illogicality of history and the intervention of the Eternal. All of these are present in his first really successful poem – although the last remains immanent only in the shape of the 'overwhelming question'.

'The Love Song of J. Alfred Prufrock' gives time wholly from the subjective position. The succession of events is registered as irrational flux: 'After the sunsets and the dooryards and the sprinkled streets, / After the novels, after the teacups, after the skirts that trail along the floor –/ And this, and so much more'. There is no clock time, as such, in the poem because there is no acknowledgement of any reality beyond subjective experience; everything is at once sensually imagistic and at the same time tenuous, vague, hypothetical. So the celebrated line 'I have measured out my life with coffee spoons' suggests not digital ordering (the number of spoons and the intervals between them is irrelevant), but habituation, within flux, by compulsive personal ritual. The effect is to make all times one – an appropriation of reality in terms of repetitive stirring, sipping, draining etc., an oral gratification (heightened by the narcotic properties of coffee), whose index is the unmoving 'hand' of the abandoned spoon in place of the moving hand of spatialised time. Both time and space are wholly psychological in 'Prufrock': they are represented in terms of metonomic details which are given no meaning beyond the relativities of experience. And yet time is here experienced in terms of a potentiality which is largely lacking in *The Waste Land* or 'The Hollow Men'. The (never-realised) possibility of action is held tantalisingly open: 'And indeed there will be time . . .'; 'And how should I begin?'; 'Shall I part my hair behind?' The whole poem enacts a teasing *coitus suspensus* between 'the idea / And the reality . . . the potency / And the existence' ('The Hollow Men'). The 'overwhelming question' is never asked, let alone answered; but its immanence haunts the discontinuities of experience, offering possible change, reordering, metamorphosis. Self-time remains a flux of trivial fragments in 'Prufrock', but the poem leaves open a half-promise that there is another kind of time (perhaps Eternal – 'Lazarus, come back from the dead'), which can erupt meaningfully into the phantasmal charade of 'mornings, evenings, afternoons'.

The major poems before 'Ash Wednesday' represent in different ways the same scenario of vacuous discontinuity and infantile habituation tics, infused here and there with the possibility of another time – which serves only to highlight the futility of the protagonist's plight. In 'Gerontion', for instance, the Eternal (in the form of 'Christ the tiger') springs into seasonal time, but the old man is too spiritually enervated, too locked in his habitual defence mechanisms, to seize the possibility – 'I have lost my passion'. He remains a 'dry brain in a dry season', his self-time a matter of fractured process: 'shifting the candles', 'vacant shuttles', the 'operations' of spider and weevil, 'gull against the wind'.

In *The Waste Land* the paradox of 'death-in-life' characterises both the clock time of the working-day and the self-time of the fleeting protagonists. The first is given in terms of lifeless chronology – 'a dead sound on the final stroke of nine'; 'reminiscent bells, that kept the hours': the second as a matter of dessicated habit: 'The hot water at ten'; 'I read much of the night, and go south in the winter'. As a quasi-epic poem, *The Waste Land* also socialises time in terms of a broad, historically layered panorama. The 'land' itself is simultaneously London, the European No Man's Land, the biblical desert, the Fisher King's blighted realm, the Nile marshes where the limbs of Osiris lie scattered and many other things. So too the river is the barge-littered modern Thames as well as the Thames of Spenser, Elizabeth and Leicester, and Pope's *Dunciad* vision. In each scenario or epiphany, the terrain bears within it a discordant variety of past 'moments' which can nowhere be rationalised into 'history'. Tradition itself is never a chronological ordering, but a resonant continuum of present potencies. Even the selves of the poem may embody the discontinuities of historical time – the neurotic modern woman of 'A Game of Chess' is both Cleopatra and Pope's Belinda; the pub voices speak back to Ophelia; Phlebas the drowned sailor is also Adonis, Osiris and a type of Christ. The overall consciousness of the poem[22] speaks a variety of discourses rooted in varying times and places, and renders the poetic self-voice as an echo chamber of transhistorical tongues. 'I can connect/Nothing with nothing' informs both the synchronic and diachronic planes of the poem: the 'voices singing out of empty cisterns and exhausted wells' unmake time as generative cause and reduce the future to bat-babies, crawling 'head downward down a blackened wall'. Once again, the Eternal is here and there infused into the texture of flux. Phlebas's watery whirlpool refines and recycles 'his age and youth' toward redemption. The church of Magnus Martyr and the 'fishmen' of Billingsgate speak a reality beyond the temporal; Augustine and Buddha evoke release from sensual process; the thunder demands a 'life-in-death' which will mean release from time's tyrannical grip. But the possibilities here remain as such: rain has not come, and the poem ends with 'shored' fragments – a frieze of time's detritus set in the midst of ceaseless change.

Between 'The Hollow Men' and 'Ash Wednesday' falls a shadow which promises the eternal 'shaft'. 'The Hollow Men' re-exploits the desert scenario of *The Waste Land* with its temporal fragments, its lost eyes ('I's?) and its compulsive ritual 'round the prickly pear' in a place where all process is broken up by the deathly 'shadow'. Eliot's 'unredeemed' time is a flux of lifeless discontinuities made tolerable only in social variants of child-ritual: 'London Bridge is falling down . . .'; 'This is the way the world ends . . .'. Thus far Eliot had the young, cynical post-war literati with him: but 'Ash Wednesday' effected a break with the views of contemporary readers[23] as spectacular as Eliot's personal renunciation of intellectual cynicism and his 'leap of faith' toward a reality beyond the world of flux. Eliot could easily have developed into a kind of proto-Beckett, creating more and yet more refined structures out of the repetition–compulsion motif. He did not: instead, by an existential act of self-unmaking and remaking, he was able to fangle a new poetic 'self' and move towards the chastened music of *Four Quartets*. In 'Ash Wednesday' he does this by the typically Eliotic strategy of effecting self-change by casting doubt on its very possibility. But the doubt, of course, is directed not as rational discourse towards a reader in normal time, but as a prayer of contrition to that which he believed to be beyond time and redemptive. Hence the last words in particular: 'And let my cry come unto Thee'.

In 'Ash Wednesday' we have a self placed in a kind of experiential time warp: a gap 'between hour and hour' and 'between birth and dying' which is also a point of *turning*. In effect, Eliot is renouncing his old fragmented self and awaiting rebirth in God through the intervention of the 'Lady'. Put another way, there is no real self in the poem – only a tension-filled space, which is at the same time a pause. The word 'I' is used 19 separate times in Section I alone: but this indicates the reverse of egotism; it is the frantic reiteration of consciousness feeling itself dissolve and losing hold of the 'my' of appropriation. It is significant that the word 'me' – signifier of the self's sense of objective identity – is used only once in the entire poem, in the hymn quotation of the penultimate line. For the rest, Eliot relies on the corporate 'us' – object position of undifferentiated sinners. The poem is in a sense personality-less; and it effects an act of penance and purgation which would be the same for any 'self'. At the same time, while the poem appears to 'progress' (in a spiralling motion), it represents a ritual appeal to the Eternal which depends on repetition, in all sincerity, for its spiritual efficacy: thus, as prayer and confession, it defies sequential time. 'Ash Wednesday' constitutes a repeatable formula of sequential words whirling about the still Word of Eternity.

Experiential time is initially given as a matter of aging, exhaustion, inability to change, and the acknowledgement of the lostness of the past: 'what is done, not to be done again'. But this weary acquiescence in unredeemed time is modified by existential affirmation: 'I rejoice, having to construct something / Upon which to rejoice'. The (self-)creation of a base from which to create constitutes a breakage of normal time links similar to Stephen's affirmation in *Portrait*, and already anticipates a 'liberation / From future as well as the past' ('Little Gidding'). Section II sketches out a form of death and possible resurrection, presided over by the 'lady of silences', the 'end of the endless / Conclusion of all that is inconclusible'. The appeal is now overtly to that which is outside of time. Section III characterises the self's attempt at pilgrimage in terms of a winding motion: the painfully forming new self turns back and sees on the stairs the discontinuities of past experience: the wrestling self, the 'dark' absence of self, the self's sensuous phantasy. In IV a lady presides over a garden where surface 'the years that walk between' – the prayer here is explicit: 'Redeem the time'. In V the 'Word' about which normal time whirls is evoked, along with a veiled 'sister', to transform lives into which the shadow falls: 'Those who are torn on the horn between season and season . . . / between . . . / word and word'. Section VI changes the causative 'because' into a tentative 'although'. The self occupies a 'brief transit / . . . between birth and dying': again the sense of self-death and resurrection is hypothetically insistent: 'the time of tension between dying and birth'. The poem ends inconclusively – on the syntactic plane at least. But it also ends with a cry to the finally Eternal. Earlier poetic 'selves' of 'vision and revision', or of 'shored' fragments, or 'driven by the Trades' have become broken down into the impersonal self of contrition, the undifferentiated self as human sinner. And, from this point, the creation of a new self depends on intercession and Grace quite apart from human personality and outside of time. 'Ash Wednesday' writes self-change as self-unmaking in the presence of the Eternal.

Four Quartets is probably the most sophisticated meditation on self-time in modern English. It uses all the resources of antinomy, ambiguity, metaphoricity and 'musical' patterning to unsettle conventional notions about selfhood in time. Though sequence is admitted, it is sequence as swirling flux rather than as rational progression. In important senses, the past is past and the future ahead (although still perhaps 'contained in time present'); but what

Discontinuous Self

joins these is less a line (let alone a causative determination) than a random sequence of impact points. As William T. Lynch has noted: 'It seems not unseemly to suppose that Eliot's imagination (and is not this a theology) is alive with points of *intersection* and *descent*. He seems to place our faith, our hope, and our love, not in the flux of time but in the points of time.'[24] What Lynch calls 'dissociation in time' is represented as the experience of at least three different subjective states: that of the hollow men ('Men and bits of paper, whirled by the cold wind/That blows before and after time'); that of the semi-enlightened ('the moment in and out of time,/The distraction fit, lost in a shaft of sunlight'); and that of the saint ('The point of intersection of the timeless/Within time'). The poem, then, constructs self-time as a montage of frozen moments (some deathly, some redeeming) – not as the flow of a Hollywood movie, but as the cumulative 'collisions' of an Eisenstein film. It is only, of course, by such dissection of flow into discrete and disparate epiphanies that Eliot is able to attempt a reconstruction of time as pattern, by setting the chosen moments into a form of dance. But the selves change in a dance, like a succession of partners: so Eliot emphasised that one aspect of the 'familiar compound ghost' of 'Little Gidding' was himself.[25] That self, being 'long dead', is a past self he meets with to learn the 'pain of reenactment'.

Memory is important in the *Quartets* because it is there that experience distils itself into discrete epiphanies; a 'memory' precisely constitutes itself as a frozen moment against which other moments can be set – as in Bloom's 'Me – and me now'. But involved in memory is not only what happened but also what might have happened. If 'what might have been' belongs only to a 'world of speculation', it remains eloquent because it separates out past possibility from past choice. Selves become themselves specifically in terms of what is chosen and what rejected at any point – 'any action is a step to the block, to the fire, down the sea's throat/or to an illegible stone: and that is where we start'. However, in a new moment a new choice amongst possibilities may be effected (hence the foundation of a new memory): so as one self may perish, another comes into being, and 'the time of death is every moment'. To imagine one can, as integral self, control or even understand past and future is illusory: one cannot even know the effect of one's actions ('things ill done and done to others' harm/Which once you took for exercise of virtue'). What matters is to act in good faith according to the self you are at any moment and ignore the 'fruits of action' – so 'fare forward, voyagers'.

Some critics have been dismissive of the 'Indian' metaphysics, in 'The Dry Salvages' especially, implying not only that Eliot had little understanding of such things, but also that they are largely nonsensical. This seems to me unjust on both counts, and ignores the degree to which the relevant lines act as effective aphorisms. Further, his use of the *Gita* operates to lend traditional authority to an essentially existentialist position. It is basic Sartre that the individual is 'condemned to be free'[26] and that we should 'act without hope',[27] and both formulations are essential to the view that the source of self-change is not causality but freedom. As in Lawrence (surprisingly enough), it is the inauthentic person who believes himself causally determined – and so becomes that: a dead, fixed, unchangeable unitary self. On the other hand, the authentic man (divinely quickened in Eliot) *can* be free of the 'place of disaffection'; can choose and act and change ('all shall be well . . . / By the purification of the motive'). The self is discontinuous because it constantly rechooses what to be in differing situations. That such a view ultimately reduces the self to a constant procession of different selves, which can themselves be only arbitrarily defined, had been faced by Eliot some twenty and more years earlier. In his doctoral dissertation he terms Bradley's units of 'immediate experience' 'finite centres' or 'points of view' – which are 'selves' in this discontinuous sense. He writes: 'wherever a point of view [self?] may be distinguished, I say, there a point of view is'.[28] But 'while one soul [self] may experience within itself many finite centres [discontinuous selves?], the soul itself may be considered in a loose sense as a finite centre'.[29] Such are the linguistic strategies necessary for one who would challenge the conventional doctrine of the 'substantial unity of the soul'![30] A final quotation from the thesis is relevant here, since it elucidates the treatment of both memory and choice in the *Quartets*. I have substituted 'self' for 'point of view' to make my construction more evident: 'What constitutes the difference, therefore, between the two [selves], is the difference which each is capable of making to the other'.[31] It is in the interaction of such differences that the discontinuous self of the poem plays out its ontological tensions:

Lying awake, calculating the future,
Trying to unweave, unwind, unravel
And piece together the past and the future,
Between midnight and dawn, when the past is all deception . . .
Sudden in a shaft of sunlight
Even while the dust moves
There rises the hidden laughter
Of children in the foliage
Quick now, here, now, always –

But such sudden fractures in self-time are also set against 'time not our time'. There is, for instance, the time of the sea-bell: the 'point of intersection of the timeless'; the intervention of the 'dove descending'; and what is represented early on as 'the still point of the turning world'. Such formulations conflict (and interact) with each other – one result of the 'intolerable wrestle/With words and meanings'. But common to all is their transcendence of both sequence and flux, so that they operate together as a further form of discontinuity in time. The pilgrim-self may experience at least an image of the Eternal: but this does not reinstate for him a predominantly developmental time ('the enchainment of past and future'); rather it renders self-time as perpetual change: 'every moment . . . a new and shocking/Valuation of all we have been'. And this suggests the nature of 're-enactment': reenactment is the experiencing and evaluation of a past self by a new self. If the new self has had some glimpse of the Eternal, this may be all the more painful, if possibly redemptive. For the self which admits the Eternal relevance of Incarnation ('the Word') sees all past selves in terms of repentance. Nor can the new self see a fixed meaning in its past from this point, for the pattern will keep changing. All it *can* do is trust in the eventuality of a final (Eternal) pattern and meaning – a matter of faith not knowledge. So the 'redeemed' self endures discontinuity in the expectation of a higher order revealed outside of time: 'All shall be well . . . /When the tongues of flame are in-folded/Into the crowned knot of fire/And the fire and the rose are one'.

We see that the notions of 'one'-ness, order, higher continuity remain in Eliot's verse as a nostalgia converted into faith and hope. But the experience of selfhood remains written as radical metamorphosis. This is pithily stated in the reworking of a cliché: 'time is no healer: the patient is no longer here'. It is also formulated in 'The Dry Salvages' as a paradox speaking back to Whitman's expansive optimism:

> 'Fare forward, you who think that you are voyaging;
> You are not those who saw the harbour
> Receding, or those who will disembark. . .'

'Old men should be explorers', we are told. And what they explore are the changing manifestations of selfhood, as they move either into the final dissolution of flux or towards the eternal redemption from time in love. The persuasive optimism at the end of 'Little Gidding' comes from the conviction that we can live with self-discontinuity because there is an absolute and unchanging Self beyond 'our time' and beyond human personality, into whom, and by whom, the repentant, self-acknowledging self can be subsumed. It is a mark of our sceptical and fragmenting culture that such an optimism, based on faith, is not something many of us can share.

'I CHANGED AND CHANGED'

If *Four Quartets* reminds us, quite frequently, of Virginia Woolf's treatment of time, then Woolf's own writing – and especially *The Waves* – seems heavily influenced by Eliot's representation of 'unredeemed' time in the early poems. This, I suspect, as much as the putative Bergsonian influence,[32] informs the way self-process and change are written in works like *Mrs Dalloway*, *To the Lighthouse* and *The Waves*. It is not only a question of clock time versus experienced time; it is also a question of the nature of experienced time. What effects has the persistence of memory? What of self endures and what alters? How can self-metamorphosis be understood or written? How far can experienced time be shared by different selves (as characters)? How can we 'make one moment merge into the next',[33] and what if we cannot? Can there be moments of Eternity in time? Is death only an ending? These are some of the questions Virginia Woolf's novels press. And, as with Eliot, the result of such questioning is to cast into radical doubt any model of a coherent, continuing self. Though memories endure, the self can be both multiple and discontinuous, and in relationships we can seem to merge, if only temporarily, into another's self.

Discontinuous Self 159

Virginia Woolf's later fiction is haunted by the experiential reality of a sudden, deathly gap in self-time – a chasm in the self, a disruptive moment of unmaking which also remakes all self-experience. This time-rift may be as small and private as the inability to cross a puddle or as vast and socially portentous as the advent of world war. It is inscribed in the novels through a variety of unusual fictional devices: the abrupt disappearance of the hero of *Jacob's Room*; the backfire moment in *Mrs Dalloway* which precipitates Septimus Warren Smith back into the instant of literal shell shock; the shuttered house and suspended life as sectional pivot of *To the Lighthouse*; or the death of Percival in *The Waves*, which effects a gulf in the self-experiences of the six speakers. Like Eliot's 'shadow', this rent in continuity becomes a metaphor whose implications threaten all linear connections in the texts. For the self-aware characters, it is a perpetual immanence which renders fragile, even absurd, the self-projects they commit themselves to. All attempts to construct selfhood in Woolf are founded on a fault line in continuity.

In *Mrs Dalloway*, self-change is explored by showing the impact of past experience on the varying events of a single day. This is achieved in terms of the consciousnesses of those characters who are shown essentially from the 'inside' – most notably Clarissa, Peter and Septimus. A single epiphanic memory – like the 'scene' at Bourton – operates as an enduring index of what the characters involved have become, their later 'selves' – in this case Clarissa the lonely, confused socialite, Peter the self-indulgent, impractical romancer. As in Eliot, the memory immortalises the poignance of possibilities lost (i.e. alternative selves). It also tantalises the reader with future possibilities: 'What is this terror? What is this ecstasy?' feels Peter in Clarissa's approach at the end of the book, thus raising the prospect of future self-changes sprung by their remeeting. So, while the book emphasises the immutability of certain experiences in memory, it also writes self-change as a matter of choice rather than temporal determination, and emphasises discontinuity. Clarissa's impulsive break with Peter at Bourton represents a bid for the peaceful marriage she now queries constantly. And Peter's love for the girl in India is something he will have to reconsider in the light of Clarissa's reception of his news. Elizabeth, riding the bus to the Strand, was 'delighted to be free'; savouring her self-possibilities (doctor? farmer? politician? – 'every profession is open to the women of your generation'),[34] as she exults in the activity of the streets below. However, there is a brooding quality to the book and it is mainly focused on past choice and the impact of changed selves on each other in the present. The two surprises of the day culminate in the reencounter of Clarissa, Peter and Sally (now Lady Rossiter) at the party, and stress the ruptures that time has effected in all their lives. Time and change are to be endured rather than understood, and *Mrs Dalloway*, for all its moments of sudden ecstasy, generates a sombre, finally elegiac, stoicism – 'Fear no more the heat of the sun.'

To the Lighthouse expresses self-change in terms of narrative interruption, and hence contrast. Again, feelings, memories, habits may persist across the interval, but the self which 'contains' these has changed qualitatively; a temporal gulf has intervened between old self and new: 'as if the link that usually bound things together had been cut'.[35] Both the war years and the death of Mrs Ramsay focus such self-discontinuity, while the voyage to the lighthouse (first imagined, then experienced) provides a scenario through which past and present may be contrasted. The third section operates as a kind of *peripeteia* whereby the realisation of self-change is effected. The voyage appears at first to move towards a culmination in which James's and Cam's childhood hatred of their father, and Mr Ramsay's old aggressive authoritarianism, will meet in oppositional climax. In fact, something very different happens, and it happens because, largely unknown to them, they have changed from what they were. So Cam discovers she loves her father, and James becomes confirmed in his father's praise. Both the lighthouse of remembered vision and the one now seen are real[36] – but in the interval the mother's boy has become the young man approved by his father. And Mr Ramsay, for all the persistence of his eccentricities, has softened, playing now 'the part of a desolate man, widowed, bereft'. As he tells Lily Briscoe: 'You find us much changed'.[37] Lily, at first, sees only an exacerbation of Mr Ramsay's emotional demands, but after her vision of the lost relationship between the Ramsays she changes her attitude, and in doing so, modifies her own sense of selfhood. Thus she is able to finish her painting – with a sudden bold line, which perhaps represents that dark gulf in time which both rends and mediates self-experience. At this point the book ends – itself a fictional artefact which also creates pattern out of fragmentation and discontinuity.

The Waves constitutes Virginia Woolf's most sustained exploration of the self in time. It provides, in its structure, a broken chronology of life time which takes us from primary childhood awareness to the oncoming of death. At the same time, the mythos of the single day is given in interspersed poetic passages which trace the rising and falling of the sun. Six characters speak their attempts to create and sustain a consistent selfhood in the face of fluxive change and sudden disaster (Percival's death). At the end, the chief narrator, Bernard, reviews the whole process of 'selfing', experiencing multi-selves, sensing selves under selves (some 'unborn',[38] one the 'hairy man' of physicality that persists throughout), 'un-selfing' (as a kind of death) and the tentative merging of self into its surrounding world. It is, then, a book which deals comprehensively and complexly with the fiction of the 'integral' self as it experiences the disintegrative impact of process.

Four of the characters – Louis, Neville, Bernard and Rhoda – experience discontinuity as a primary mode of being, though their strategies for coping with this vary. The other two – Susan and Jinny – construct for themselves inauthentic[39] personae through which they seek to deny discontinuity – Susan as earth mother and Jinny as promiscuous adventuress. All six are almost mystically united by the figure of Percival, who never speaks. Percival, in fact, represents the myth of the integral, continuous self – and it is crucially emblematic that he dies half-way through the novel. Percival is represented as the man of action, a non-self-conscious hero figure whose confident gestures others imitate without ever achieving their authenticity. The very Boys' Magazine quality of this character (and his likeness to the 'bravest and best' myth of the war generation) indicates his status as a lost ideal of selfhood. It is in relation to this ideal that the other characters measure their experiences and bewail their fragmentary incompleteness.

In his book *The Unknown Virginia Woolf*[40] Roger Poole sees Rhoda as the chief representative of Woolf herself, because some of her experiences (e.g. the terror in crossing a puddle) are recorded as Woolf's own in *Moments of Being*.[41] Be that as it may, Rhoda certainly seems to experience self-fragmentation in a more radical and distressing way than any of the other characters. Her identity is constantly threatened by others – friends as well as strangers – and also by objects in the physical world. 'Alone', she confesses, 'I often fall down into nothingness' (p. 36). And this anxiety about her experience is at its most acute with respect to time. Her fear is that 'nothing persists' (p. 111). She says:

> I cannot make one moment merge into the next. To me they are all violent, all separate . . . I do not know how to run minute to minute and hour to hour, solving them by some natural force until they make the whole and indivisible mass that you call life.
>
> (p. 111)

Rhoda is an extreme case of the self constantly torn apart by the contrastive succession of experiences. Or, put another way, she is an extreme case of the impossibility of finally identifying a unity in the disparate moments, situations and encounters that constitute self-life ('life is . . . a luminous halo . . .'). Her selfhood has no more solidity than the atom in post-quantum physics. Hence, too, what 'happens' to her in the novel – her affair with Louis or her visit to Spain – has no significance in normal fictional terms. Love does not establish her, experience does not 'mature' her, death, one feels (its circumstances are not described), cannot complete her. For she is not a 'person' in the normal sense. She 'has no face' (p. 35). The anguish of fragmentation is with her from moment to moment, in womanhood as in girlhood, and is only confirmed over and again by the lived experience of time. The implications of her self-discontinuity inform the novel as a whole, whose revolutionary structure expresses all experienced time as absurd flux.

The contrast between Rhoda and Susan demonstrates the range of Woolf's exploration of selfhood. Already in childhood Susan demonstrates a conventional ability to define herself – 'I love and . . . I hate' (p. 12) – and establishes herself in terms of 'purpose'. As she grows up she sees the world in terms of possession based on acknowledged self-need. Hence, 'I cannot be divided, or kept apart'. She too suffers disappointment in love, but it does not break up her sense of self. Instead, she marries a squire, owns land and brings up children. 'So life fills my veins', she cries, 'so life pours through my limbs.' In traditional fictional terms, Susan is a success. But in this book, although Woolf does not comment directly, it is evident that she has achieved and retained her sense of self by self-ignorance and self-deception. Other characters speak of her disparagingly once she is settled, and she herself realises, later in life, that she is rather a fraud. Her last utterance concerns 'something that has escaped me'. Even more than Jinny, whose creation of a self incorporates something of the reality of discontinuity (i.e. her promiscuous pursuit of ever-new lovers), Susan, for most of the book, stands in strong contrast to those more central characters who question identity at its core.

Bernard is the chief of these characters, though less disoriented than Rhoda, and his summing-up ends the book. As such, his experience subsumes the questioning of both Louis and Neville, who, though important in themselves, are shown to cling eventually to artificial identity props: Neville carrying his secret authenticating 'documents' about with him; Louis signing his name on perpetual business letters – 'clear, firm, unequivocal'. It is only Bernard in *The Waves* who undergoes a late transformation and new awareness of self-experience. From childhood Bernard establishes himself as story teller, at home in any social situation. He is able to do this by a chameleon-like tolerance of self-change which he is soon to articulate at college: 'I have to effect different transitions; have to cover the entrances and exits of several different men who alternatively act their part as Bernard' (p. 64). The theatrical metaphor is important for it stresses the dynamic nature of Bernard's metamorphoses. He is actively self-fragmentary where Rhoda is passively self-fragmented. Bernard, especially in youth, imposes his own fluxive energy on experience through a changing sequence of masks and roles: 'I changed and changed; was Hamlet, was Shelley, was the hero, whose name I forget, of a novel by Dostoevsky; was for a whole term, incredibly, Napoleon; but was Byron chiefly' (p. 214). Similarly, his jotting of phrases into notebooks and his trying-out of stories are both modes of exercising power by utilising the varied potentialities of self. However, eventually, and for a long time, he too succumbs to the reductive conventionality of the unitary self: 'I rose and walked away – I, I, I; not Byron, Shelley, Dostoevsky, but I, Bernard' (p. 217).

It is this unitary Bernard which is finally broken down in the last section of the book. Earlier he had resisted Neville's accusation that 'you are not Byron; you are yourself' by refusing to be 'contracted by another person into a single being' (p. 76). He had asserted: 'I am more selves than Neville thinks'. Though repressed in later life in the interests of survival, this sense of the self's fluidity – beyond mere student posing – is retained to undergo a deepening of experience in old age. The familiar self of 'many tremendous adventures' (p. 244) suddenly vanishes:

This self now as I leant over the gate looking down over fields rolling in waves of colour beneath me made no answer. He threw up no opposition. He attempted no phrase. His fist did not form. I waited. I listened. Nothing came, nothing. I cried then with a sudden conviction of complete desertion. Now there is nothing. No fin breaks the waste of this immeasurable sea. Life has destroyed me.

(p. 244)

Bernard experiences this moment as a kind of death, as an 'eclipse of the sun': he has become a 'man without a self'. And when the 'light' returns, he feels a mystical unity with nature, savouring 'the world seen without a self'. This sense of the end of 'being' remains with him at the stated moment of telling ('So I hung up my coat, tapped you on the shoulder, and said, "Sit with me"' (p. 248)). Bernard feels both that he is nobody and that he may be all six of the book's characters. He is also haunted by 'shadows of people one might have been; unborn selves' (p. 249). His state has become like Rhoda's – one of constant discontinuity ('while I sat here I have been changing', p. 253). At the end, aware that the restaurant is closing, he is forced back to a socially given sense of self ('I, I, I, tired as I am . . . even I, an elderly man . . . must take myself off and catch some last train', p. 255). But as dawn breaks he remains part of the process, beyond self – 'the eternal renewal, the incessant rise and fall and fall and rise again' – and it is this process which 'swells' in him to effect a last persona – the knight, modelled on Percival, who will fling himself upon death. Bernard, then, constitutes Woolf's most sustained characterisation of discontinuous selfhood.

It is significant that Bernard's eventual loss of self is associated with his final abandonment of his book-writing project. From youth, he had collected phrases and aimed to create a synthesis of his perceptions in a novel. But at the end of *The Waves* he leaves the uncompleted book on the floor to be swept up by the charwoman. He also dismisses his lifelong phantasy of having his experiences described (and given meaning?) by a biographer. The experience of breaking out of the myth of self teaches him also the arbitrariness of discourse. So 'I need a little language such as lovers use. I need a howl; a cry' (p. 254); 'There are no words . . . How describe or say anything in articulate words again' (p. 247); 'How much better is silence' (p. 254). Although, of course, he still (paradoxically) *says* this (and Woolf writes him saying it), the perception of the final inauthenticity of language is vital to the novel and what it has to say about the self. Bernard's abandonment of phrases (let alone narrative) contrasts strongly with Lily Briscoe's completion of her painting. Woolf's perception has moved on a whole stage. She herself finishes her project, but uses enough experimental devices here (double time-scale, dramatic voices, poetic phraseology, musical repetition and variation on theme) to expose the nature of normal narrative. And, through Bernard, she finally admits the limitations in her own attempt to speak selfhood. It is as if she is aware that the illusion of a continuous self is grounded in the successive continuity of language – most particularly the pre-plotted linearity (phrase after phrase, page by page, chapter upon chapter) of printed textuality. Her exploration of discontinuity in selfhood at last lights on the fact that the coherent, developing self is above all a textual construction. So, in the end, her language gestures out towards that complexity of experience which is beyond words. If Bernard is indeed partially modelled on the would-be novelist Desmond MacCarthy,[42] *The Waves* perhaps attests to Woolf's mature perception that her friend's failure may evidence a greater authenticity than her own success. In the end, the reality of selfhood in time cannot be communicated: it is something that can only be known in self-aware personal living.

'EGO SCRIPTOR'

It is a moot point how far we should consider the *Cantos* – Pound's 'tale of the tribe' – as a 'personal' poem. In insistent ways, it speaks itself as a Modernist epic, and its chief allusive referents – the *Odyssey*, *Sordello*, the *Divine Comedy* – all suggest a social and historical intention. Nevertheless, an authorial 'self', if variable and expressed through mask, is indelibly written into part of the poem, emerging most strongly in the Pisan *Cantos*. This is a highly self-conscious presence, sometimes given in terms of the chronicler's 'ego scriptor' – socialised and Latinised, a screen for the individuality of 'virtù'. It can also be dramatically versatile – staggering clown-like through hell-mud ('inch by inch / the matter resisting') or playing the respectful student ('And I said "I dunno sir"'). It is the represented source of a number of conflicting rhetorical postures – frenzied denunciation or Confucian calm or folksy anecdotage – and combines the roles of teacher, elegist, priest, scholar, lover and so on. But the very insistence of the 'scriptor' to mediate parts of the content, and the variety of masks and speaking postures, signal the poem's dependence on a compulsive if variable sense of self. It looks back to the Romantic 'egotistical sublime' through the 'prismatic hues' of Browning's partial relativism: via the Browningesque 'swerve'[43] of dramatisation, it continues the Romantic project concerning the 'poet's mind'. From Canto III ('I sat on the Dogana's steps') to CXVI ('Charity I have had sometimes'), the poem traces in its contents a self-in-process. And a key tension in the poem is generated by the way the Romantic notion of 'growth' is undermined by radical discontinuities; the self here harks after organic development but finds, in the experience of its own history, radical disjunctions. The self is alienated from itself by the passage of time.

Donald Hall has some interesting comments about meeting Pound shortly before the poet's death:

> 'Mr. Hall,' he said to me in the doorway, 'you-find-me-in fragments.' As he spoke he separated the words into little bunches, like bursts of typing from an inexperienced typist. 'You have driven-all the way – from England-to find a man-who is only fragments.'[44]

and again:

> then suddenly it happened, horribly in front of my eyes: again I saw vigor and energy drain out of him, like air from a pricked balloon. The strong body visibly sagged into old age; he disintegrated in front of me, smashed into a thousand unconnected and disorderly pieces.[45]

Of course, this can be construed purely as an old man's exhaustion, but Pound's use of the word 'fragments' is telling – very different from saying 'you find me worn out', where the 'me' would remain intact. As Hall notes: 'one mistake . . . is to underestimate the diversity and discontinuity of the psyche'. It is such 'diversity and discontinuity' which the *Cantos* charts, unmaking the ideal Poundian project of making it all 'flow through'. In twentieth-century experience, it seems, one *can* 'wring lilies from the acorn'.

From the beginning of his career, Pound had been preoccupied by the problem of selfhood and its relation to writing. As he noted in 1914:

Discontinuous Self

> In the 'search for oneself', in the search for 'sincere self-expression', one gropes, one finds some seeming verity. One says 'I am' this, that, or the other, and with the words scarcely uttered one ceases to be that thing.
>
> I began this search for the real in a book called *Personae*, casting off, as it were, complete masks of the self in each poem. I continued in a long series of translations, which were but more elaborate masks.[46]

Poems like 'Cino' and 'The Ballad of the Goodly Fere' are examples of the earlier type, 'The Seafarer' and 'Exile's Letter' of the later, and in *The Poetic Achievement of Ezra Pound* Michael Alexander[47] has shown how much of Pound's personal feelings and situation may be detected even in his translation from Anglo-Saxon. However, the masks also vary considerably; so that even at this time Pound's 'self' resembles that of the lady in his 'Near Perigord': 'a shifting change, / A bundle of broken mirrors'. In his most characteristic Imagist poems, Pound attempts to ignore the problems of selfhood by diffusing personal emotions in reified images – 'direct treatment of the "thing" whether subjective or objective'.[48] But in 'Hugh Selwyn Mauberley', that strange and largely misrepresented poem, he diffuses self-conflict throughout the sections in an extraordinary way, which is rarely under firm ironic control. Briefly, it is a poem of self-splitting, self-parody, self-castigation and virtual self-castration, under the thin guise of the careers of two poets called 'E.P.' and 'Mauberley' – both of whom he 'buries'. Whether the two are supposed to represent two phases of Pound's career (say 1908–12 and 1912–15), or two aspects of him throughout the period, the sense of confusion about himself and his role, and a generalised sense of inadequacy, are given bizarre expression in a poem ostensibly about the artist's place in modern society. Perhaps strangest of all is the way the feminine inclination (as expressed in the muse poems 'Envoi' and 'Medallion') is rebuked by the censorious discourse of other sections ('wrong from the start', etc.). It is as if the law of the father (expressed as public written discourse – the 'reviewing' voice) is employed to repress the celebration of mother and mate in the specifically 'poetic' end lyrics. Mauberley, in particular, is punningly unmanned (unable 'to designate his orchid') and both are killed off – as men and reputations – within the poem's short span. Two selves, as it were, are excoriated and disposed of as Pound prepares to leave London and embark on his new self-project, the *Cantos*. So a model of self-in-process is set up here which will recur at a key point in the *Cantos*: not the 'growth of a poet's mind', but the disintegration and decease of 'self', written from a position which asserts the resurrection of a new self. We have not linear continuity but painful metamorphosis.

In many ways the project of the *Cantos* is to transcend the Wordsworthian preoccupation with the poetic subject – to erect a monument in words where the self is almost wholly dissolved in the discourses of history and world-mythology. However, from quite early on there are moments when a variable but distinctive self-voice breaks into the texture as witness or elegist, in a way that looks forward to the Pisan *Cantos* and last fragments. Such a moment occurs in VII as a meditation on time past:

> We also made ghostly visits, and the stair
> That knew us, found us again on the turn of it,
> Knocking at empty rooms, seeking for buried beauty;
> But the sun-tanned, gracious and well-formed fingers
> Lift no latch of bent bronze, no Empire handle
> Twists for the knocker's fall; no voice to answer.
> A strange concierge, in place of the gouty-footed.
> Sceptic against all this one seeks the living,
> Stubborn against the fact. The wilted flowers
> Brushed out a seven year since, of no effect.
> Damn the partition! Paper, dark-brown and stretched,
> Flimsy and damned partition.
>   Ione, dead the long year
> My lintel and Liu Che'e's.
> Time blacked out with the rubber.[49]

The slightly Eliotic tone here summons up the ideals of the 'men of 1914' through memory; the figure of the turning stair, as in 'Ash Wednesday', effects a discontinuous mode of process; the flowers are now wilted, and the paper (textual?) partition stretches between self and self. Hence the evocation of an earlier poem marks change beyond even the attempt to express it – 'Where Ione / Walked once, and now does not walk / But seems like a person just gone'.[50] The past of the self is both held and yet is 'of no effect' and 'blacked out with the rubber'. So the progression to define what is 'in "time"'[51] – 'to-day against the past'[52] – and to acknowledge what persists from 'self' to 'self': 'The passion endures.'[53]

As the cantos continue, Pound's meditations on time are worked out on a largely impersonal canvas – the battle of notions of order which arise out of flux to master it and create a coherent history. But as such, and perhaps inevitably, the poem ends up confirming the power of flux over the very ideals Pound seeks to set in marble. Malatesta, Jefferson and Adams, Confucius and Ming – all these float in the turbulent wake of history, and the poet's energetic attempt to recycle them for modern use, to reshape history, inevitably falls back into the tidal cross-currents of the fluid element, Poseidon. Man can navigate through, but not control, time. With the end of World War II, and Pound's personal experience of defeated ideals and social retribution, the poem recapitulates the struggle with process on a largely personal plane. In the Pisan *Cantos* the self comes to the centre of the stage. But I do not find, with Alan Durrant, that 'the identity of the self . . . is restored to a prevailing position of centrality and self-sufficiency',[54] since the nature of the self is thrown into radical doubt here, and 'sufficiency' – beyond the occasional defiance – is the last thing we can expect to find. The tragedy of the Pisan *Cantos* is that Pound becomes thrown forcibly out of the world of historico-economic theory into an existential anguish which he cannot rationalise into any kind of order. In the realm of his own experience, he can find neither unity nor consistency. So the 'self' of these cantos is rendered as a vortex of memories and sensations, inscribed as shorthand jottings, which at no point add up to anything like a meaningful identity. The predominant message is the inability to connect:

>   Le Paradis n'est pas artifiel
>   but spezzato apparently
>   it exists only in fragments unexpected sausage,
>   the smell of mint, for example.   (Canto LXXIV)
>
>   What thou lov'st well is thy true heritage
>   Whose world, or mine or theirs
>   or is it of none?   (Canto LXXXI)
>
>   . . . but I will come out of this knowing no one
>   neither they me.   (Canto LXXXIII)

Michael Alexander takes LXXIV as 'a microcosm of the *Pisan Cantos*',[55] and it will serve as a representative site where the implications of self-fragmentation-as-process are played out. The canto is exactly and poignantly situated: 'from the death-cells of Mt. Taishan @ Pisa' – a point of stillness, suffering, recollection. Pound himself felt 'twice crucified' (by two world wars?). So the 'drama is wholly subjective' – brokenly at that. The canto proceeds as a collaged diversity of discourse fragments, unfolding not a narrative but a resonant mental continuum. But in spite of the overall randomness of reference, a distinctive, if at times ambivalent, double torsion can be perceived – a spiralling struggle between the sense of flux and the desire for order, development, rationalised process. Both the staccato, agglutinative style of the canto, and the existential shock it inscribes, ensure that, unlike the Confucian or Jefferson-Adams sections, centrality is given to the notion of discontinuity – and fitful attempts are made to come to terms with the double reality of disjunctive time and the metamorphic self. Images of liquidity and detritus assert a norm against the impossible ideal – marble, precision, the carved trace. 'Ends have their beginnings' we are assured – but this is nowhere demonstrated: rather "ΡΕΙ ΠΑΝΤΑ' ('all things flow'), 'as the winds veer and the raft is driven', and both wind and rain are part of 'the process'. For most of the canto, flux is given as something deathly: 'magna NUX animae' – the dark night of the soul. The Disciplinary Training Centre experience is written as crucifixion, hell, destruction ('with a bang not with a whimper'). So 'time is not. Time is evil', and within it 'ghosts move about me', '"patched with histories"'. Out of his confusion, Pound still clings to the dream – a single ordered history where everything has 'its proper season'. But the canto insists on another reality – that paradise exists only in fragments and that 'liquid is certainly a/property of the mind'.

For Pound, the implications of this torsion are figured in terms of money and economic value. What he most fears and loathes is the 'Usurer's hell-a-dice' – which can stand as an image also of history and self-process. Hell, for the dreamer of order, is chance, the unpredictable, the uncontrollable – money, as it were, surrendered to flux, gambling, the 'invisible hand' over market forces. So his two indictments of capitalism are: 'the alteration/of the value of money', and that money value is 'made out of nothing'. He sees this usurious norm as confirmed by the verdict of the second war – against both Mussolini, and a possibly reconstructed Stalin who is named, along with Lenin, in the canto. The American triumph (under which he suffers here) ensures the continuance of a value standard which is both originless ('out of nothing' – unfathered by causative authenticity) and unstable (subject to 'alteration' and hence chaotic). The relation of this to the sense of self is signalled both across and 'under' the text. Maud Ellmann has mused fruitfully on the word-chime Ezra-Usura.[56] And, if we see Pound's almost hysterical economic strictures as partly due to displaced anxiety about the nature and value of the self-in-process, then Usura signifies the radical unmaking of Ezra, in terms of origins (patriarchal, national, literary) and self-continuity (the America, London, Paris, Rapallo years and then the DTC: or, say, Cino, Bertrans de Born, Rihaku, E. P., Mauberley, the various postures of Ego Scriptor). This devaluation of the Pound[57] is connected directly with his Odyssean un-naming as 'ΟΥ ΤΙΣ' ('no man'), or 'a man on whom the sun has gone down'. The identity and value of the self is not continuous through time: rather like coinage, it is unfounded and variable, itself a flux permeated and constantly altered by the chaotic currents of historical process.

The loss of a coherent sense of time and self is evident in both the form and matter of individual passages of Canto LXXIV. Here is one such:

> that wd/have been in the time of Rais Uli
>   when I rode out to Elson's
>   near the villa of Perdicaris
>   or four years before that
> elemental he thought the souls of the children, if any,
> but had rented a shelter for travellers
>   by foot from Siria, some of them
> nor is it for nothing that the chrysalids mate in the air
>   colour di luce,
> green splendour and as the sun through pale fingers
> Lordly men are to earth o'ergiven
>   these the companions:
> Fordie that wrote of giants
>   and William who dreamed of nobility
>   and Jim the comedian singing:
>   'Blarrney castle me darlin'
>   You're nothing now but a stOWne'. . .

There is a wayward privacy of reference and association in such lines which admits the reader directly into the unmediated vortex of Pound's mind continuum. People we might know about – Ford Madox Ford, W. B. Yeats and James Joyce – are given not by their public names but in terms of private reference – Fordie, William and Jim – and connected up, by internal reference, with a certain Elson and literary references important to Pound – 'colour di luce', or his own translation from the Saxon: 'lordly men are to earth o'ergiven'. Even external time markers, where we have them, are vague – 'That wd/have been . . . / or four years before that'. It is like an individual computer searching its memory-bank randomly for a program key that never emerges. And behind the references is no sense of public tradition in Eliot's provisional sense of monuments-in-order. Even with the 'great', it is the small and largely irrelevant personal quirks that are registered – if Yeats's snobbery rather overinforms his verse, Ford is not celebrated for writing about giants, nor is Joyce's chief claim to fame his comic renditions of Irish songs. Pound is trapped in the unravelling of his discontinuous memories, producing a self in writing that is nothing but 'a heap of broken images' 'shelved/shored' against 'his ruin' – and yet the ruin is evident in the very process.

Even though such passages communicate meanings, in their own fashion, there is a sense in which they both signify and embody a destruction of writing. By syntactic breakage, by the rhetorical linking of unlikes, by the dissolution of familiar time–space conventions and by collage of very private allusions in a spasmodic stream-of-consciousness, the Pisan *Cantos*, in particular, deconstruct even the *possibility* of the kind of meaningful order Pound desires, on the crucial plane of discourse. It is not just that the existential absurdity of the DTC situation invades the writing, mimetically, or that Pound is making a Prestructuralist point about the self-as-signifier, from some known ground outside language. The two twinned realities are there together: the discontinuity of the 'self' both as lived and as written; with the inbuilt double bind that we perhaps largely experience things through a language paradigm at the same time that we transform discourse according to experiential biases. Here Pound unmakes writing; and writing unmakes him – renders him as a collage of discourses. This is fitting, in that the whole notion of a coherent and consistent self is a legacy of the alphabetically linear, analytical and iterative nature of writing, which had haunted Western thought from its initial (written) inception. Pound's notorious pursuit of the ideogrammic does not so much establish a reordered poetic discourse as create a weird and rather wonderful poetry out of the disintegration of discourse. The discourse is fractured as the 'self' is, in terms of non-origination, juxtaposition and discontinuity. Put one way, Pound has no style – any more than he has a self; rather the waywardness of a powerful, but variable, 'virtú' is impressed upon language as a variety of stances, discourses, styles; just as the poet's past and present consist of strong but variable energies at play within the diverse fauna of experience. It was an early project of Pound, enshrined in some insightful review-writing, to 'gather the limbs of Osiris'.[58] The Pisan *Cantos* demonstrate that it cannot be done in Pound's world. The self becomes broken up by the workings of time, and there are no honest words, no authentic rhetorical connectives which can put Humpty-Dumpty together again. Pound acquiesces in this – for all the sudden moments of rebellion ('I surrender neither the empire nor the temples' or 'I believe in the resurrection of Italy quia impossibile est'). The dislocated syntax of Pound's mature poetry speaks a dislocated self-world. And his metaphors of mediation between flux and ideal order suggest a pattern that the cantos do not give us: neither the ball dancing in the fountain nor the magnetic 'rose in the steel dust'. The integrity and the fascination of the *Cantos* lies then, simply, in the intensity and beauty of the prolonged balancing act whereby the poet battles to furnish 'oak' from the 'acorn' in a world of flux where all metaphors are broken down. As the *Prelude* is the key self-document of nineteenth-century poetry, so is the *Cantos* of the twentieth century. Its own ending as 'drafts and fragments', in possible self-confessed failure, precisely authenticates rather than minimises the project. It is not a failed eccentric, but the communal voice of modern selfhood, which concludes in honesty and with dignity: 'I cannot make it cohere'.

7

Conclusion

'I, say I. Unbelieving'[1]

If the last drafts of Pound's *Cantos* carried the Modernist project into the 1970s, the main impetus of the movement had spent itself by the mid-thirties. The discourse of self-fragmentation was well established by then, and a new generation of writers was emerging whose interests were in social rather than personal issues. The selfhood of an 'unknown citizen' was more a matter for sociological analysis than psychological investigation. At the same time, it is difficult to see what, in that decade, the new generation could have added to such radical presentations as 'Tiresias', Leopold Bloom or Mrs Dalloway. Joyce's contemporaneous 'Work in Progress' served to indicate how strait the road might be for those who wished to continue Modernist experimentation, and Beckett, who did, contributed nothing distinctive to its discourse until the fifties. Although Auden, in particular, assimilated much of the mood, and some of the mode, of Modernism, thirties writing, overall, appears something of a reaction against the preoccupations and textual complexities of the previous movement. The 'I' that becomes 'a camera' has suppressed the problems of selfhood and its representation to focus on the realities of the social nexus.

The Second World War effected a watershed in English writing. If the Great War had helped precipitate the best young writers into a ferment of international experimentation, its successor did quite the reverse. Its effect was to produce nationalist isolation and imaginative timidity. The best of such writing – say of Waugh or Orwell – prepared the way for the new generation of the fifties, which simply ignored (or sometimes rejected) the achievement of Modernism. In poetry this phenomenon was centred on the Movement. It was not just a matter of breaking with the Romanticised neo-Modernism of Dylan Thomas and the New Apocalypse: it represented a retreat to the conventions of Georgianism. Philip Larkin, the most talented of the new poets, consciously rejected the influence of Yeats and Eliot and invoked instead the 'English' tradition of Hardy and Edward Thomas. The result was a return to the unexamined unitary self – as little-Englander suburbanite:

> . . . I'm a better hand
> At knowing what I can stand
> Without them sending a van –
> Or I suppose I can.[2]

So, in 'Self's the Man' Larkin compares himself (not unfavourably) with a certain Arnold, and, for all the half-disclaimer of that last line, it will be the 'supposed self' – the integral, common-sense, defensive self – which will lie at the heart of his poetry. In 'Whitsun Weddings', for instance, the 'I' which sits on the southward-speeding train, gathering the conclusion of the poem out of a variety of detailed observations, is as whole and self-sufficient as Robinson Crusoe on his island. The appeal of the Larkin self is in its enbattled ordinariness – 'I work all day, and get half drunk at night'.[3] Its final unsatisfactoriness lies in its defensiveness, its denial of the deepest conflicts and its assertion of a single unproblematical 'voice'. Larkin neither developed nor contended with Modernist selfhood; he wrote as if it has never existed. And his example has been centrally influential in British poetry up until now. Although there are exceptions, post-war British poetry has been dominated by the myth of the coherent self and its originating mono-ideolective 'voice'. The 'I' of, say, Peter Porter, Seamus Heaney, Tony Harrison,[4] Andrew Motion, Craig Raine or James Fenton are all like Larkin's in this: they are all pretty sure about who they are and just what it is they feel, and they all seem naively at home in the form of language that 'constructs' them. Mainstream contemporary English poetry has learned little, if anything, from Modernism in this regard.

The picture in mainstream post-war fiction is much the same. While there have been some gains in the new areas of life explored – 'working-class' fiction, women's writing, Third World novels etc. – there has been little attempt to follow up the modes of new characterisation which were pioneered by James, Conrad, Ford, Lawrence, Joyce, Richardson and Woolf. The fifties was perhaps the grimmest period, with the realist melodrama *Room at the Top* and the realist farce *Lucky Jim* contending for significance with the Jansenist allegory, *Lord of the Flies*. None of these said anything about selfhood which expressed a specifically twentieth-century awareness of the complexities of self-experience. In the sixties there were hints of existentialism (in say Iris Murdoch), metaphysical self-probing (John Fowles) and psychoanalytic awareness (Doris Lessing), but nothing amounting to a shared project of discourse. And the seventies, if anything, reverted to conventional simplicities. Malcolm Bradbury's popular *The History Man*, for instance, served to reconstruct such expanded self-exploration as the sixties afforded in terms of aggressive and greedy egoism – the unitary self as satiric type. Only in some of the recent Booker Prize decisions[5] does there seem hope that fiction in the eighties might be more adventurous and probe the mysteries of the self's experience in new and illuminating ways. But for the most part, British fiction since World War Two has agreed with poetry that the Modernist challenge should be virtually ignored.

This situation is bizarre in comparison with other literature of the period. The French, the Germans, the Italians and the South Americans, for instance, have all produced important post-war writers who engage with specifically Modernist issues. And, in English, the Americans have achieved almost a continuity with the movement, especially in poetry. If William Carlos Williams and Louis Zukofsky act as link-men, there is quite a direct line from Pound to such poets as Charles Olson, Allen Ginsberg, Robert Duncan, Robert Creeley and perhaps even John Ashberry. At the same time Confessional poets like Robert Lowell, John Berryman, Theodore Roethke, Anne Sexton and Sylvia Plath have elevated self-fragmentation into something like a poetic genre. America has also produced contemporary novelists who are far more adventurous than almost all their English counterparts. Norman Mailer, Saul Bellow, Thomas Pynchon, Kurt Vonnegut, William Burroughs, John Hawkes and William H. Gass, for instance, are all, in a real sense, products of the Modernist urge to experimentation. The fact is that, with the exception of drama, American writers (like the American critics who did so much to construct the Modernist canon) have been far more aware of the importance and implication of the Modernist movement. And in so far as there has been a shift of literary centrality from England to America in the last 45 or so years, the failure of English writers (and publishers) to live up to the challenge of Modernism must have had much to do with the matter. In literary, as in commercial, affairs the Americans have been far more willing to invest in new ideas, new techniques and new modes of organisation. Their reward has been a more vital and intellectually interesting post-war literature.

And yet the situation in England has not been absolutely bleak. If the cult of integral selfhood has remained the norm – a fallen god exercising its fatal attraction on most of our best talents – there have been some who have learnt from Modernism rather than ignored it. The example of Beckett is central, although it would be contentious to claim him as English. His fictional work, for instance, has continued that self-aware deconstruction of selfhood we associate with Joyce and Eliot:

> I hope this preamble will soon come to an end and the statement begin that will dispose of me. Unfortunately I am afraid, as always, of going on. For to go on means going from here, means finding me, losing me, vanishing and beginning again, a stranger first, then little by little the same as always, in another place, where I shall say I have always been, of which I shall know nothing . . .
> (*The Unnamable*, 1958)

> . . . That then is the proposition. To one on his back in the dark a voice tells of a past. With occasional allusion to a present and more rarely to a future as for example, You will end as you now are. And in another dark or in the same another devising it all for company. Quick leave him.
> (*Company*, 1980)[6]

Multiplication of the self's names and identities, the fictionality of all memories and anticipations, an uncertain shifting between pronoun positions, radical linguistic scepticism, the impossibility of speech and the obligation not to remain silent – these are all properties we associate with Beckett's writing. But it is no Poststructuralist game. The self's suffering and moments of strange ecstasy are expressed in everything he has done. Beckett's plays have been put on in England repeatedly since the fifties; his fiction has been widely disseminated; some of his work has appeared on television. If there is a single figure who has stood for literary intelligence and integrity here since the war, it is him – his gaunt photo-image the supreme icon of the writer–intellectual. What he has represented is a continuity from the great Modernist works, the persisting necessity of truly experimental discourse, and the twentieth-century reality of extreme self-fragmentariness.

Beckett first became widely known as a dramatist, and in England it has been drama rather than poetry or fiction that has kept some of the issues of Modernism alive. While the norm of theatrical Realism has remained dominant, it has been only since the Second World War that the Modernist movement has made a real contribution to English drama, influenced variously by Theatre of the Absurd and Theatre of Cruelty, by Brecht and Ionesco and Artaud. On the one hand, there has been a new awareness of the theatrical artificiality of stage-representations which has enabled writers such as N. F. Simpson, James Saunders, Peter Nichol, Joe Orton and Tom Stoppard to break down the unitary coherence of 'realistic' characterisation. On the other, the psychological emphasis of method-acting has helped writers like John Arden, Harold Pinter, Peter Shaffer or David Rudkin to characterise selfhood as layered, contradictory and ultimately mysterious. Such dramatic experimentalism, together with some 'fringe'[7] poetry and fiction (Eric Mottram and B. S. Johnson spring to mind) has helped keep alive – if not greatly expand on – the Modernist probing of the complexities of self-experience within the narrowly neo-Positivist climate of recent British intellectual life.

But an ontologically simplistic and psychologically naive neo-Positivism has remained the pervasive norm until quite recently, and has had a restrictive influence on literary awareness and criticism. Just as Freud and Jung have had little place in academic psychology, or Heidegger, Sartre and Merleau-Ponty (to cite only one non-Positivist School) in institutionalised philosophy, so key Modernist works such as *Tarr*, the *Cantos*, *Parade's End*, *Finnegans Wake* or *In Parenthesis* have scarcely yet found their true place in the study of twentieth-century English literature. Indeed much influential post-war criticism – Leavisite, vulgar Marxist or old-fashioned humanist – has been specifically negative about the masterwork of Joyce and Pound and has scarcely mentioned the names of Lewis, Ford or Jones. The 'Copernican' revolution in the discourse of selfhood has not so far achieved its proper place even in critical discussion – some 80 years after the onset of Modernism. In the Postmodern situation, the full implications of fragmenting self remain to be incorporated into British intellectual awareness.

The importance of Poststructuralist theory in aiding a fuller understanding of the importance of the Modernist project has already been mentioned. It has challenged critical assumptions, helped uncover the radical implications of Modernism and pioneered a more self-aware critical method and discourse. But feminist critical theory is also now crucial in deconstructing deep-seated assumptions and in privileging a counter-discourse more relevant to the subtleties of self-experience. It is debatable whether we should speak of the integral mode of selfhood as purely 'male' – especially in the light of the predominantly male struggle chronicled in this book. Nevertheless, this egoic construction – with its emphasis on rational integration, linear continuity and authoritarian self-possession – takes a place quite clearly within a masculinist tradition of intellectual control.[8] To be 'master of my fate', or 'I; faltering forward, / . . . And the woman calling' or to 'keep your head' in order to 'be a man, my son' are specifically patriarchal ideals at the end of a long line of such male self-representations. It is intriguing that some recent feminist criticism should invite us to see Modernist literary experimentation (by both men and women) as part of a revolutionary 'écriture féminine'. In this regard, fragmenting self becomes very much a deconstruction of male presumption and the new discourse of selfhood appears as a 'feminised' or 'androgynous' style expressive of fluidity, versatility and holistic inclusiveness. This is certainly a version that some feminists have claimed as their own project:

We intend to find ourselves. In the burning city.

The holistic sense of life without the exclusionary wholeness of art . . . Holistic work: great tonal shifts, from polemic to essay to lyric. A self-questioning, the writer built into the centre of the work, the questions at the centre of the writer, the discourse doubling, retelling the same, differently . . .

Exploration not in service of reconciling self to world, but creating a new world for a new self.[9]

If in England this aim is coupled with the example of three of our most precious literary imports – H. D., Sylvia Plath and Doris Lessing – it seems likely that the continuity from Modernism will, in future, be in the hands of women writers and critics rather than men.

However, the representation of selfhood is no longer confined to the domain of writing – or even of language. The electronic age has greatly increased and diversified the means by which selfhood and the self's experience can be expressed. But the advent of new media has not occurred overnight. The Modernists themselves were highly aware of the importance of the new modes of communication already available. Imagism was implicitly predicated on the authority of the photographic image, the organisation of *Ulysses* and *Mrs Dalloway* was based on the date-line of tabloid newspapers, *The Waste Land* and, at times, the *Cantos* replicate cinematic effects and much of Modernist technique is informed by the methods of montage. This awareness also shows itself in small details – the headlines in *Ulysses* ('Aeolus'), the 'prose kinema' in 'Hugh Selwyn Mauberley', the typist's gramophone in *The Waste Land*, the sky-writing aeroplane in *Mrs Dalloway* or the telephonic messages at the front line in *In Parenthesis*. Arguably the very dislocation of genre and disruption of syntax in Modernist texts acknowledge the break-up of the old hegemony of writing as a means of representation.

Certainly since the Second World War the electronic media have occupied the foreground of human consciousness, and their distinctive modes of representation have only quite recently been studied seriously and systematically. But it is interesting that in England, at least, the new media have often learnt from the techniques of Modernism in ways the main writers have not. There is something distinctly neo-Modernist about the Surreal phantasies of 'The Goon Show' or 'Monty Python's Flying Circus', the 'open-field' format of 'That Was The Week That Was' and 'Saturday Live' or the word-sound collages of the Beatles' 'Revolution 9' and David Bowie's 'cut-up' lyrics and Laurie Anderson's 'O Superman'. Indeed, in the case of the 'electronic' lyric alone (forgetting for the moment the vital counterpoint of sound), pop troubadours like John Lennon, Bob Dylan, Jim Morrison, Elton John and David Bowie have been far more adventurous in expressing the complexities or ambiguities of the self than most mainstream English poets. It is not surprising, then, that Lennon's prose reads more like pop-Joyce than, say, pop-Amis, that Dylan could invoke 'Ezra Pound and T. S. Eliot . . . fighting in the captain's tower' or that Bowie adapted the 'cut-up' technique from Brion Gysin and William Burroughs.

Yet the main point here does not concern how consciously the new media have adapted Modernist attitudes and techniques. It is simply that representation itself is now far more than a literary issue. Our sense of selfhood, for instance, is now developed not only out of Larkin's poetry or Lessing's prose but also out of, say, Resnais' 'Last Year at Marienbad' and Bergman's 'Cries and Whispers' (not to mention Chaplin, Keaton and the whole Hollywood tradition); out of Lennon's 'Don't Believe' and Elton John's 'Someone Saved My Life Tonight' and Culture Club's 'Karma Chameleon'; out of style advertisements and photographs of starved Africans; out of radio reminiscences and television interviews; out of Agony Aunt columns and soap operas and videoed poetry readings and comments made on phone-in radio. All this has enormously expanded our sense of what selfhood is: it has populated our minds with a myriad figures who are, in a sense, part of us. It has thus reaffirmed the multiplicity of selfhood and given us a representational plethora of possibilities in terms of aspiration and role play. And in fragmenting our mythical self-cores it has also connected us up, in imagination, with the teeming diversity of selves in the entire 'global village'.[10]

In this situation it seems absurd to revert, in literary or philosophical discussion, to the construct of a finally unified and coherent self – even when it makes discussion easier. We have to be far more tentative, far more psychoanalytically and Poststructuralistically aware, far more open to admit and negotiate the relativities involved in any sense of selfhood or any statements about self. We can no longer take refuge in the old egoic, rationalist (and 'male'?) model of selfhood – so implicated itself in the pressures of 'grammatology'[11] towards hard, precise conceptualisation. The Modernist project was salutary and prophetic in this; and the Postmodernist argument carries the issues into the future.[12] We are not single units, or cores or coherences and we damage ourselves in trying to live as if we were. We are more like 'nations' as Derek Parfit has suggested: we are plenitudes and there is always more to us than we can know – let alone say or film or act or sing or write. As selves we exist in infinite complexity, outside of conceptualisation and finally outside of ideology or linguistic representation.[13] The language we use to discuss selfhood, then, should not try to construct it as what it is not, but strive, with all the connotative resources which 'rational' discourse has repressed, to bear witness to the diverse complexities that we, in fact, are.

As we have seen, Modernist writers have gone a long way in helping us achieve this by revolutionising our sense of selfhood and creating new modes of discourse to express it. Turn-of-the-century literature began to break up the substance of the integral self, and, by the use of devices such as Symbolist ambiguity and syntactical disruption, rewrote selfhood in terms of tentative and self-reflexive formulations. The literature of the Great War attested to the reality of self-fragmentation in extreme situations and transcended narrative control to explore the contrastive sub-languages, and the evasions and silences, through which radical experience is uttered. The main canonical works of Modernism represented the self as inherently fragmentary (or multiple) and developed experimentalist discourses to give expression to the diversity and complexity of self-experience. Such writings inevitably probed the tangle of self-deceptions and self-conflicts within real selfhood and evolved modes of writing in which contradictory assertions, deceitful avowals, and false denials are a normative expression of inner conflict. And later Modernist texts specialised in evidencing the discontinuities of the self's life – the gaps, metamorphoses, cessations and sudden advents which characterise experience through time – and pioneered discourses where fluxive discontinuity and random transformation characterise the flow of the words themselves. In Modernism, then, selfhood has been rewritten as heterogeneous, multiple, metamorphic, conflictual and multi-voiced. Modernism has established self as a complex, 'open-field' site of interaction in place of the bounded and mono-directional atom of traditional discourse. And its experimental stylistics has opened infinite possibilities for a fuller expression of that rich plethora which is the self's experience seeking identity.

The Modernist project thus holds out the promise of a new, far fuller and more honest humanist selfhood. It has allowed humanism to own to the realities of being human. Thus a Postmodernist humanism will assent to the infinite variety and complexity that is the self – as well as the multiplicity of relativistically legitimated representational 'games' which express it – and seek to promote its balanced fulfilment. And in this it has a social as well as a personal role. For part of the selves we all are precisely constitutes other, sometimes contradictory, selves – the woman in the man, the anarchist in the Marxist, the 'Gerontion' in the young intellectual, the admirer in the antagonist, the shell-shocked soldier in the Bloomsbury woman aesthete, the millionaire in the pauper, the 'white' philosopher in the black poet. The positive element in Modernism suggests that we should abandon the old egoic dream of competitive self-sufficiency and acknowledge and develop an open selfhood which can live in harmony with others, as with its own self-parts. As Virginia Woolf, in particular, has shown, we need other people because, psychologically, they are part of us and we part of them. In the nuclear age, this new Postmodernist humanism is surely more important, in the end, than any political theory or specific course of action. If now we 'must love one another or die', we can begin by loving those others who are, in important ways, part of ourselves.

Yet can we accept such heterogeneity in selfhood without imperilling our sanity? Modernist texts would certainly suggest that the fragmentary self is in danger of radical breakdown. I think here we must remember the position of the Modernist movement – both with respect to the revolutionary nature of its project and its relation to the Great War. Most of the texts we have considered are riven through with the horror of the war and haunted by the unprecedented spectre of shell shock. Their discourse is inevitably embued with the terrors of that historical era. At the same time, the fragmenting of an assumed self-unity was always likely to be associated with deep elements of anxiety and fear. As we have seen, the Modernists hankered nostalgically for the comfort of a lost sense of wholeness – even as they were demonstrating the falseness of the old model of selfhood. But such demolition work, and the anxieties associated with it, are now part of history, as are the experiences of the Great War. We start from different ground. Further, the later writings of Joyce, Eliot and Woolf, for instance, evidence a movement away from painful self-disintegration towards the affirmation of a liberated self-plenitude. And that is part of the ground we start from. To accept that we are many things simultaneously and that we can change dramatically seems a greater safeguard for sanity than to put trust in any one egoic posture, which will always be susceptible to falsification by the test of unusual experience.

The Modernist representation of selfhood, then, remains directly relevant to our present and future self-awareness, but we can now begin our explorations from the ground Modernism has prepared. Future representations, in whatever medium, must be liberated from the persisting ghost of unitariness and develop the Modernists' insights into the live plenitude of the self. In literature (now a less central mode of representation) we need to evolve new ways of expressing the realities of selfhood which start from the position of the self's multiplicity. As Modernism has shown, this cannot be in terms of the old 'rationalist' discourse, since that is itself implicated in a narrow and obsolete conceptualisation of selfhood. The way forward is to extend and modify the most telling techniques of Modernist discourse and expand them outside the field of high literature, as feminists and Poststructuralists would have us do. This would not only entail a greater adventurousness in middle-brow writing, it would also necessitate a more 'aesthetic' *écriture* for critical, philosophical and psychological discussion. To pursue the exploration of self-experience in the Postmodern era we need a new, more experimentalist procedure, a new, more rhetorically daring discourse, and a new, more intuitive awareness. At which point my argument, and my current complicity in this mode of discourse, comes to an end:

> Where now? Who now? When now? Unquestioning. I, say I. Unbelieving. Questions, hypotheses, call them that. Keep going, going on, call that going, call that on.[14]

Notes

Chapter 1: Introduction

1. Ezra Pound, from Notes for Canto CXVII *et seq.*, *The Cantos* (Faber and Faber, 1986), p. 802.
2. As will be seen, I do not believe Tiresias 'unifies' *The Waste Land*. However, because of Eliot's footnote to line 218 I have tended to use the name Tiresias as signifier of the dramatic consciousness which expresses the poem. For my view of the poem see below, pp. 91–9.
3. That is, the highly variable 'I' represented in the *Cantos*, sometimes given in this Latin formula.
4. 'The point of view which I am struggling to attack is perhaps related to the metaphysical theory of the substantial unity of the soul'. T. S. Eliot, *Selected Essays* (Faber and Faber, 1958), p. 19.
5. I am not suggesting that the Elizabethan representation of self is the same as the Modernist, but simply that it can be more variable and complex than that in seventeenth-century literature.
6. 'When I Consider How My Light Is Spent', *The Poems of John Milton*, edited by John Carey and Alastair Fowler (Longman, 1968), p. 330.
7. 'Epistle to Dr Arbuthnot', *The Poems of Alexander Pope*, edited by John Butt (Methuen, 1965), lines 261–4, p. 606.
8. Daniel Defoe, *Robinson Crusoe* (Signet, 1961), pp. 65–6.
9. Robert Langbaum, *The Mysteries of Identity: A Theme in Modern Literature* (University of Chicago Press, 1977). Karl Miller, *Doubles: Studies in Literary History* (Oxford University Press, 1985).
10. Langbaum, p. 46.
11. To Richard Woodhouse, 27 October 1818, in *The Letters of John Keats*, vol. 1, edited by Hyder Edward Rollins (Cambridge University Press, 1958), p. 387.
12. For example, the Autumnal uncertainties of Andrea del Sarto, the terminal self-dissolution of the Bishop of St Praxted's and the primitive linguistic self-positioning of Caliban in 'Caliban Upon Setebos'.
13. See Browning's 'Essay on Shelley'.
14. From *The Disappearance of God* (1963), included in *Browning: 'Men and Women' and Other Poems*, a casebook edited by J. R. Watson (Macmillan, 1974), pp. 155–6.
15. Gillian Beer, *Darwin's Plots: Evolutionary Narrative in Darwin, George Eliot, and Nineteenth Century Fiction* (Routledge and Kegan Paul, 1983), p. 14.
16. Joseph Conrad, *Nostromo: A Tale of the Seaboard* (Penguin, 1963), p. 259.
17. Virginia Woolf, *The Waves* (Penguin, 1964), p. 172.
18. Quoted by Jeffrey Meyers in *The Enemy: A Biography of Wyndham Lewis* (Routledge and Kegan Paul, 1980), pp. 108 and 109.

19. Antony Easthope, 'Why Most Contemporary Poetry is So Bad and How Post-Structuralism May be Able to Help', *PN Review*, 48, Nov–Dec 1985, p. 36. See also Antony Easthope's *Poetry as Discourse* (Methuen, 1983), especially Chapter 9. While my book was in press Maud Ellmann's *The Poetics of Impersonality: T. S. Eliot and Ezra Pound* (Harvester Press, 1987) was published. I wish I could have read this book while formulating my arguments; it provides fine insights into the deconstruction of selfhood in Eliot and Pound.
20. Emile Benveniste, from *Problems in General Linguistics*, quoted by Catherine Belsey in *Critical Practice* (Methuen, 1980), p. 59.
21. Jacques Lacan, from 'Of Structure', quoted by Robert Young in *Untying the Text* . . ., (Routledge and Kegan Paul, 1981), p. 13.
22. Jacques Derrida, from '*Differance*', quoted by Catherine Belsey, *Critical Practice*, p. 59.
23. 'Epimenides the Cretan said that all Cretans were liars, and all other statements made by Cretans were certainly lies. Was this a lie?' Alfred North Whitehead and Bertrand Russell, *Principia Mathematica* (Cambridge University Press, 1967), p. 60.
24. Derrida's invented word. See, for instance, his 'Freud and the Scene of Writing', in *Writing and Difference*, translated by Alan Bass (Routledge and Kegan Paul, 1981).
25. From 'The Love Song of J. Alfred Prufrock', T. S. Eliot, *Collected Poems 1909–1962* (Faber and Faber, 1968), pp. 16–17. All quotations from Eliot's poetry will be taken from this edition.
26. James Joyce, *Ulysses* (Penguin, 1969), p. 262.
27. Virginia Woolf, *The Waves*, p. 254.
28. See *Aion: The Phenomenology of Self* in *The Portable Jung*, edited by Joseph Campbell, translated by R. F. C. Hull (Penguin, 1978), pp. 139–62.
29. Including, of course, Irishmen like Yeats and Joyce, and Americans like Eliot and Pound.
30. Freud's analogy. See *Introductory Lectures on Psychoanalysis*, translated by James Strachey (Penguin, 1978), p. 326.

Chapter 2: Dissolving Self

1. A description of Mauberley on the Moluccas islands. See Ezra Pound, *Selected Poems* (Faber and Faber, 1981), p. 111.
2. Ibid., p. 110.
3. Ibid., p. 63.
4. Quotations from Sir Henry Newbolt, Rudyard Kipling and T. E. Henley.
5. Quotations from Thomas Hardy, A. E. Housman and W. B. Yeats.
6. In a letter to Edward Garnett, quoted by Walter Allen in *The English Novel* (Penguin, 1958), p. 361.
7. In 'Mr Bennett and Mrs Brown', quoted by Walter Allen, ibid., p. 341.
8. Yeats, quoted by Robert Langbaum in *The Mysteries of Identity*, p. 148.
9. Quoted by Langbaum, ibid., pp. 159–60. See also 'The Centre Cannot Hold', below, pp. 124–30.

10. See 'A Coat', W. B. Yeats, *The Collected Poems* (Macmillan, 1967), p. 142.
11. All quotations from Henry James, *The Ambassadors* (Signet, 1960).
12. For example, Canto VII.
13. See William James, *The Principles of Psychology*, vol. 1 (New York: Dover Publications, 1953).
14. Joseph Conrad, *Nostromo*. First published in 1904.
15. All quotations from D. H. Lawrence, *Sons and Lovers* (Penguin, 1967).
16. All quotations from Ford Madox Ford, *The Good Soldier: A Tale of Passion* (Penguin, 1982).
17. See Ford's 'Dedicatory Letter to Stella Ford', ibid., p. 8.
18. See T. E. Hulme, *Speculations*, edited by Herbert Read (Routledge and Kegan Paul, 1965), p. 48 and pp. 217–45.
19. *Selected Poems*, p. 35.
20. Ibid.
21. Having worked at these poems in France, Eliot completed them in Boston. It is most unlikely he knew of English Imagism at this time (1912).
22. Quotations from T. S. Eliot, *Collected Poems*.
23. First published in *Blackwood's Magazine*, CLXV (February, March, April 1899). First published in book form in 1902. All quotations from Joseph Conrad, *Heart of Darkness* (Penguin, 1975).
24. It has something in common, however, with American writers' work, such as that of Hawthorne and Melville.
25. See Marlow's remarks on the Romans, ibid., pp. 9–10.
26. 'His Majesty, the Ego' seems in Kurtz more like Ubu Roi than Oedipus Rex – animal-like and wholly unpredictable.
27. Nevertheless, they reinforce Conrad's satiric version of Western selfhood.
28. See below, pp. 88–90 and 134–6.
29. But, unlike F. R. Leavis, I do not see this as a stylistic flaw. See below, p. 118.
30. 'Heart of Darkness: A Choice of Nightmares', in C. B. Cox, *Joseph Conrad: The Modern Imagination* (Dent, 1974).
31. Ibid., pp. 47 and 49.
32. Cox writes: 'Kurtz releases his *Id* from European restraint; he is a pioneer in a psychic wilderness'; ibid., p. 56. I agree with the second clause.
33. I regard such terms as pragmatic tools for discussing mental phenomena rather than the names of interior realities. At least the ego–id–super-ego model transcends the old binary division of self.
34. *Heart of Darkness*, p. 8.
35. See 'Conrad's Uneasiness – and Ours', in Frederick Crews, *Out of My System: Psychoanalysis, Ideology and Critical Method* (New York: Oxford University Press, 1975). According to Skura, Crews later retracted his earlier views. See Meredith Anne Skura, *The Literary Use of the Psychoanalytic Process* (Yale University Press, 1981), p. 76.
36. See, for instance, Terry Eagleton, *Criticism and Ideology* (Verso, 1980), pp. 134–7.

37. Crews's reading is persuasive here. See note 13.
38. Eliot's celebrated description of the poet's mind. See T. S. Eliot, *Selected Essays*, pp. 17–19.
39. Browning's phrase for his dramatic method. See his preface to *Strafford*.
40. Compare the limbo-men of *The Waste Land* and Eliot's own comment that 'so far as we do evil or good, we are human; and it is better in a paradoxical way to do evil than to do nothing: at least we exist'. T. S. Eliot, *Selected Essays* (Faber and Faber, 1958), p. 429.
41. Eliot bought a copy of *Appearance and Reality* in June 1913, according to Herbert Howarth, *Notes on Some Figures Behind T. S. Eliot* (London, 1965), p. 206. But according to the same writer he was planning a thesis on Meinong and Bradley in 1911. Presumably he was already acquainted with Bradley's philosophical ideas.
42. See Henri Bergson, *An Introduction to Metaphysics*, translated by Mabelle L. Andison (Littlefield, Adams and Co., New Jersey, 1965), pp. 165–6.
43. 'Let us call it the stream of thought, of consciousness, or of subjective life', *Principles of Psychology*, vol. 1, p. 239. 'Looking back, then, over this review, we see that the mind is at every stage a theatre of simultaneous possibilities. Consciousness consists in the comparison of these with each other, the selection of some, and the suppression of the rest by the reinforcing and inhibiting agency of attention', ibid., p. 288.
44. See *Selected Essays*, p. 19.
45. See Virginia Woolf, *Moments of Being*, edited by Jeanne Schulkind (Granada, 1982), p. 90.
46. T. S. Eliot, *Knowledge and Experience in the Philosophy of F. H. Bradley* (Faber and Faber, 1964).
47. See Jean-Paul Sartre, *Being and Nothingness: An Essay on Phenomenological Ontology*, translated by Hazel E. Barnes (Methuen, 1977), pp. 364ff.
48. Terry Eagleton expounds the post-Derridean view of the linguistic system of differences: 'If every sign is what it is because it is not all the other signs, every sign would seem to be made up of a potentially infinite tissue of differences', Terry Eagleton, *Literary Theory: An Introduction* (Basil Blackwell, 1983), p. 127.
49. 'East Coker', II, *Collected Poems*, p. 198.
50. See F. H. Bradley, 'On Immediate Experience', *Essays on Truth and Reality* (Oxford University Press, 1968). Eliot frequently refers to this concept in *Knowledge and Experience*, and, I believe, seeks to express it in many of his poems.
51. Rejected by Eliot as a kind of 'divine intervention'. See his article 'Leibniz' Monads and Bradley's Finite Centre', Appendix II, *Knowledge and Experience*, pp. 198–207.
52. 'The conclusion to which I am brought is that a relational way of thought – any one that moves by the machinery of terms and relations – must give appearance, and not truth', F. H. Bradley, *Appearance and Reality: A Metaphysical Essay* (Oxford University Press, 1969), p. 28.
53. 'The facts in logical space are the world', Ludwig Wittgenstein,

Tractatus Logico-Philosophicus, translated by D. F. Pears and B. F. McGuinness (Routledge and Kegan Paul, 1961), l. 13, p. 7.
54. See especially Jacques Derrida, *Of Grammatology*, translated by G. C. Spivak (Johns Hopkins, 1976) and *Writing and Difference*, translated by Alan Bass (Routledge and Kegan Paul, 1978).
55. All quotations from James Joyce, *A Portrait of the Artist as a Young Man* (Penguin, 1976).
56. Compare Sartre: 'I am condemned to exist for ever beyond my essence, beyond the causes and motives of my act. I am condemned to be free. This means that no limits to my freedom can be found except freedom itself' (*Being and Nothingness*, p. 439); 'The anguish which, when this possibility is revealed, manifests our freedom to our consciousness is witness to this perpetual modifiability of our initial project', ibid., p. 464. In Existentialist terms, Stephen is represented as one of the most fully authentic characters in modern fiction.
57. For example, 'The next day brought death and judgement . . . He felt the death chill touch the extremities and creep onwards towards the heart, the film of death veiling the eyes, the bright centres of the brain extinguished one by one like lamps . . .', p. 112.
58. Maud Ellmann has some perceptive things to say about this scene in 'Disremembering Dedalus', *Untying the Text*, edited by Robert Young (Routledge and Kegan Paul, 1981), pp. 189–206.
59. See the discussion on the novel's textuality in Colin MacCabe, *James Joyce and the Revolution of the Word* (Macmillan, 1979).

Chapter 3: Self at War

1. T. E. Lawrence, *Seven Pillars of Wisdom: A Triumph* (Penguin, 1969), p. 461.
2. Paul Dubrulle on bombardment at Verdun, quoted in Richard Holmes, *Firing Line* (Jonathan Cape, 1985), pp. 232–3.
3. Richard Holmes, ibid., p. 256.
4. Holmes, ibid. He also comments: 'Psychiatric casualties were undoubtedly relatively uncommon prior to the twentieth century' (ibid.). For an earlier discussion of combat neurosis in the Great War, see Eric J. Leed, *No Man's Land: Combat and Identity in World War I* (Cambridge University Press, 1979).
5. Holmes, *Firing Line*, p. 257.
6. Quoted from *First World War Poetry*, edited by Jon Silkin (Penguin, 1981), p. 118.
7. Silkin, ibid., p. 195.
8. The Preface, *The Collected Poems of Wilfred Owen* (Chatto and Windus, 1968), p. 31.
9. This is especially true of memoirs like Graves's *Goodbye To All That* where the author is distancing himself from his war experiences and trying to clear a way for a new kind of life – in Graves's case, a poetic life in Mallorca.

10. In Eliot's *The Waste Land* and Pound's *Cantos*, for instance.
11. From 'Hugh Selwyn Mauberley', Ezra Pound, *Selected Poems*, pp. 100–1.
12. The life–death polarity within the novel is generated by wartime tensions: actual moments of aggression, like Hermione's attack upon Birkin or Gudrun's destruction of Gerald are pertinent, as are descriptions like that of Birkin stoning the moon's reflection in Willey Water. For a fuller discussion of this see the chapter on *Women in Love* in Anne Wright, *The Literature of Crisis* (Macmillan, 1984).
13. T. S. Eliot, *Collected Poems*, p. 67.
14. Virginia Woolf, *Mrs Dalloway* (Penguin, 1967).
15. It seems to me likely that both Eliot and Woolf were directly influenced by war poems. In the case of Sassoon's possible influence, see above, p. 57 and footnote 40, and p. 105. Pound's play on 'Dulce et decorum est' in 'Hugh Selwyn Mauberley' is almost certainly speaking to Owen's poem of that name.
16. Robert Graves, *Poems Selected by Himself* (Penguin, 1966), pp. 29–30, 33–4, 35–7.
17. Quoted from Graves's introduction to *The Common Asphodel* by William David Thomas in 'The Impact of World War I on the Early Poetry of Robert Graves', *The Malahat Review*, 35 (July 1975), p. 129. The whole article is of relevance to the subject. See also Chapters 3 to 8 in Martin Seymour-Smith, *Robert Graves: His Life and Work* (Abacus, 1982).
18. *Poems*, p. 49.
19. Andrew Rutherford, *The Literature of War* (Macmillan, 1978). His chapter on Lawrence is entitled 'The Intellectual as Hero: Lawrence of Arabia', pp. 38–63.
20. Quoted by Rutherford, ibid., pp. 38 and 51.
21. *Seven Pillars*, pp. 27–30.
22. Leed's term. See his *No Man's Land*, pp. 113 and 198.
23. See Leed, ibid., p. 94.
24. Ford Madox Ford, *No More Parades* in *Parade's End* (The Bodley Head, volume IV, 1980), p. 16. Compare Conrad's 'by all the stars! these were . . . devils, that swayed and drove men – men, I tell you', *Heart of Darkness*, p. 23.
25. Richard Aldington, *Death of a Hero* (Hogarth, 1984; first published 1929), pp. 22 and 297.
26. Ibid., p. 308.
27. It is worth noting that the end of the war did not call an end to the incidence of battle neurosis. Leed writes that, on the contrary, it was a condition 'more prevalent in "peace" than in war', *No Man's Land*, p. 158. Further, many men who had shown no marked neurotic symptoms during the war succumbed afterwards to the graver conditions of psychosis. See ibid., p. 189.
28. Jon Silkin, *Out of Battle: The Poetry of the Great War* (Oxford University Press, 1972), p. 130.
29. All quotations from Siegfried Sassoon, *The War Poems*, arranged and introduced by Rupert Hart-Davis (Faber, 1983).
30. See the after-note to the poem, ibid., p. 41.

31. See the after-note, ibid., pp. 46–7.
32. Rupert Hart-Davis terms him 'psychologist and anthropologist . . . now a temporary captain in the Royal Army Medical Corps' (ibid., p. 131, footnote 3). In terms of his sessions with Sassoon we should nowadays, I think, term him a psychotherapist, or at least a therapeutic counsellor.
33. *Sherston's Progress*, in *The Complete Memoirs of George Sherston*, Siegfried Sassoon (Faber, 1972; first published 1937), p. 534.
34. Compare 'Letter to Robert Graves':

> But yesterday afternoon my reasoning Rivers ran solemnly in,
> With peace in the pools of his spectacled eyes and a wisely omnipotent grin;
> And I fished in that steady grey stream and decided that I
> After all am no longer the Worm that refuses to die.
>
> (ibid., p. 131.)

See, too, what I say about rain in 'Repression of War Experience' above, and the quotation from 'Letter to Robert Graves', p. 115.
35. On page 453 of *Memoirs*, for instance:

> From the munitions factory across the road, machinery throbbed and droned and crashed like the treading of giants; the noise got on my nerves. I was being worried by bad dreams. More than once I wasn't sure whether I was awake or asleep; the ward was half shadow and half sinking firelight, and the beds were quiet with huddled sleepers. Shapes of mulitated soldiers came crawling across the floor; the floor seemed to be littered with fragments of mangled flesh. Faces glared upward; hands clutched at neck or belly; a livid grinning face with bristly moustache peered at me above the edge of my bed; his hands clawed at the sheets . . .

36. In 'Mr Sassoon's War Verses', first published in *Nation* (13 July 1918), reprinted in *Poetry of the First World War*, a casebook edited by Dominic Hibberd (Macmillan, 1981), p. 50.
37. According to Henry Williamson in *Test to Destruction*, quoted in Bernard Bergonzi's 'Counter-Attack and Other Poems' reprinted in *Poetry of the First World War*, p. 194.
38. Jon Silkin, *Out of Battle*, pp. 165–6.
39. *Siegfried Sassoon: Poet's Pilgrimage*, assembled with an introduction by D. Felicitas Corrigan (Gollancz, 1973), p. 85.
40. Eliot knew Sassoon: see, for instance, Peter Ackroyd, *T. S. Eliot* (Hamish Hamilton, 1984), pp. 119 and 135. He also read enough war poetry to generalise about it in 'Reflections on Contemporary Poetry', *Egoist* (July 1919), reprinted in Dominic Hibbert, *Poetry of the First World War*, p. 52. It seems quite likely that he knew 'Repression'. The atmospherics involved in the thunder-storm fantasy might well have impressed a poet as obsessed as Eliot with dryness, and himself in a state of breakdown. If good poets 'steal', it is possible that the most

famous scenario of rain crisis in modern literature owes a debt to Sassoon's Weirleigh poem.
41. Footnote to my edition, ibid., p. 85. The lecture was reprinted in W. H. R. Rivers, *Instinct and the Unconscious* (1920).
42. See the song 'I talk to the trees', and the Goons' emendation of the second line to 'That's why they put me away'.
43. 'Two Soldier Poets', *Times Literary Supplement* (11 July 1918), reprinted in D. Hibberd, *Poetry of the First World War*, pp. 45–6.
44. See especially: 'The trees waved, brandished. We welcome, the world seemed to say . . . But the branches parted. A man in grey was actually walking towards them. It was Evans! But no mud was on him: no wounds . . .', *Mrs Dalloway*, pp. 77–8.
45. The Bodley Head edition of Ford's works does not print *Last Post*. In his Introduction Graham Greene cites Ford's expressed wish that it be excluded from the sequence. See *Ford Madox Ford*, vol. III, *Parade's End*, Part I (The Bodley Head, 1980), p. 5. For a view that *Last Post* is integral to the sequence see Robie Macaulay, 'Parade's End' in M. Schorer (ed.), *Modern British Fiction* (New York: Oxford University Press, 1961), pp. 158–9. I incline to the latter view, but the first three novels are most relevant to the argument of the book. I have used the Bodley Head edition for quotations. *Some Do Not* and *A Man Could Stand Up* are in volume IV (1980), as *Parade's End* occupies volume III.
46. See below, Chapter 6, p. 261.
47. See *A Man Could Stand Up*, vol. IV, pp. 415 and 443. There are, of course, passages where strong psychophysical feelings are shown between them. The question is how far Tietjens, in particular, is represented as able to own to and express these.
48. 'That immense army was . . . depressed by the idea that those who controlled it overseas would – I will not use the word "betray" since that implies volition – but "let us down"'. Quoted by Macaulay, 'Parade's End', p. 151.
49. All references to David Jones, *In Parenthesis* (Faber, 1963).
50. 'I do hope it is something – I terribly want outside judgement. Sometimes when I read it it seems to have a shape, at other times it sounds awful balls and full of bad jokes and strained meanings.' Letter to Reńe Hague, 2 December 1935, in R. Hague (ed.), *Dai Great-Coat: A Self-Portrait of David Jones in his Letters* (Faber, 1980), p. 80.
51. Jones referred to his depressions as 'Rosie' (neurosis). See *Dai Great-Coat*, throughout.
52. For a discussion of Jones' aesthetic, see Patrick Grant, *Six Modern Authors and Problems of Belief* (Macmillan, 1979), Chapter 4, 'Belief in Religion: The Poetry of David Jones', pp. 67–92.
53. Jon Silkin discusses Hague's description in *Out of Battle*, p. 320.
54. Compare Major Knacksbull on p. 177. The surname plays with both the colloquial 'nackers' and 'ball'. 'Bull' here replaces 'ball' as John Ball replaces John Bull. Was this one of Jones's 'bad jokes' (see note 50)?
55. 'Reńe's reading to me *Anna Livia* did not influence the "form" of I.P.' From a letter in *Dai Great-Coat*, p. 190.

Notes 193

56. *Out of Battle*, p. 324.
57. Ezra Pound, *Literary Essays*, edited by T. S. Eliot (Faber, 1968), p. 46 and from 'The Approach to Paris – V', *The New Age*, XIII, 23, (20 October 1913), p. 662.
58. It should be remembered that most heroic works contain their own anti-heroic components: e.g. Roland's absurd arguments with Oliver about when to blow the trumpet in *The Song of Roland* or Henry V's Falstaff and co. Jones's allusions do not simply glorify the modern soldier, they set him within a complex historical debate about the meaning of heroism and dishonour.

Chapter 4: Fragmentary Self

1. From 'Modern Fiction', reprinted in *The Common Reader* (1925), quoted here from Miriam Allot, *Novelists on the Novel* (Columbia, 1966), p. 77.
2. Wyndham Lewis's phrase. See Wyndham Lewis, *Blasting and Bombardiering*, (John Calder, 1982), pp. 252–6.
3. The new title was *The Egoist*. Dora Marsden founded the *New Freewoman* in 1913, but changed its title after pressure from Pound and others. In 1914 Richard Aldington took over from Rebecca West as assistant editor.
4. Freud's analogy. See, e.g., *Introductory Lectures*, p. 326.
5. Quoted from Miriam Allott, *Novelists on the Novel*, p. 289.
6. D. H. Lawrence, *Women in Love* (Penguin, 1981), p. 381.
7. H. G. Wells, *The New Machiavelli* (Penguin, 1966), pp. 220–1.
8. Wyndham Lewis, *Tarr* (Penguin, 1982), p. 55.
9. An attack on the time theories of Bergson, Einstein and others (including writers such as Gertrude Stein and Joyce) was the main theme of Lewis's *Time and Western Man* (1927).
10. Quoted in Michael Alexander, *The Poetic Achievement of Ezra Pound* (Faber and Faber, 1979), p. 135.
11. 'The real reason for writing and reading history, namely that the past should be a light for the future . . .', from Pound's review of John Buchan's *Cromwell*, published in *The New English Weekly* on 6 June 1935. Reprinted in *Selected Prose*, pp. 235–6.
12. W. B. Yeats, *Collected Poems*, pp. 210–11.
13. Compare the poem 'The Wild Old Wicked Man', ibid., pp. 356–8.
14. 'The best lack all conviction, while the worst/Are full of passionate intensity', ibid., p. 211.
15. First published in 1919. My edition, George Bernard Shaw, *Heartbreak House* (Penguin, 1980).
16. It is interesting that Lewis thought that Joyce's 'Circe' chapter in *Ulysses* 'was derived from his own innovative technique in *Enemy of the Stars*'. See Jeffrey Meyers, *The Enemy: A Biography of Wyndham Lewis* (Routledge and Kegan Paul, 1980), p. 139.
17. It seems to me that *Heartbreak House* can be theorised as dream-work in the same way that I have theorised *The Waste Land* (see this chapter, pp. 94–9). Keith M. May performs a similar operation on Joyce's

'Circe' in *Out of the Maëlstrom: Psychology and the Novel in the Twentieth Century* (London: Paul Elek, 1977), pp. 27–34.
18. Recently reissued by Virago Press. See Dorothy Richardson, *Pilgrimage*, in four volumes with an introduction by Gill Hanscombe (Virago, 1979).
19. I am indebted to my colleague Jean Radford for drawing my attention to these sentences.
20. Leon Edel, *Stuff of Sleep and Dreams: Experiments in Literary Psychology* (Chatto and Windus, 1982), p. 108.
21. Ibid., p. 109.
22. James Joyce, *Finnegans Wake* (Faber, 1982; first published in 1939), p. 364.
23. *Ulysses*, p. 701.
24. See Keith M. May, *Out of the Maëlstrom*, p. 28.
25. Quoted by Robert Humphrey in *Stream of Consciousness in the Modern Novel* (University of California Press, 1965), p. 1.
26. In the earlier chapters of the book, before the urge towards continual stylistic parody takes over.
27. For example, 'Because life is a stream', ibid., p. 153; 'Stream of life', ibid., p. 155.
28. Humphrey, *Stream of Consciousness*, p. 42.
29. The chapter is called 'Proteus', of course.
30. 'I remember / Those are pearls that were his eyes' (124–5); 'O O O O that Shakespeherian Rag' (127).
31. *A Portrait of the Artist*, p. 215.
32. Ibid.
33. See Peter Ackroyd: 'He was reading the later chapters of *Ulysses* and was explaining to Joyce that, although he wholly admired the achievement, he rather wished, for his own sake, that he had not read it.' *T. S. Eliot*, p. 112.
34. See 'Tradition and the Individual Talent', *Selected Essays*, pp. 13–22. Of course, part of what Eliot is denying here is the metaphysical unity of the self.
35. Quoted by Ackroyd, *T. S. Eliot*, p. 127.
36. In a 'trance'. See Ackroyd, ibid., p. 116.
37. See Robert Fussell, *The Great War and Modern Memory* (Oxford University Press, 1975).
38. See the note to line 218.
39. The title of his early working draft. See *The Waste Land: A Facsimile and Transcript of the Original Drafts Including the Annotations of Ezra Pound*, edited by Valerie Eliot (Faber, 1971).
40. See Grover Smith, *The Waste Land* (Allen and Unwin, 1983), pp. xi and 12.
41. *Basic Psychoanalytic Concepts on the Theory of Dreams*, edited by Humberto Nagera, The Hampstead Clinic Psychoanalytic Library, vol. II (Maresfield Reprints, 1981), p. 79. I have used this handbook because it usefully collates Freud's ideas about dreaming – including his later thoughts.
42. Ibid., pp. 85–6.

43. Quoted by Grover Smith, *The Waste Land*, p. 133.
44. 'The poet must be aware that the mind of Europe – the mind of his own country – a mind which he learns in time to be much more important than his own private mind – is a mind which changes, and that this change is a development which abandons nothing *en route.*' *Selected Essays*, p. 16.
45. 'The work of art cannot be interpreted; there is nothing to interpret'; T. S. Eliot, *The Sacred Wood: Essays on Poetry and Criticism* (Faber, 1969), p. 96. 'Comparison and analysis . . . are the chief tools of the critic'; 'The Function of Criticism', *Selected Essays*, pp. 32–3. 'To understand a poem it is also necessary . . . to grasp its entelechy', *On Poetry and Poets* (Faber, 1957), p. 110.
46. 'The reader's interpretation may differ from the author's and be equally valid . . . it may even be better', *On Poetry and Poets*, pp. 30–1.
47. 'The use of "myth" is simply a way of controlling, of ordering, of giving a shape and a significance to the immense panorama of futility and anarchy which is contemporary history', from '*Ulysses*, Order and Myth', *The Dial*, 75 (November 1923), p. 483.
48. Of course, Eliot was himself dismissive about the significance of the notes.
49. Virginia Woolf, *Mrs Dalloway*, p. 109.
50. See *A Writer's Diary: Being Extracts from the Diary of Virginia Woolf*, edited by Leonard Woolf (Hogarth, 1969), p. 48. 'Sometimes I like being Virginia, but only when I'm scattered and various and gregarious' (Tuesday, 22 August 1922). See 'Yes, I'm 20 people', ibid., p. 35.
51. Many of her remarks about *Ulysses* are negative. For example: 'The book is diffuse. It is brackish. It is pretentious. It is underbred . . .' *Writer's Diary*, p. 49 (Wednesday, 6 September 1922). But compare 'I reflected how what I'm doing is probably being better done by Mr. Joyce', p. 28 (Sunday, 26 September 1920).
52. Ibid., especially Wednesday, August 16, Wednesday, 6 September and Thursday, 26 September 1922.
53. Ibid., pp. 23 and 47.
54. From 'Modern Fiction', quoted again from Miriam Allott, *Novelists on the Novel*, p. 77.
55. *Writer's Diary*, p. 47 (Wednesday, 26 July 1922).
56. The completion of Lily Briscoe's painting in *To the Lighthouse*, for instance, symbolises such creative reconciliation of contraries.
57. Riesman's phrase. See David Riesman, with Nathan Glazer and Reuel Denney, *The Lonely Crowd: A Study of the Changing American Character* (Yale University Press, 1971), *passim*.
58. See *The Diary of Virginia Woolf*, vols I–IV (Hogarth, 1978).
59. Gurney died in a mental institution.
60. See 'Hugh Selwyn Mauberley', Ezra Pound, *Selected Poems*.

Chapter 5: Self-deception and Self-conflict

1. Joseph Conrad, *Lord Jim* (Penguin, 1965), p. 103.
2. Ibid., p. 94.
3. Jean-Paul Sartre, *Being and Nothingness*, p. 49.
4. Herbert Fingarette, *Self-Deception* (Routledge and Kegan Paul, 1977).
5. In 'Agency of the Letter in the Unconscious or Reason since Freud', Jacques Lacan, *Ecrits: A Selection*, translated by Alan Sheridan (Tavistock, 1977), p. 166.
6. Derek Parfit, *Reasons and Persons* (Oxford University Press, 1984).
7. May Sinclair, *Life and Death of Harriett Frean*, edited by Jean Radford (Virago, 1980).
8. Siegfried Sassoon, *The War Poems*, pp. 130–2.
9. Ezra Pound, *Selected Poems*, pp. 191–2.
10. Peter Brooker cites the Pound interviews with Allen Ginsberg and Daniel Cory as evidence that Pound thought the poem merely a 'botch'. See Peter Brooker, *A Students' Guide to the Selected Poems of Ezra Pound* (Faber, 1979), pp. 362–3.
11. See above pp. 2–3.
12. This is brought out convincingly in Bernard C. Meyer, *Joseph Conrad: A Psychoanalytic Biography* (New Jersey: Princeton University Press, 1967).
13. In a letter to Cunningham Graham, 14 January 1898, quoted by Meyer, ibid., p. 128.
14. In a letter of (?) 25 July 1894, quoted by Meyer, ibid., p. 101.
15. Of Decoud in *Nostromo*, quoted by Meyer, ibid., p. 104.
16. I am indebted for this idea to my student Paul Beck who argued the case in his MA thesis, 'Obsession and Narrative Technique in the Novels of Joseph Conrad', Hatfield Polytechnic, 1984.
17. See F. R. Leavis, *The Great Tradition* (Penguin, 1962), pp. 196–202.
18. Conrad on a doctor's report: 'The last he does not say in so many words, but I can see an implication through a wall of words'. Letter to Edward Sanderson, 19 July 1897: quoted by Meyer, *Joseph Conrad*, p. 126.
19. *Lord Jim*, pp. 12–13.
20. All quotations from ibid., p. 13.
21. Ibid., p. 10.
22. Ibid., p. 29.
23. Ibid., p. 48.
24. See Albert J. Guerard, *Conrad the Novelist* (New York: Atheneum, 1967) Chapters 4 and 5.
25. 'Marlow has repeatedly taken us in', ibid., p. 153. See, too, the whole of Chapter 5.
26. Ibid., p. 313.
27. W. B. Yeats, *Autobiographies* (Macmillan, 1961), p. 189.
28. W. B. Yeats, *A Vision* (Macmillan, 1950), pp. 299–300.
29. W. B. Yeats, *Essays and Introductions* (Macmillan, 1961), p. 155.
30. W. B. Yeats, ibid., p. 28.
31. There are some interesting speculations on the psychological origins

of Yeats's self-conflict in the early part of David Lynch's book, *Yeats: The Poetics of the Self* (University of Chicago Press, 1979).
32. Quoted by T. R. Henn, *The Lonely Tower* (Methuen, 1966), p. 36.
33. Ibid.
34. Denis Donoghue, *Yeats* (Fontana, 1971), p. 41.
35. Ibid., p. 40.
36. Donoghue's first chapter is entitled 'A Kind of Power'.
37. Richard Ellmann, *The Identity of Yeats* (Faber and Faber, 1964), p. xi.
38. 'The scientific movement brought with it a literature which was always tending to lose itself in externalities of all kinds, in opinion, in declamation, in picturesque writing, in word-painting or in what Mr. Symons has called an attempt "to build in brick and mortar inside the covers of a book"', *Essays and Introductions*, p. 155.
39. James Joyce, *Ulysses*, p. 164.
40. Keats's 'negative capability' represents one of the most striking premodern formulations of the centrelessness of self. See John Keats's letter to Richard Woodhouse, 27 October 1818, in H. E. Rollins (ed.), *The Letters of John Keats 1814–1821* (Cambridge, Mass.: Harvard University Press, 1958), I, pp. 386–7. See, too, the letter to George and Tom Keats, 21, 27 (?) December 1817, ibid., pp. 193–4.
41. Marilyn French, *The Book as World: James Joyce's Ulysses* (Abacus, 1982), pp. 67–8.
42. Seen from a deconstructionist point of view, however, Molly represents the situation we are *all* in when attempting to face the realities of our subjectivity – a subjectivity experienced only in terms of the conditions of its discursive production. In Molly's case, her sense of herself issues particularly out of the way her subjectivity as woman has been produced in terms of ideological gender differentiation. So, while her spiel is, in a sense, both a rebuke to and deconstruction of such normative discursive gendering, it also evidences the power of ideological gendering in creating experiential confusions out of its fragmenting contradictions. In this regard, see the chapter 'Language and Subjectivity' in Chris Weedon's *Feminist Practice and Poststructuralist Theory* (Blackwell, 1987). See also the arguments about language and gender in Toril Moi (ed.), *The Kristeva Reader* (Blackwell, 1987).
43. Joyce thought Odysseus the greatest of classical heroes and the one seen in most breadth: not only as warrior and schemer but also as 'pacifist, father, wanderer, musician and artist'. See Richard Ellmann, *James Joyce* (Oxford University Press, 1968), p. 430.

Chapter 6: Discontinuous Self

1. The conclusion to *The Renaissance* gives the Greek. See L. Trilling and H. Bloom (eds), *Victorian Prose and Poetry* (Oxford University Press, 1973), p. 317, note 1 for Pater's translation.
2. Henri Bergson, 'Introduction to Metaphysics', translated by Mabelle L. Andison, in *A Study in Metaphysics* (Totowa, NJ: Littlefield, Adams & Co., 1965), p. 162.
3. *Ulysses*, p. 176.

4. Derek Parfit, *Reasons and Persons*, pp. 289–93.
5. Canto CXVI, *Selected Poems*, p. 192.
6. T. S. Eliot, *Collected Poems*, p. 40.
7. Canto III, *Selected Poems*, p. 16.
8. Canto IX, ibid., p. 38.
9. Canto XIII, ibid., p. 64.
10. William Wordsworth, *The Prelude or Growth of a Poet's Mind* . . .
11. Book 1, edited by Thomas Hutchinson, revised by Ernest de Selincourt, *Wordsworth: Poetical Works* (Oxford University Press, 1974), p. 499.
12. The whole chapter is relevant. See Maud Ellmann, 'Disremembering Dedalus', pp. 189–206.
13. I base this description on the *Confessions* as a whole, but Augustine's use of quotation at the beginning of Book VIII is apposite: 'Lord there is none like you. You have broken the chains that bound me; I will sacrifice in your honour. I shall tell how it was that you broke them . . .' Saint Augustine, *Confessions*, translated by R. S. Pinecoffin (Penguin, 1984), p. 157. The 'chains' very much include those of temporal development.
14. W. B. Yeats, 'Nineteen Hundred and Nineteen', *Collected Poems*, p. 234; Ezra Pound, Canto LXXVI, *Cantos*, p. 487.
15. Virginia Woolf, *Mrs Dalloway*, p. 165.
16. I find it hard to believe that either 'Nineteen Hundred and Nineteen' or 'The Second Coming' are solely concerned with Irish matters, to the exclusion of the Great War. Both the 'Platonic Year' and 'Animus Mundi' are involved in world events at large.
17. See Wyndham Lewis, *Blasting and Bombardiering*, reprinted by John Calder in 1982.
18. From Eliot's review 'Ulysses, Order and Myth', p. 483.
19. See 'Tradition and the Individual Talent', *Selected Essays*, pp. 13–22.
20. F. H. Bradley, *Appearance and Reality*, p. 194.
21. In 'Francis Herbert Bradley' (1927), *Selected Essays*, p. 455.
22. See my distinction between Tiresias and the Eliotic awareness on page 93.
23. Stephen Spender notes: 'On one occasion I was having tea with Leonard and Virginia Woolf when Eliot was also a fellow-guest. At their most "Bloomsbury-agnostic" they started needling him about his religious beliefs. "Tom, do you really go to church?" "Yes". "Do you hand round the collection?" "Yes". "Oh, really! . . ."' Stephen Spender, *Eliot* (Fontana, 1975), pp. 129–30.
24. William F. Lynch, SJ, 'Dissociation in Time', in B. Bergonzi (ed.), *T. S. Eliot: Four Quartets* (Macmillan, 1969), pp. 249–50.
25. See Hugh Kenner, *The Invisible Poet: T. S. Eliot* (Methuen, 1963), p. 274, note 1. Compare, 'When he gave two readings at Columbia University and the University of Texas, on both occasions he made the same disclaimer – that he had almost lost contact with the young man who had written the earlier poetry. It might be more accurate to say that he had escaped from him.' Peter Ackroyd, *T. S. Eliot* (Hamish Hamilton, 1984), pp. 323–4.
26. Jean-Paul Sartre, *Existentialism and Humanism*, translated by Philip Mairet (Eyre Methuen, 1978), p. 34.

Notes

27. Ibid., p. 39.
28. T. S. Eliot, *Knowledge and Experience in the Philosophy of F. H. Bradley*, p. 148.
29. Ibid.
30. See 'Tradition and the Individual Talent', *Selected Essays*, p. 19.
31. Ibid., p. 148.
32. Eliot's early poems were, of course, themselves partly influenced by Bergson's thought. See, for instance, Peter Ackroyd, *T. S. Eliot* pp. 40–1.
33. Rhoda's problem in *The Waves*; see p. 111.
34. Virginia Woolf, *Mrs Dalloway*, p. 151.
35. *To the Lighthouse* (Granada, 1979), p. 138.
36. Ibid., p. 172.
37. Ibid., p. 139.
38. *The Waves*, p. 249.
39. My judgement, (perhaps unfair to Jinny, see this chapter, page 162): Virginia Woolf is content to let the characters speak themselves, by and large.
40. Roger Poole, *The Unknown Virginia Woolf* (Cambridge University Press, 1978).
41. Virginia Woolf, *Moments of Being*, p. 90.
42. See Mitchell A. Leaska, *The Novels of Virginia Woolf: From Beginning to End* (City University of New York, 1977), footnote 11, pp. 188–9.
43. I am using the term in Harold Bloom's sense. See *The Anxiety of Influence: A Theory of Poetry* (Oxford University Press, 1973).
44. Donald Hall, *Remembering Poets: Reminiscences and Opinions* (Harper Colophon, 1979), p. 114.
45. Ibid., p. 156.
46. 'Vorticism', *Fortnightly Review*, vol. XCVI, no. 573 (1 September 1914), pp. 463–4.
47. Michael Alexander, *Poetic Achievement*, pp. 61–79.
48. F. S. Flint's formulation reproduced by Pound in T. S. Eliot (ed.), *Literary Essays*, p. 3.
49. *Cantos*, p. 29.
50. 'Ione, Dead the Long Year', *Selected Poems*, p. 54.
51. From four lines later, ibid., p. 29.
52. Ibid.
53. Ibid.
54. Alan Durant, *Ezra Pound: Identity in Crisis* (Harvester, 1981), p. 61.
55. *The Poetic Achievement*, p. 198.
56. In a paper given at the Ezra Pound Conference, Middlesex Polytechnic, 1982. See also her 'Floating the Pound . . .', *Oxford Literary Review*, 3:3 (1979), pp. 16–27.
57. See the title in note 56.
58. Originally published in *The New Age* (7 December 1911–16 February 1912) these are now collected in W. Cookson (ed.), *Ezra Pound: Selected Prose, 1909–1965* (Faber and Faber, 1978), pp. 21–43.

Chapter 7: Conclusion

1. Samuel Beckett, *The Unnamable*, in *Three Novels by Samuel Beckett* (New York: Grove Press, 1965), p. 291.
2. Philip Larkin, *The Whitsun Weddings* (Faber and Faber, 1973), p. 25. Since writing these brief words on the Movement I have read C. K. Stead's new book *Pound, Yeats, Eliot and the Modernist Movement* (Macmillan, 1986). The developing opinions of Donald Davie discussed in Chapter 10 cast an interesting light on my own views in the conclusion and, indeed, this book as a whole.
3. From 'Aubade', *Times Literary Supplement*, December 1977, reprinted in *The Observer*, Arts and Books Review, 8 December 1985, p. 22.
4. But Harrison does exploit the self-conflict attendant on class divisions and problematises a poetic voice situated between dialect and literary English.
5. For instance the placing of Salman Rushdie's *Midnight's Children* and D. M. Thomas's *The White Hotel* in 1981, J. M. Coetzee's *The Life and Times of Michael K.* in 1983 and Keri Hulme's *The Bone People* in 1985.
6. *The Unnamable*, p. 302. *Company* (Picador, 1980), p. 8.
7. Jeff Nuttall's book *Bomb Culture* (Paladin, 1968) eloquently records the frustrations of trying to get non-conventional writing through the system in the post-war period. In this context it may be remembered that most of the Modernists' texts (now gold-mines for publishers through the education industry) were only launched in the first place by private money, small reviews and special publishing houses.
8. Compare '"I am the unified, self-controlled center of the universe" man . . . has claimed', and 'I am a unified, coherent being, and what is significant in the world reflects my male image': Elaine Marks and Luce Irigary, quoted by Ann Rosalind Jones in 'Writing the Body: Toward an Understanding of l'Écriture Féminine', in *The New Feminist Criticism*, edited by Elaine Showalter (Virago, 1986), pp. 362 and 364.
9. Rachel Blau DuPlessis, 'For the Etruscans', *The New Feminist Criticism*, pp. 279 and 288.
10. Marshall McLuhan's phrase, of course. See *Understanding Media: The Extensions of Man* (Sphere Books, 1967).
11. See Jacques Derrida, *Of Grammatology*. See also the argument about the biases of written language in Walter J. Ong, *Orality and Literacy: The Technologizing of the Word* (Methuen, 1982).
12. See, for example, Jean-François Lyotard, *The Postmodern Condition: A Report on Knowledge*, translated by Geoff Bennington and Brian Massami (Manchester University Press, 1984) and *Postmodernism and Politics*, edited by Jonathan Arac (Manchester University Press, 1986).
13. This remains true even if, in Lacan's sense, our 'selves' are largely constructed in terms of linguistic initiation.
14. Samuel Beckett, *The Unnamable*, p. 291.

Index

Aldington, Richard, 51, 65; *Death of a Hero*, 51
Alexander, Michael, 167, 170; *The Poetic Achievement of Ezra Pound*, 167
Althusser, Louis, 7, 28
Anderson, Laurie, 180; 'O Superman', 180
Arden, John, 178
Artaud, Antonin, 178
Ashberry, John, 176
Auden, Wystan Hugh, 174
Augustine of Hippo, 145; *Confessions*, 145
Authenticity, 23, 36, 41–2, 55, 58, 73, 103, 104, 105, 107, 111, 113–17, 119, 120, 123, 124, 128, 135, 136, 137, 146, 147, 156, 157, 158, 161, 165, 171, 173, 177, 182

Barthes, Roland, 7
Beatles, The, 180; 'Revolution 9', 180
Beckett, Samuel, 81, 153, 174, 177, 178; *The Unnamable*, 177, 184; *Company*, 177
Beer, Gillian, 6; *Darwin's Plots*, 6
Bellow, Saul, 176
Bennett, Arnold, 15
Benveniste, Emile, 7
Bergman, Ingmar, 181; 'Cries and Whispers', 181
Bergson, Henri, 31, 141
Berryman, John, 176
Blake, William, 6, 125, 126, 129
Blunden, Edmund, 50; *Undertones of War*, 50
Boehme, Jacob, 125
Bowie, David, 180
Bradbury, Malcolm, 176; *The History Man*, 176

Bradley, Francis Herbert, 31, 36, 150, 156; *Appearance and Reality*, 31
Breakdown, 12, 15, 17–20, 29, 43–8, 54, 57, 58, 61–5, 67, 76, 81, 92, 105, 106, 183
Brecht, Bertolt, 178
Brooke, Rupert, 105
Browning, Robert, 5, 6, 30, 166; 'My Last Duchess', 5; *Sordello*, 165
Burroughs, William, 176, 180

Carlyle, Thomas, 76; *Sartor Resartus*, 76
Chaplin, Charlie, 181
Chaucer, Geoffrey, 97
Chekhov, Anton Pavlovich, 80
Churchill, Sir Winston Leonard Spencer, 55
Clough, Arthur Hugh, 4; 'Dipsychus', 4
Conrad, Joseph, 1, 3, 16–18, 24–6, 28, 29, 42, 43, 44, 58, 74, 82, 94, 111, 117–19, 122–3, 124, 147, 175; *Heart of Darkness*, 5, 10, 16, 17, 22–9, 30, 36, 94, 119, 142; *Lord Jim*, 11, 17, 22, 25, 111, 117–124, 131, 142; *Nostromo*, 6, 17, 118, 119; *Secret Agent, The*, 119; 'Secret Sharer, The', 22
Cox, C. B., 25
Creeley, Robert, 176
Crews, Frederick C., 28
Culture Club, 181; 'Karma Chameleon', 181

Dante, Alighieri, 96; *Divine Comedy*, 165
Derrida, Jacques, 7, 8, 36
Descartes, René, 110
Dickens, Charles, 4, 17, 108

Index

Discourse, ix, 1, 2, 4, 6, 7, 8, 9, 10, 11, 12, 14, 15, 16, 19, 20, 21, 25, 28, 29, 30, 33–6, 38, 40, 41, 45, 52, 58, 67–70, 74–8, 81, 82, 86, 90, 91, 92, 96, 97, 98, 101, 106, 107, 108, 109, 110, 112, 113, 118, 125, 126, 128–30, 136, 140, 143, 145, 152, 153, 164, 167, 168, 170, 172, 173, 174, 176, 177, 178, 179, 181, 182, 183, 184
Donne, John, 2
Donoghue, Denis, 129
Doolittle, Hilda, 74, 179
Dostoyevsky, Fyodor Mikhailovich, 17
Dream, 22, 23, 26, 27, 29, 37, 47, 50, 52, 53, 54, 80, 82, 83, 92, 94–9
Duncan, Robert, 176
Durrant, Alan, 169
Dylan, Bob, 180

Easthope, Anthony, 6–7
Edel, Leon, 82
Eliot, Thomas Stearns, 1, 2, 5, 8, 15, 16, 21, 30–6, 42, 43, 46, 57, 58, 70, 87, 91–8, 99, 109, 110, 112, 113, 129, 141, 143, 144, 147, 148, 149–50, 153, 155–7, 158, 159, 172, 174, 177, 180, 183; 'Ash Wednesday', 151, 152, 153, 154, 168; *Four Quartets*, 1, 11, 12, 81, 142, 144, 148, 153, 154–8; 'Dry Salvages, The', 156–7, 157–8; 'Little Gidding', 149, 154, 155, 158; 'Gerontion', 57, 143, 149, 151; 'Hollow Men, The', 31, 151, 152; *Knowledge and Experience in the Philosophy of F. H. Bradley*, 32; 'Love Song of J. Alfred Prufrock, The', 5, 9, 10, 12, 30–6, 112–13, 142, 150–1; 'Poems Written in Early Youth', 150; 'Portrait of a Lady', 21; 'Preludes', 22; 'Rhapsody on a Windy Night', 21–2; 'Tradition and the Individual Talent', 2; *Waste Land, The*, 1, 4, 8, 10, 21, 46, 57, 68, 70, 71, 76, 77, 81, 87, 91–9, 142, 143, 144, 148, 151, 152, 180
Ellmann, Maud, 145, 171
Ellmann, Richard, 129
Existentialism, 18, 30–2, 36, 41–2, 43, 103, 118, 123, 126, 128, 131, 145, 146, 148, 153, 154, 156, 169, 170, 172, 176

Faulkner, William Harrison, 11
Fenton, James, 175
Fingarette, Herbert, 110, 111; *Self-Deception*, 110, 111
Ford, Ford Maddox, 1, 2, 10, 19–20, 21, 50, 58–61, 63–5, 69, 82, 147, 148, 172, 175, 178; *Good Soldier, The*, 12, 19, 20; *Parade's End*, 10, 19, 46, 50–1, 58–9, 65–6, 147–8, 178; *A Man Could Stand Up*, 58, 61, 62; *Last Post, The*, 59, 148; *No More Parades*, 58, 60, 62, 64; *Some Do Not*, 58, 61, 63–4, 148; *Saddest Story, The*, 20
Fowles, John, 176
French, Marilyn, 132, 134, 135; *The Book as World*, 133, 134–5
Freud, Sigmund, 44, 94, 95, 97, 178; *The Case of Dora*, 12
Fussell, Robert, 92; *The Great War and Modern Memory*, 92

Garnett, Edward, 74
Gass, William H., 176
Gaudier–Brzeska, Henri, 45
Ginsberg, Allen, 176
'Goon Show, The', 180
Graves, Robert, 46–8, 51, 52, 58; 'Castle, The', 47; 'Down', 46, 47; 'In Procession', 46, 47; 'Pier Glass, The', 46, 47
Guerard, Albert J., 121, 122
Gurney, Ivor, 44, 45, 54, 106; 'Strange Hells', 44
Gysin, Brion, 180

Haggard, Sir H. Rider, 44
Hall, Donald, 166
Hardy, Thomas, 15, 175
Harrison, Tony, 175

Index

Hawkes, John, 176
Hawthorne, Nathaniel, 76; *Young Goodman Brown*, 76
Heaney, Seamus, 175
Heidegger, Martin, 141, 178
Heraclitus, 141, 150
Hogg, James, 4, 5; *Confessions of a Justified Sinner*, 4
Holmes, Richard, 43, 70; *Firing Line*, 43, 70
Hulme, Thomas Ernest, 20, 45
Hume, David, 4, 6
Humphrey, Robert, 86

Imagism, 20–1, 31, 32, 47, 54, 69, 76, 83, 91, 95, 107, 116, 151, 167, 180
Ionesco, Eugene, 178

James, Henry, 1, 16, 30, 74, 82, 112, 175; *The Ambassadors*, 16
James, William, 16, 31, 83
Janet, Pierre Marie Felix, 16
John, Elton, 180, 181; 'Someone Saved My Life Tonight', 181
Johnson, Bryan, 178
Jones, David Michael, 1, 10, 66–7, 69–70, 72–3, 92, 178; *Anathemata, The*, 69; *In Parenthesis*, 10, 46, 50, 66–73, 178, 180
Joyce, James, 1, 2, 7, 15, 17, 21, 36, 39–42, 43, 67, 70, 81, 82–3, 86, 89–91, 100, 109, 110, 113, 131–2, 134, 136, 138, 140, 145, 172, 174, 175, 177, 178, 183; *Finnegans Wake*, 12, 81–2, 178; *Portrait of the Artist as a Young Man*, 10, 17, 18, 36–42, 113, 133, 144–5, 154; *Ulysses*, 1, 10, 11, 12, 41, 68, 70, 76, 81, 82–90, 91, 97, 98, 99, 131–40, 142, 143, 144, 146, 148, 180; 'Work in Progress', 67, 174
Jung, Carl Gustav, 10, 178

Keaton, Buster, 181
Keats, John, 4, 6, 35, 126
Kipling, Rudyard, 44

Lacan, Jacques, 7–8, 12, 110; *Ecrits*, 12
Laforgue, Jules, 30
Langbaum, Robert, 4; *Mysteries of Identity*, 4
Larkin, Philip, 174, 175, 181; 'The Whitsun Weddings', 175; 'Self's the Man', 175
Lawrence, David Herbert, 12, 15, 18–19, 45, 61, 65, 74–6, 77, 109, 111, 114, 136, 146, 156, 175; *Psychoanalysis and the Unconscious*, 12; *Rainbow, The*, 76; *Sons and Lovers*, 18–19, 76, 113; *Women in Love*, 12, 45, 61, 75–6, 114, 146
Lawrence, Thomas Edward, 48, 49; *Seven Pillars of Wisdom*, 48, 49; *Revolt in the Desert*, 48
Leavis, Frederick Raymond, 118
Leed, Eric J., 50; *No Man's Land*, 50
Lennon, John, 180, 181; 'Don't Believe', 181
Lessing, Doris, 176, 179, 181
Lewis, Percy Wyndham, 6, 77, 79, 141, 178; *Enemy of the Stars*, 79; *Tarr*, 77, 178; *Time and Western Man*, 141
Locke, John, 4
Lord of the Flies (William Golding), 175
Lowell, Robert, 176
Lucky Jim (Kingsley Amis), 175
Lynch, William T., 155

MacCarthy, Desmond, 165
Mailer, Norman, 176
Marinetti, Filippo Tommaso, 75
Marx, Karl, 28
Merleau-Ponty, Maurice, 178
Metamorphosis, 11, 41, 79, 80, 82, 89, 97, 140, 145, 148, 151, 153, 154, 155, 157, 158, 160, 163, 168, 170, 182
Miller, J. Hillis, 5
Miller, Karl, 4; *Doubles*, 4
Milton, John, 2, 117; 'When I Consider How My Light is Spent', 2, 117

Index

Modernism, ix, 1, 2, 4, 5–14, 17, 22, 30, 42, 46, 47, 51, 52, 58, 66, 69–72, 74, 76, 79, 81, 98, 108–14, 117, 130, 140, 141–2, 144–9, 165, 174–84
'Monty Python's Flying Circus', 180
Morrison, Jim, 180
Motion, Andrew, 175
Mottram, Eric, 178
Murdoch, Iris, 176
Murry, John Middleton, 55

Nagera, Humberto, 96, 98; *Basic Psychoanalytic Concepts*, 96, 98
New Freewoman, The, 74
Nichol, Peter, 178
Nietzsche, Friedrich, 109, 141

Odyssey, The, 165
Olson, Charles, 176
Orton, Joe, 178
Orwell, George, 174
Owen, Wilfred, 44–5, 47, 51, 54, 55, 70, 105; 'Disabled', 54; 'Mental Cases', 44, 54, 55; 'Strange Encounter', 47

Parfit, Derek, 110, 141, 181; *Reasons and Persons*, 110
Pater, Walter, 141
Persona, 6, 15, 16, 17, 20, 30, 52, 69, 72, 91, 93, 94, 95, 97, 124–6, 130, 131, 138, 139, 141, 144, 152, 161–7, 171
Pinter, Harold, 178
Plath, Sylvia, 176, 179
Poole, Roger, 161; *The Unknown Virginia Woolf*, 161
Pope, Alexander, 152; 'Dunciad, The', 152; 'Epistle to Dr. Arbuthnot', 3
Porter, Peter, 175
Poststructuralism, ix, 6–9, 28, 35–6, 55, 177, 178, 181, 184
Pound, Ezra, 1, 2, 5, 14, 16, 21, 30, 45, 70, 77–8, 91, 93, 109, 115–17, 142, 143, 144, 148, 165–73, 174, 176, 178, 180; 'An Object', 21; 'Ballad of the Goodly Fere, The', 167; *Cantos, The*, 1, 4, 11, 16, 21, 78, 81, 115–17, 142, 143, 148, 165–6, 168–73, 174, 178, 180; 'Canto I (Draft of)', 78; 'Canto II', 78; 'Canto III', 166; 'Canto VII', 168; 'Canto LXXIV', 169, 170, 171–2; 'Canto LXXXI', 169; 'Canto LXXXIII', 169; 'Canto CXVI', 115, 166; 'Cino', 167; 'Envoi', 167; 'Exile's Letter', 167; 'Hugh Selwyn Mauberley', 12, 14, 45, 142, 167, 180; 'Medallion', 167; 'Near Perigord', 14, 167; 'Portrait d'une Femme', 21; 'Seafarer, The', 167
Proust, Marcel, 11, 141
Psychoanalysis, 1, 6, 11, 12, 16, 18, 19, 22, 26–9, 33, 37, 41, 43, 44, 52–8, 60, 64, 66, 80, 81, 83, 85, 94–9, 109, 115, 118, 121–2, 127, 132–3, 137–8, 145, 147, 176, 178, 181
Pynchon, Thomas, 176

Raine, Craig, 175
Reader involvement, 33, 38, 55, 63, 65, 113, 116, 117, 119, 121, 122, 130, 134, 135–6, 140, 153, 159
Relativism, 5–6, 9, 12, 18, 29, 35, 39, 58, 86, 93, 102, 108, 110, 112, 116, 117, 118, 124, 129, 130–2, 140, 151, 162, 166, 181, 182
Repression, 13, 17, 36, 39, 42, 50, 55–9, 63, 64, 83, 85, 114, 126, 136, 151, 163
Resnais, Alain, 181; 'Last Year at Marienbad', 181
Richardson, Dorothy, 74, 80, 81, 83, 100, 175; *Pilgrimage*, 80; *Pointed Roofs*, 80–1
Rivers, Dr. W. H. R., 44, 53, 54, 57
Robinson Crusoe (Daniel Defoe), 3, 4
Roethke, Theodore, 176
Room at the Top (John Braine), 175
Rudkin, David, 178
Russell, Bertrand, 92
Rutherford, Andrew, 48

Index

Sartre, Jean-Paul, 109, 110, 156, 178; *Being and Nothingness*, 109–10
Sassoon, Siegfried, 10, 44, 46, 51–8, 69, 70, 105, 109, 115; 'Absolution', 52; 'A Letter Home', 52; 'A Night Attack', 53; 'At Carnoy', 52; 'Christ and the Soldier', 53; *Complete Memoirs of George Sherston, The*, 54; *Memoirs of a Fox-Hunting Man*, 52; *Sherston's Progress*, 53, 55; 'Counter-Attack', 55; 'Died of Wounds', 52; 'Letter to Robert Graves', 53–4, 55, 115; 'Repression of War Experience', 54, 55, 66, 105, 115; 'Road, The', 53; 'Statement Against the Continuation of War', 53; 'Stretcher Case', 53; 'Survivors', 54, 55, 56
'Saturday Live', 180
Saunders, James, 178
Self-conflict, 5, 10, 15–17, 25–7, 37–8, 52, 55–7, 70, 72, 74, 89, 91, 101, 108–40, 142, 167, 182; -deception, 10, 17, 33, 45, 60, 65, 74, 101, 108–40, 142, 146–7, 161–2, 182; -discontinuity, 2, 11, 50, 70–3, 81–3, 86, 93, 102, 103, 107, 110, 126, 130, 138–40, 141–73, 182; -dissolution, 6, 10, 14–42, 43, 45, 67, 69, 72, 73, 77, 80, 93, 98, 106, 139, 141, 149, 152–3, 168; -division, 4–5, 8, 14–16, 20, 22, 25, 48–9, 51, 58, 78, 80, 90, 111, 117, 125–6, 167; -expression, 5, 36, 39, 40–2, 90, 103, 106, 113, 133, 145, 180; -fragmentation, ix, 1–2, 5–8, 10–13, 15, 16, 17, 18, 20, 21, 24–30, 33, 37, 41, 43, 45–8, 50–5, 58–61, 63, 65–9, 72–3, 74–107, 108, 110–12, 117, 118, 125–6, 128–9, 135–6, 140, 142, 144, 148, 149, 153, 160–3, 166, 170, 172–3, 173–4, 176–9, 181–3; -integration, ix, 2–8, 10, 12–13, 14, 15, 16, 17, 19, 20, 22–5, 28, 30–1, 33, 35, 36, 37, 40, 41, 43, 52, 59, 61–5, 74, 75, 79, 95, 98, 99, 101, 102, 104, 105, 110, 111, 117, 125, 128, 129, 130, 131, 134, 139, 141, 143, 144, 146, 147, 155, 156, 161, 163, 169, 173, 175–9, 181–3; -liberation, 12–13, 17, 18, 24, 26, 36, 38–42, 89, 103, 113, 125, 141, 146, 154–8, 164, 186; -multiplicity, 8, 13, 16, 31, 33, 36, 40, 72, 81, 82, 88–91, 99, 101, 107, 110–12, 131, 138, 139, 142, 143, 156–8, 161, 163–6, 177, 181–3
Sexton, Anne, 176
Shaffer, Peter, 178
Shakespeare, William, 90, 133; *Hamlet*, 2, 133; *King Lear*, 2, 92
Shaw, George Bernard, 79, 80; *Heartbreak House*, 79–80
Shelley, Percy Bysshe, 5, 126
Shell-shock, 10, 15, 20, 43–7, 52–4, 57–8, 61–2, 67, 72, 92, 105, 147, 148, 159, 183
Silkin, Jon, 51, 56, 70
Simpson, Norman Frederick, 178
Sinclair, May, 74, 114; *Life and Death of Harriet Frean*, 114
Spenser, Edmund, 152
Sterne, Laurence, 6
Stevenson, Robert Louis, 4
Stoppard, Tom, 178
Stream of Consciousness, 31, 37, 62, 80–91, 99–107, 131, 136, 172
Strindberg, John August, 80

Tennyson, Alfred, 4, 30, 35; 'Two Voices', 4
'That Was The Week That Was', 180
Thomas, Dylan, 174
Thomas, Edward, 175
Time, 31, 34, 72, 141–5, 147–61, 161, 166, 169, 170

Vonnegut, Kurt, 176

War (The Great), 1, 10, 18, 20, 43–73, 74, 78–80, 91–2, 99, 105, 147–8, 159–61; 174, 182, 183
Waugh, Evelyn, 65, 174
Webster, John, 96

Wells, Herbert George, 15, 76–7; *The New Machiavelli*, 76–7
Whitman, Walt, 97, 157
Wilde, Oscar, 16
Williams, William Carlos, 176
Wittgenstein, Ludwig, 36; *Philosophical Investigations*, 36
Woolf, Virginia, 1, 2, 6, 9, 15, 31, 46, 57, 59, 74, 77, 81, 83, 99–107, 109, 110, 138, 141, 147, 158–62, 164–5, 175, 183; *Jacob's Room*, 159; 'Modern Fiction', 77, 100; *Moments of Being*, 161; *Mrs Dalloway*, 10, 12, 46, 57, 81, 99–107, 142, 148, 158, 159–60, 180; *To the Lighthouse*, 148, 158, 159, 160; *Waves, The*, 1, 2, 6, 11, 59, 81, 142, 148, 158, 159, 160–5
Wordsworth, William, 4, 5, 44, 145; 'Prelude, The', 145, 173; 'Strange Fits of Passion', 9

Yeats, William Butler, 2, 5, 11, 15, 16, 74, 78–9, 109, 124–30, 131, 138, 142, 148, 172, 174; *A Vision*, 126; 'Among Schoolchildren', 130; Autobiographies, 124–5; 'Circus Animals' Desertion, The', 130; 'Crazy Jane Talks With the Bishop', 127; 'Dominus Ego Tuus', 78, 125; 'Lapis Lazuli', 124; 'Leda and the Swan', 130; 'Nineteen Hundred and Nineteen', 124; *Per Amica Silentia Lunae*', 125; *Responsibilities*, 5; 'Sailing to Byzantium', 126–7; 'Second Coming, The', 78, 79; 'Spur, The', 130; 'Those Images', 124; *The Tower*, 79, 128; 'Under Ben Bulben', 124

Zukofsky, Louis, 176